GRANTA 55, AUTUMN 1996

EDITOR Ian Jack
DEPUTY EDITOR Ursula Doyle
MANAGING EDITOR Claire Wrathall
EDITORIAL ASSISTANT Karen Whitfield

CONTRIBUTING EDITORS Neil Belton, Pete de Bolla, Frances Coady, Will Hobson, Liz Jobey, Blake Morrison, Andrew O'Hagan

Granta, 2–3 Hanover Yard, Noel Road, London N1 8BE
TEL (0171) 704 9776, FAX (0171) 704 0474
SUBSCRIPTIONS (0171) 704 0470

SALES AND BUSINESS MANAGER Kate Griffin, FINANCE Geoffrey Gordon, ASSOCIATE PUBLISHER Sally Lewis, SUBSCRIPTIONS John Kirkby, SUBSCRIPTIONS ASSISTANT Rhiannon Thomas, OFFICE ASSISTANT Angela Rose

Granta US, 250 West 57th Street, Suite 1316, New York, NY 10107, USA
US PUBLISHER Matt Freidson

PUBLISHER Rea S. Hederman

SUBSCRIPTION DETAILS: a one-year subscription (four issues) costs £21.95 (UK), £29.95 (rest of Europe) and £36.95 (rest of the world).

Granta is printed in the United States of America. The paper used in this publication meets the minimum requirements of American National Standard for Information Sciences—Permanence of Paper for Printed Library Materials, ANSI Z39.48-1984. ♾

Granta is published by Granta Publications Ltd and distributed in the United Kingdom by Bloomsbury, 2 Soho Square, London W1V 5DE; and in the United States by Penguin Books USA Inc, 375 Hudson Street, New York, NY 10014, USA.

Cover photographs: Danny Bright/SOA (front); Corbis-Bettmann (back)
Cover design by The Senate

ISBN 0 903141 02 7

animal
planet
SCOTT
BRADFIELD
'A brilliant satire . . . Bradfield has done a
remarkable thing in writing a deliriously funny
book . . . to be relished'
Observer
'Hyper-alert writing
that never lets up
for a moment'
Independent
Available now
in Hardback
PICADOR

THE FABER LIBRARY

Books which speak for themselves

1 Siegfried Sassoon *Memoirs of an Infantry Officer*
2 T. S. Eliot *Four Quartets*
3 William Golding *Lord of the Flies*,
4 George Steiner *The Death of Tragedy*
5 Ted Hughes *Crow*
6 Milan Kundera *The Unbearable Lightness of Being*
7 Louis MacNeice *Autumn Journal*
8 Philip Larkin *Jill*
9 John Osborne *Look Back in Anger*
10 Flannery O'Connor *A Good Man is Hard to Find*
11 Seamus Heaney *North*
12 Kazuo Ishiguro *The Remains of the Day*

13 Djuna Barnes *Nightwood* £9.95

14 W. H. Auden *New Year Letter* £8.95

15 Randall Jarrell *Poetry and the Age* £10.95

16 Sylvia Plath *The Bell Jar* £10.95

17 Tom Stoppard *Jumpers* £8.95

18 Peter Carey *Illywhacker* £11.95

The Faber Library Box Set 3 (titles 13–18) £50.00

All titles are available at good bookshops or directly from Faber and Faber (postage and packing free). Contact Faber and Faber Promotions Department on 0171 465 0045 for further details.

CHILDREN

ADAM MARS-JONES

BLIND BITTER HAPPINESS

My mother was born on 20 August 1923 and christened Sheila Mary Felicity Cobon. At some stage she was told the supposed meaning of these names, or looked them up in a book. Her forenames meant by derivation Blind Bitter Happiness. As an adult Sheila found this augury ruefully amusing, or faintly annoying, in its mixture of the appropriate and the hopelessly wrong.

Sheila was both a wanted and an unwanted child. Charles and Gladys Cobon already had a daughter, three-year-old Margaret ('Peggy'). What they wanted was not Sheila the eventual alto but a boy, who would in time sing treble in the same choir as his father. There was a name prepared for the invited guest: Derek. Sheila was a failed Derek, a fact that was not entirely kept from her.

Sheila was keenly aware of the difference in status, as far as her father was concerned, between herself and her sister. The family lived in Wembley, in north-west London, while Charles worked for a firm of marine engineers in Rotherhithe, on the river to the east of the city. As a matter of routine, Peggy would meet Charles's train after work on a Saturday. When Sheila was old enough to deputize for her sister in this coveted duty, Charles's first question would always be: 'Is Peggy ill?' This was before parenting skills. He didn't have the sense to wrap it up. To say: Lovely to see you, Sheila. Kind of you to come and meet your old man. How's your mother? Good, good. And Peggy?

As children, Peggy and Sheila competed over such important matters as who could eat slowest. Peggy was particularly skilled at hiding, say, a straggling line of peas in the shadow of a folded knife and fork, so as to thwart Sheila's triumph and eat the stragglers with a relish out of all proportion to their deliciousness.

As a girl, Sheila's candidates for the title of Naughtiest Words in the World were *bosom* and *spasm*. She would say them in her head continuously, until the laughter burst out of her. Bosom spasm bosom spasm. A litany of taboos. A wicked prayer.

Sheila was ten when Gladys died, after a stroke, and it was Sheila who found her stricken, incapable, labouring for breath.

Ever after, Sheila was hysterically distressed by physical impairment, by paralysis and mutilation, even the malformation of a London pigeon's feet. A pigeon with fused feet was still a wounded symbol to her, a fly-specked mirror held up to her of bedraggled suffering, loss of self. Her reaction was complex, being made up of both identification and disgust, the desire for things to be whole and for them to be dead. If anyone asked about this phobic affinity, she would refer to the conspicuous presence in her childhood of veterans injured in the war, but not everyone of her generation was so deeply affected.

In the months after her mother died, a new routine established itself. Sheila would come home from school first and let herself in, but was not trusted to make a fire on her own or for her own benefit. She would have to wait for Peggy's return before she could think of getting warm.

When Charles himself came home, he would cook supper, which would be chops, or else steak, and boiled potatoes. Sheila was in a phase of revulsion against meat and ate only the potatoes. At weekends the girls' Aunt Mimi, who lived in Rotherhithe, would cook Sunday lunch and prepare sandwiches for them to eat at school the next day, using the meat left over. On the way home Sheila would be repulsed all over again, seeing the wrapped sandwiches in the glove compartment of the car. She was prone to carsickness anyway, but the closeness of the meat made things worse. At school she would throw the meat away, convinced it smelt of petrol, and eat only the bread.

Those around her did not for some time connect the fact of her developing boils with her near-exclusive diet of bread and potatoes.

Charles was not a worldly man. His father had been an organist and had published a *Te Deum*; Charles himself not only sang in the choir, but was a lay preacher. If he had a passion besides God and marine engineering it was trains. He didn't share his bereavement with his daughters, but then bereavement is not for sharing. If it can be shared, it is something other than bereavement. Still, Charles can't be accused of anticipating his children's needs with overmuch imagination. He did know, though, that girls need a mother. He found one for them.

Lilian, his second wife, was a schoolteacher in her forties. Her motives for the union are more obscure than her new husband's. Perhaps there was sly triumph in the casting off of a maiden name at a time of life when the label old maid was firmly attached to her. Perhaps, too, as a teacher who had met the Cobon girls in their mother's lifetime, she responded to Charles's appeal on their behalf, and to the challenge of shaping a child's character more directly than she could in the classroom.

It was 'a child' she had ambitions to shape, rather than children, and her first choice was Peggy. She would have had more of a chance if she had played her cards better. It was a mistake to insist that the girls both wear ankle socks and frilled red velvet dresses at the wedding. Peggy at fourteen thought herself too grown-up to be dressed as a child, almost a doll, and never forgave the ankle socks.

It was also a mistake to expect to be called Mummie, or at least to make an issue of it. Peggy would never call Lilian Mummie. Sheila would.

Now at least there was someone who noticed whether she ate properly or not. Boils stood no chance against Lilian. Lilian was also determined that Sheila should have a proper education and in due course be financially independent.

This was in part a recognition that Sheila was bright, but also reflected a colder agenda. It was Lilian's feeling that women should always be financially independent, because women should have as little as possible to do with men in any way.

By the time she was fourteen, Sheila had been told by Lilian that she had never let Charles come near her in 'that way'. No carnal congress for Lilian, thank you very much. No bosom spasm.

What did Lilian think she was doing by passing on so grotesquely inappropriate a confidence? There are a number of possibilities. To establish as a general principle that Men Are Beasts. Or to offer reassurance that she was playing by the rules of the marriage: the girls' new mother, not Charles's new wife. Perhaps, too, it was a way of striking a bargain. Showing that she had no secrets from Sheila—a rare sort of trust. And trust must be returned.

By being mother of a sort to at least one of his children, without being functionally Charles's wife, Lilian effectively split the family in two. At one point she had a maid who performed some duties also for Sheila, but had instructions not to attend on

Charles or Peggy. From there it was only a small step to separate the two half-households.

In her early teens Sheila was not expected to choose what clothes to wear—she would put on what was laid out for her, schoolday or holiday. So there could be no question of her being allowed to choose which person to live with. Lilian always said that when Sheila was sixteen, she would be able to exercise a choice, but it was clear that Lilian had fixed expectations of the choice.

Looking back as an adult (and a legally trained adult to boot), Sheila realized that Lilian was careful all this time to avoid making herself vulnerable to a charge of deserting Charles. What she wanted was to negotiate her demands from within the married state, not risk a departure from it. So Sheila would spend the time after school at Lilian's mother's house, 92 Upward Road, and then be brought back to sleep in the family home, the house with the grandly pretty name of Foxes Dale.

The prospect of being allowed to choose somehow suggested to Sheila that she was considered relatively unimportant. Charles hardly seemed anxious to claim her. Sheila didn't even particularly look like a Cobon, unlike Peggy with her bony face and prominent eyes.

Sheila had masses of dark curly hair, cause for pride, and a nose she felt was beaky, cause for shame. There were other things about which she felt self-conscious. Her feet were so narrow that she would leave school-issue shoes behind, even when tightly laced, if she ran upstairs.

There wasn't actually a moment, for Sheila, of decision between guardians. Before she was ever sixteen, rights over her had imperceptibly been transferred to Lilian. She had been kidnapped piecemeal.

Sheila was too young to wonder whether the bisection of the family was a legally sanctioned or an informal arrangement. In later life she assumed it was informal, and therefore that Lilian took her because Charles didn't want to. It was not in Lilian's interest to tell her that Charles contributed to her maintenance, and that both parties had put their signatures to an Agreement assigning custody.

Lilian's care, which had from the start contained an element of over-identification, of vicarious living, shaded bit by bit into abuse. Sheila never used that word about her experience of subjection, even when it became so ubiquitous in the culture that people could be routinely described as abusing alcohol, or a racquet during a tennis match. It was 'only' emotional abuse, moreover: but abuse it was. Lilian pumped the breathable air out of the house and replaced it with oxides of rancour, her grudge against the world.

Lilian would give her stepdaughter the silent treatment for three uninterrupted days, until Sheila begged to be told what her crime had been. It would turn out to be misbehaviour on the level of failing, at a school concert, to let the applause die down fully before coming on stage to announce the next item. Just *bouncing* on to the stage, full of herself in a common way.

By this method Sheila's mild extroversion was obliterated. Yet she never thought of Lilian's behaviour as normal. She had memories enough of the time before her mother's death to know that it was Lilian's coldly boiling rage which was disordered. She developed a hatred of confrontations and of 'atmospheres' which would last all her life.

Lilian had no real prospect of imposing a hatred of men on this adolescent girl. The part of Sheila's sensibility which had been so tickled by *bosom spasm bosom spasm* would later take joy in a school joke that Lilian would certainly have found smutty:

> *Girl's Father*: I should inform you, young man, that the lights go out in this house at nine-thirty sharp.
> *Young Man*: I say, Sir, that's awfully sporting!

If this was smut, it was more wholesome than what Lilian dished up daily.

Though Sheila wasn't temperamentally able to assert herself against Lilian, she wasn't altogether biddable either. On one occasion she ran away, and fulfilled an ambition fuelled by her teenage reading by sleeping in a haystack. She loved to read. Once she'd been so wrapped up, perched halfway up a tree reading *Lorna Doone*, that she missed lunch and didn't even mind.

From Lilian's reign onwards, although Sheila was widely regarded as bright, anyone who wanted to make her feel stupid could do so, and there were those who produced the same effect without intending to or noticing, purely in passing.

One day, staying with a schoolfriend, she picked up a book which her hostess's older brother was studying as part of his university course. She had been given his bedroom to sleep in, and law books were everywhere. This particular volume was called *Winfield on Tort*. She opened the book at random, and her eyes fell on a bracketed phrase: '(Married Women and Tortfeasors)'. There was something irresistibly comic about this combination—a tortfeasor sounded as if it should mean a small spherical sweet, honeycomb with a coating of chocolate. *I'll have a box of Tortfeasors, please—they're the torts with the less fattening centres.* (It happened that Maltesers were her favourite sweets.) It seemed plain to her that somewhere lurking in the legal system was a great dry sense of humour. She read on and found herself, if not exactly rocking with laughter, then certainly intrigued by the system that the book spelt out.

Sheila was a good student, and Lilian could hardly object, in view of her stated ambitions for her stepdaughter, to the plan of reading law in due time at London University, relocated in wartime to Cambridge. Sheila and her lodgings-mate smoked five cigarettes a week each, on principle. They were sending smoke signals. This was their way of signalling that they were approachable, not nuns or prudes but Modern Women.

In the evenings Sheila helped at a canteen set up for forces personnel doing courses; the bolder men called her The Girl with the Gypsy Eyes.

The war brought both enlargements of horizon and setbacks to Sheila. She had especially been looking forward to the appearance of American troops in the global conflict, but in the event she was disappointed. Their buttocks were large and slack; they looked nothing like the men in the movies. Could that be why they were called Doughboys?

In June 1943, when Sheila was nineteen, Lilian made some sort of appeal to Charles, desiring him to reinforce her authority with his. It was odd that she should make such an approach, when she had hitherto been so steadfast in separating father and daughter.

Charles had come to regret the Agreement that gave Lilian

her power, and seems to have made the suggestion that Sheila should return to his care, if she was proving troublesome. Lilian's response to Charles's solicitors was sharp. She would of course continue to respect the Agreement and to offer Sheila parental affection as and when she proved worthy of it. It was not possible however to offer care to a headstrong young woman who was abetted in her opposition by outsiders. She was disgusted by the motive of Mr Cobon's interference. If she had known he would seek to exploit the situation she would never have thought of involving him.

Charles asked his solicitors if there was any prospect of having the Agreement set aside. They told him this would only be possible by mutual consent, while in this matter the parties hardly seemed to be *ad idem*. By professional reflex they translated the idea of being in agreement into the dignified extinction of Latin. They did however object to Mrs Cobon's withholding information about Sheila's whereabouts, information to which he was certainly entitled.

After that Charles adopted a more conciliatory, even a wheedling approach. He started his letters 'Dear Lily', and wrote a rough draft so that he could add a little more soap to the final version. He was grateful that she was doing so much for Sheila. He would send any gifts or pocket money to Lily rather than Sheila, for her to pass on as she saw fit. He would be grateful for an opportunity of seeing Sheila, in London if that was more agreeable to Lily. Perhaps he could take her to a show. He would of course meet all expenses.

Between the ages of fifteen and twenty-five, Sheila saw her father twice and her sister not at all. The estrangement extended even to birthday and Christmas cards. The second lunch, when she was nineteen or so, was perhaps the rendezvous requested in the letter to Lilian. Charles surprised his daughter by treating her as a grown-up. This recognition was conveyed by the offer of a glass of light ale.

After Part One of her degree, Sheila joined the Wrens, and was duly posted to a Wrennery in London. The premises were very grand, a town house in Cheyne Walk, and she slept in the ballroom, but she shared it with thirty-one other Wrens. Sixteen of them would want the windows open at night, and sixteen wanted them shut, so half of them were always simmeringly resentful. They were a mixed group: one girl never changed her clothes, until eventually they had to be taken from her by a little deputation of hygienic Wrens. A kangaroo court come to lynch a dirty shirt.

There was drudgery, admittedly, in the effort to keep smart. You had to wash your white shirt every night and iron it in the morning, either getting up at crack of dawn or queueing for the iron. Then after breakfast Sheila would walk across the bridge to Battersea and learn how to assemble radios. Luckily her hair was short: girls with long hair were always having it brush against the soldering iron. The smell of burnt hair became familiar, almost consoling. In the evenings she would do her Bates exercises, for perfect sight without glasses, before washing her shirt again. If the exercises had worked for Aldous Huxley, who had been as good as blind, why not for her?

Lilian's plan to make Sheila a career woman independent of men had the inherent drawback that the world of work was full of them. After the war and the completion of her degree, she was called to Gray's Inn as a barrister. By the time she met Bill Mars-Jones in 1946, it was no novelty to be romanced by a stranger.

He projected on to her a strongly romantic account of their future together. But he also—and this *was* a novelty—seemed bothered by his lost virginity and introduced the subject with a jarring urgency into their early conversations. Why in the world does he think I care one way or the other? she thought. She also found it odd, if virginity was so important to him, that he seemed to entertain no doubts whatever about her own. This was almost unflattering enough to pique an interest. Did he think she'd had no offers?

Still, he had merits. One of them was that although he had served, and even earned a rather smart little gong, he didn't go on and on about the war the way so many men did. Maybe that was an advantage of the Navy, that either everyone went down together or they were all more or less OK. You could see action without seeing casualties directly, without being scarred or turned into some dreary hero. Bill had had his share of dangerous duty, on Russian convoys, but his closest brush with death proper came when he was posted to *HMS Hood*, sunk before he could take up the post.

It was almost a shock when Bill turned out to be Welsh. He'd lost the accent in pretty short order. His voice was musical, but he sounded more like someone on the Home Service than a country boy who was going to say 'look you' at the drop of a hat. Perhaps she had met the only Welshman in London at that time who didn't dream of being mistaken for Dylan Thomas.

Bill was still thrilled to be living in London, which made Sheila feel almost old, but in a nice way. Bill was still, deep down, the teenager who had hidden his face in fear at a screening of *King Kong* on his first visit to London, grateful to have his father sitting next to him—not because the old man made him feel strong by example, rather the opposite. His dad gave little suppressed yelps during the great ape's appearances and prayed under his breath in Welsh.

Bill was smartly dressed, even a bit of a dandy, what with his tie always in a tubby Windsor knot, but it was pretty clear he wasn't a wolf. From the way he told her about his past philandering it was clear that a philanderer was what he was not.

It was only much later, on her first visit to Bill's family in North Wales, that she understood some of the fuss about his fallen sexual state. He came from a different world. She had been briefed to do without make-up and cigarettes, at least until Bill's widowed father got to know her. It was bad enough her being English rather than Welsh, without being *painted* and English, and the smoke signals that spelt out Modern Womanhood in Cambridge would convey the same all-too-inflammatory message here.

In Bill's world, the woman you married would be as pure as your mother had been—and he had mourned his mother intensely. Bill would have it that his intended recapitulated his mother's virtues. She was entitled to expect a virgin, and he broke the bad news to her as soon as possible, before he lost his nerve. Never mind that his seduction technique with local girls had been not only rather successful, but rather calculating: day trips by rail to Manchester with their parents' permission, without chaperonage since no night away was involved. A brisk poke in an unshared compartment, with no fear—on a train without a corridor—of being seen. Getting into trouble precluded by a protective from Denbigh's leading dealer in rubber goods, a tradesman known to all as Lord Dunlop.

Impossible to go into these coarse details with someone of Sheila's refinement (whose railway-related adventures, by contrast, had tended to involve artificially missing the last train).

Nor did Sheila learn until much later that there had been a particular urgency in Bill's desire to get married. Looking at his hairbrush one day, he found it matted with shed fibres and convinced himself he was going rapidly bald. He was already thirty, after all, and his younger brother David had gone bald in his twenties (admittedly David had made matters worse by forever wearing a cap).

Bill thought he'd better get married, just to be on the safe side. Better get a girl down the aisle while there was still some thatch remaining. So he looked through his address book in search of women who were potentially marriageable, women in other words who had turned him down sexually. It wasn't much of a list.

If in fact Bill's hair had given him cause for concern, it must have been that he was going through some sort of seasonal moult. He continued to produce scalp fur in large quantities. Or perhaps it was that being married acted as a hair restorative. In later life Sheila, watching him brush it with daily devotedness, would experience a rueful twinge. Hospitalized for an intestinal abscess in 1995, Bill would sweetly ignore requests to do physiotherapy but would brush his hair for hours.

As a young man Bill was known for his charm. He played the guitar and would improvise comical calypsos at parties. At university (Aberystwyth and then Cambridge) he had done as much acting as studying: his advocacy was a professionally promising mixture of careful preparation and theatrical flair.

He seemed so very sure that he had found the right woman, and who was Sheila to say he was wrong? Her extroversion was a shadow of its former self after the Lilian years, and she would never find it easy to make the first move. With Bill she might never have to. Very early on in their relationship, Bill started relying on her to prompt his patchy memory, to remember the names and histories of his friends—including those she hadn't met. She experienced a twinge of irritation flooded out by the joy of being needed, a combination of emotions she recognized as promisingly marital.

If Bill's father had taken to Sheila despite Bill's fears, no such rapport could be expected between Bill and Lilian. Learning that Bill's father was a lifelong teetotaller, she wrote to him warning him that his son had a serious drinking problem. She did however agree, when this revelation seemed to have no effect on the proposed union, to take on the traditional duties of the bride's mother.

Her motive, though, was to sabotage them. She consented to Sheila's father attending, but Peggy received no invitation. The list of Bill's guests was firmly restricted.

Sheila trembled so badly during the ceremony that she thought everyone must notice. She was sure her wedding dress was shaking right down to its train. When the ceremony was safely over, and she arrived at the reception, a waiter offered her a mixed drink. Accepting, she asked what it was. The drink was so potent and so timely that it took away all her tension, but as it did so it took away also the name of this utterly necessary, utterly restoring drink. She was never able to remember what it was.

At the reception Bill's father, a teetotaller but not a fool, fixed Lilian in the eye while he drank a glass of champagne without visible distress. But perhaps the sparkling wine in his glass was changed, as he drank it, into untroubling water: a reversed miracle-at-Cana, reworked with abstainers in mind.

Sheila hated the photographs of herself at the wedding and destroyed them. She did however permit the pictures of the couple in going-away clothes after the reception to continue to exist.

The newly-weds honeymooned in Ireland. For the first time Sheila ate potatoes that had been boiled in their jackets, a simple pleasure. They went to the Abbey Theatre, a sophisticated one.

Bill had been in charge of the arrangements and had got the dates wrong, so the marriage got under way not in the intended suite, but in the only room their Dublin hotel had free for the first night: an attic room whose bed had comically squeaky springs. A bed like a prop in a bad farce, not the sort of theatrical fare for people who bought tickets for the Abbey.

On the way back from Ireland the two of them spent two nights with Bill's father and (fair's fair) two nights with Lilian.

Lilian however had moved from attempted sabotage to a sort of flailing revenge, and claimed back from Sheila every present she had given her over the previous decade and a half. There was a particularly undignified squabble over a pair of ice-skates that were too small for Sheila anyway, but had not become quite worthless to either party.

Lilian unleashed revenge on a new front by sending the invoices for the wedding and reception expenses to the groom. Bill got the bill. This was a particular imposition since the newly-weds' assets at the time of their marriage amounted to (this is the statutory phrasing) two briefcases, two umbrellas and a thousand-pound overdraft. As an index of the ominousness of that figure: the rent at Clare Court, their first home, was three pounds a week.

Bill had stayed with a friend for a few days before his wedding, learning how to cook. What he learned how to cook was bacon and eggs, which he prepared for Sheila on Sunday mornings in the first year of their marriage.

Despite everything, Sheila didn't cleanly break with Lilian. Perhaps she felt free enough of that influence to be magnanimous. Perhaps she was beginning, even, to feel pity. Lilian came to call while Bill was away on circuit and warned her fiercely of the danger she was in from poisoning. She must avoid eating anything that Bill had prepared or even touched.

Luckily one weekend Bill was so tired that Sheila cooked breakfast for him, and he never offered again. The danger of poisoning at his hands, never great, dwindled to nothing.

In the summer of 1949 Bill and Sheila took a holiday in Spain. Sheila was the linguist of the couple, but had only basic Italian to make stretch, so as to fit this rather different country. She had brought with her a new bathing suit which was smart by British standards but, as she saw on her first visit to the swimming beach, potentially a scandal in Franco's Spain. It wasn't remotely a bikini but it *was* a two-piece, and Fascist beachwear had not yet taken that path. The *señoras* chose to veil their mid-sections, while Sheila felt much more self-conscious about her (as she thought) knobbly knees than about her firm young midriff.

She felt less conspicuous when she was actually in the water, and undertook to teach Bill the long-overdue lesson of floating. Bill swam short distances with vigour, especially if women were watching, but had not yet learned to suppress the panic reflex that prevents relaxed floating, particularly when he was out of his depth. She tried to persuade him to put his trust in the basic unsinkability of the body.

Rather than run into town and buy a less challenging costume, Sheila and Bill decided the next day to find another beach. Sheila thought she had seen a party of nuns take to the water in the next bay. They would swim there. With them went a hotel acquaintance who had been a champion swimmer not so long ago.

The sea was rough, and thanks to the unfamiliar pleasure of being knocked off balance by big, brusque waves, they didn't immediately realize that they were being swept out and were out of their depth almost at once. As it turned out, the beach was notorious locally for its appetite, and the nuns glimpsed the day before were optical illusions, or else only paddling.

The hotel acquaintance resolved to swim back to shore and raise the alarm. Bill and Sheila needed only to stay afloat. They were soon separated in the water, however, and Sheila, knowing that floating was a very shallowly rooted skill in Bill's repertoire, gave him up for dead. Mentally she was widowed as she trod water in the heavy swell, waiting for death or rescue. She had time to absorb the full meaning of the phrase *lost at sea.*

The third member of the party managed with difficulty to reach the shore. He tried to explain the situation to the few people on the beach. One of them was a young man called Xavier Cremades who, as soon as he had understood, seized a child's inflatable boat—a tiny thing, only a toy—and charged into the water. He let himself be swept out in his turn, reasoning that this would bring him to the approximate position of the floundering English.

If Sheila had been visualizing rescue, it was not in the form of what looked like a teenager holding on to an inflated toy boat rather smaller than an air-bed. She had left her glasses with her towel and her book on the beach, but she had no difficulty seeing him approach. Her first thought was, What a clot! What a clot to be out in this sea with that cockleshell.

Then he swam up to her, and she realized that if this was a clot she should be thankful for it. He was nodding and smiling, having no English, and prevented from gesticulating by the need to hold on to the infant lifeboat. Sheila gestured wildly in all directions at the heaving sea, shouting hoarsely *Il marito!* This was Italian, and she conscientiously repeated her distress signal in what she hoped was the corresponding Spanish idiom: *el marido!* Xavier Cremades had understood the first time, and the two of them started to search together.

Of course he wasn't Xavier Cremades to her then, simply a figure as unlikely and as inherently sunlit as a boy on a dolphin.

Each of them now held on to the little boat, and when a swell lifted them briefly up they tried to stare at different sectors of what was revealed to them. Sheila's eyes were less sharp than Xavier's, but she had the advantage of having a clearer mental image of what they were looking for: his dear hair matted with seaweed, the view of his pale back under the water that would mean he had forgotten yesterday's lesson in floating.

Bill was actually only a little distance away, unconscious and blue in the face, but undeniably floating. Without being able to communicate verbally, Sheila and Xavier nevertheless managed a very tricky piece of manoeuvring. At this point the boat expands from its previously stated dimensions, and becomes big enough for a woman and a boy to heave an unconscious man on to. So be it. Or compromise by saying that what they were doing, despite the emphasis on *teamwork* and *heaving*, was closer to slipping the boat underneath Bill, with the same happy result of flotation.

Sheila didn't dare to hope that Bill would be all right, even now. She had no way of knowing how much water he had swallowed, but at least he was breathing. On he breathed. She wanted him to cough, to clear his lungs of what they had taken in, and she managed with Xavier's help to turn him face down so he could safely vomit. For any more ambitious rendering of first aid, the little boat would have had to go through another, more drastic expansion, to the size of the vessel that eventually rescued them, a ship of the Spanish navy.

Bill was the one who had been despaired of, but Sheila took much longer to recover. Bill after all had known nothing of being despaired of, while Sheila's despair as she trod water out of sight of land, her sense of being rescued from Lilian and then abandoned all over again, had been an overwhelming mental event.

Back in London, with Bill away on circuit, Sheila started to show the early symptoms of some sort of breakdown. She was prey to obsessional thoughts. Sitting on a bus, she would be aware of people looking at her oddly, and only then realize that she had been silently weeping for some considerable time.

Medical advice was sought on her behalf: her state of anxiety was diagnosed, perhaps unsurprisingly, as an anxiety state. Being given a description and a name for what she was experiencing did her some small good in itself. The suggestion was made that she was reliving, in an oblique way, the marine despair she had experienced before Xavier Cremades paddled into view, of which she had no direct memory. Time would bring a cure, time that steals all wounds.

It became increasingly difficult for Sheila to let Bill out of her sight, and for a while she stayed with him on circuit. Bill's professional life, though, with its institutionalized male camaraderie of Circuit Mess and Circuit Dinners, its heavy smoking and drinking and sessions of frantic preparation through the night, was essentially a bachelor zone in a married life, and Sheila couldn't indefinitely share it.

Her symptoms gradually abated, though she would always think of a time 'before Spain' and a time afterward, almost as if she had seen action with the International Brigade. The simmering of her brain as it cooled percolated through to her skin, and a few months after Spain she started to suffer from psoriasis. Stress is recognized to play a part in this condition. From then on her quest for clear skin took over from any direct quest for emotional peace. Over the years, she tried a number of remedies, from acupuncture and PUVA-plus-sunlamp to (in the 1970s) methotrexate, which proved the most effective treatment for a condition which was never as obvious to others as it was to her. But why is that always offered as a consolation? To say the same thing with a different emphasis: it was a condition that impinged on her sense of herself as much as it affected her dermis.

Sheila had never wanted children, partly because every baby whose pram she had ever leaned over lost no time in bursting into tears. Bill, however, had always made clear that he had a paternal destiny and wanted four sons. Eventually, after a few years of marriage, Sheila leaned over a friend's pram and was greeted with a gurgle rather than a howl. It seemed to her that a jinx had been lifted. Perhaps children of her own would gurgle too.

Though she had never wanted children, it hadn't occurred to Sheila that they wouldn't come when they were called. They tried. They monitored cycles and ringed dates in the calendar. On one occasion Bill was away on circuit, appearing in an important case, for almost the entirety of Sheila's time of ripeness. He would be cutting it fine. Never short of bravado or a lawyer's access to official favours, he arranged for a police car to meet his train at Paddington. The fretful sperm travelled under police escort as it went to meet the shivering egg.

Nothing worked. Every time they had 'tried' early in the day, Bill and Sheila would catch a show, hoping to cheer themselves up. But that year in the theatre the controlling metaphor of every play seemed to be infertility. Every time they sat down in the stalls, the curtain rose to show them a childless couple symbolizing the emptiness at the heart of modern life.

Bill took tests, and so did Sheila. She knew she had only one Fallopian tube, since the other had become gangrenous during her time as a Wren and been removed. Now it turned out that the other one was blocked. She had an operation, in which the tube was blown through. Having your tube blown through conjures up a mental image of something from an old-master painting, a bright Botticelli angel in surgical smock setting sexless lips to the reproductive trumpet, sounding the high true note of fertility. It sounds like an Annunciation under anaesthetic. The reality of the operation was presumably a little different, but she fell pregnant in 1952.

Bill had wanted four sons for no better reason than that in his Denbighshire childhood he had known a farming family with four sons which had seemed ideally happy. It didn't occur to him that this family's happiness might have had other sources than brute number and gender of offspring, or indeed that happiness for a farming family may require sons rather than daughters, as it need not for a metropolitan lawyer. He wanted four sons, and so did Sheila.

Babies carry a magnetic charge which can act unpredictably on their carers, and it seems unlikely that Bill and Sheila would have treated daughters with coldness. They maintained a slush pile of tolerable female names, in case: Victoria, Hilary, Zoë. But in the event Sheila bore a son in February 1953, another in October 1954 and a third in November 1957. After that her vindicated ovary rested on its laurels.

Sheila was morbidly afraid that she would drop her first-born, surprised that the nursing home allowed her to take him with her when she left. Shouldn't they have held on to him? They knew what to do. This must be a common fear in first-time mothers, but with Sheila the fear returned only slightly diminished with her second child and full force with her first grandchild. It seemed that she needed to convince herself every time from scratch that she was not going to drop or break this leaking treasure.

Early motherhood was the happiest time of Sheila's life, expressed by her in the formula *I knew what I was supposed to be doing*. From parenthood she had expected no enhancement of self, but that was what she experienced, or at the very least a lifting of conflict.

Her thirties and early forties were lived by Sheila as her prime. She had children and some help with them, au pairs at first foreign and later Welsh. She had a successful and devoted husband, who spent much time away, but who could be relied upon for a ritually caressive phone call at least once a day.

Soon before the birth of their first child she and Bill moved into 12 Gray's Inn Square; soon before the birth of their second they moved to a much larger flat opposite, at number three. Both rents were cushioned by Gray's Inn, which had yet to feel the vulgar necessity of getting the most out of its assets.

Gray's Inn had suffered considerable damage during the war. They were the first tenants of the new 3 Gray's Inn Square, rebuilt in a paraphrase of the original's Georgian style, and could even modify some of its specifications. Above the attics was the roof, which Sheila could reach up a ladder on sunny days so as to assuage her psoriasis with a tan. On one side the flat overlooked Gray's Inn Walks: Sheila lay in the bath when big with her second child, soon after moving in, and watched sunlight through mature, even overgrown, London planes. On the other side was Gray's Inn Square, also well planted with trees, where babies could be left in their prams with no closer watch kept on them than a mother's casual eye from three floors up.

In those days the ozone layer was as plump as a fresh pillow, though the aerosols that would dent and crease it were already proudly displayed in select bathrooms and kitchens, and sunlight was still considered good for babies. Ten minutes' walk away was Coram's Fields, with playground equipment and a marginally earthier social mix.

Ten minutes' walk in the other direction were Bill's chambers in the Temple, where Sheila's maiden name (under which she had practised) was also on the door. It was possible for her to think of herself as being in the informal sense 'out of practice'. Not that she missed the Bar and her inglorious career largely devoted to uncontested divorces.

Sheila hadn't practised for long. When novice lawyers stand up in court and speak they either experience a swelling of chest and voice and brain, an ability to fill the high-ceilinged space with compelling audible logic, or they remain exactly as they were before. She was the second type of lawyer, and realized that she would never know the barrister's joy of being given a red bag to replace her blue one. This is a ritual recognition by a Queen's Counsel of a junior's outstanding contribution to a significant case, but she knew it was something more: the blue bag changing colour as it leaves the alkaline environment of mediocrity.

She was better suited to law reporting, despite the mad rush to get copy to *The Times* at Printing House Square before five o'clock. She went back to law reporting for a term after the birth of her first son, until she was offered work she could do from home, sub-editing the *Weekly Law Report*. Her workload could be, within reason, contracted and expanded. She had passable shorthand and made her sons' eyes widen, when they were only a little beyond *the cat sat on the mat*, by demonstrating her favourite

Pitman hieroglyph, the expert arbitrary squiggle that meant *necessary*.

Her lull of fulfilment as a mother allowed Sheila a discreet expansion of personality. After driving the children to school she would make herself a cup of coffee and sometimes even feel that she deserved it. She was always tense in her pleasures, as if at any moment she might be told she hadn't earned them.

It took her many more years to throw off the conviction, instilled by Lilian, that reading for pleasure by daylight was immoral, and it required some steeling of nerve on her part to take up so much as a newspaper before sunset. But she signed up for dance lessons with Bill, who took with surprising agility to that not very Welsh dance, the tango. Only the bossa nova, when that became fashionable, flummoxed them with syncopation.

Sheila had no instinct for housework, but learned to run a household by a sustained act of will. In the end she was even able to derive a penitential satisfaction from a campaign of spring cleaning waged with the proper fierceness. One legacy of the war years was that she found it psychologically very difficult to throw food away and would hang on to an egg, for instance, if it had the slightest whiff of viability about it. The memory of scarcity carried over into something subtly different: a disbelief in abundance. Far from hoarding supplies, as might be expected from someone who had experienced years of rationing, she never acquired the habit of buying in bulk, preferring to shop every day long after supermarket habits had made inroads into the lives of the middle classes.

Sheila's neighbour and best friend, Cynthia, one of those 'best friends' whose differences are savoured as much as their similarities, loved running her home and expressed her personality in intensely feminine touches like the collection of little cats on her mantelpiece. Sheila so relaxed in these years that she felt it was legitimate for her too, career woman or no, to collect something ornamental. She decided on bulls rather than cats, not realizing that cows outnumber bulls on the market stalls of the world by thousands to one. Finding a bull she liked became a challenge in the short term and a minor annoyance in the long. Finally she changed the rules of her hobby so that anything quadruped and of bovine aspect was admitted.

In her continuing education, which she pursued strongly in these years, Sheila showed both an appetite for knowledge and a strain of masochism. The City Literary Institute (City Lit) was ten minutes' walk away from Gray's Inn and offered tuition in a huge variety of subjects. Yet over the years Sheila tended to choose classes that would make her feel slightly inadequate—not French conversation but French grammar; not a continuation of long-ago piano lessons but a grounding in harmony and counterpoint. Why brush up on a Chopin prelude when you can be notating a juicy retrograde inversion? She seemed to be seeking a sort of mortification of the intellect by this recurring impulse to take a course too far.

It was as if she needed to prove to her own satisfaction that she wasn't really all that brainy, and consequently that she wasn't wasting herself in the life she had. When she started studying Welsh, she not only set herself to running the gauntlet of that language's notoriously difficult consonantal mutations, but found an area of study where she would always by definition perform less well than the native speaker she had married.

Bill and Sheila and their sons spent the famously idyllic summer of 1959 in Rhosneigr, a village on the west coast of Anglesey. Rhosneigr with its beaches and sunshine seemed to offer an even more propitious setting for the happiness of children than Gray's Inn with its square and its gardens, and the next year Bill used his inheritance from his father, who had died some little time before, to buy a house a short way outside the village. The white house he chose (always called the White House, with no presidential irony and no recourse to Welsh) had the great advantage of being separated from the main road by an extensive common, so there was a strict limit on development in the immediate area. Fourteen steps led down to the beach. In September gales, spray would blow from the breakers to strike the kitchen windows with considerable force.

The sea. One day in the early sixties Sheila was swimming with her two older sons, while Bill rolled up the trouser legs of his Prince of Wales-check suit to paddle. Suddenly Sheila saw that her boys were swimming out of their depth. As she reached them, she realized that she was barely in her own, and where she put her feet down they met not sand but rock.

She then managed the difficult task of grabbing her children and half-swimming, half-wading with them to safety. She wanted to alert Bill to a crisis without letting the boys know this was anything but a game. And in fact they had no sense of danger in the water, although they were marked with different memories of the event. One son, looking down, was mesmerized by the sight of Mother's blood swirling thinly from a gash on Sheila's leg. The other, looking to shore, was awed by the sight of his father rushing fully clothed into the water. It was only Bill's willingness to endanger his Prince of Wales-check suit, and the sodden banknotes from his wallet which dried out slowly on a radiator for the rest of the day, that made the swim seem to contain anything momentous.

If Bill and Sheila collaborated on rescue that day they were not always so secure in their teamwork. Every generation should have at least one complaint, properly filed and docketed, against the one that went before. That's good form. It prevents bad feeling. The complaint of her sons would have to be that Sheila's hatred of confrontation led her to accept a discrepancy in disciplinary styles.

She didn't punish physically, and Bill did. Bill's punishment normally had the spontaneity that is its excuse or mitigation, but he sometimes fell back into a lawyer's habits. He might cross-examine, looking for inconsistencies, and in the face of denial he would gather evidence. By the time punishment came to be delivered, there was a coldness to it, made worse by his saying, 'This is for hurting your mother,' when the sons knew that if she was there she would extend her mercy.

Between them Bill and Sheila wrote a script by which the male parent acquired a certain vengefulness. Indirectly therefore they also shaped their sons' particular versions of the sentence starting 'If I have children I will never ever . . . ', and often running to many thousands of clauses, which constitutes the mental life of a teenager. A sentence like the tie-breaking slogan for a newspaper competition.

Sheila's hatred of atmospheres could sometimes prevent her

from intervening. Otherwise her life offers no support for a trickle-down theory of trauma. In general the damage done to her trickled down only into herself and wasn't allowed to spill out over others. Is it a characteristic of women as opposed to men, or of the abused as against the respected, that they absorb injuries rather than pass them on as they should? Great abuse, of course, breaks the pattern by exceeding any power to absorb.

In 1969 Bill, after an escalating series of recorderships (Birkenhead, Swansea, Cardiff), was made a High Court judge. Such an appointment carries with it a knighthood. Bill glowed with prestige and talked sweetly to Sheila about having made a Lady of her at long last.

Sheila was wary about having a title, often too shy to include it when asked her name. She was moving now in a world of compliments and stylized attention for which nothing in her background had prepared her. Lilian had not used compliments; she preferred the other weapon. Sheila came to assume that most of the attention she was receiving was either mildly or intensely false, and greeted it with a smile of blankness. One of the things she enjoyed about the winter-sports holidays in Austria which the family took at this period was that social life *après*-ski for once had no connection with legal London and its tortuous skirmishings.

In her forties Sheila undertook two small pieces of editing on herself: she deleted her glasses and she rephrased her nose. She had already tried contact lenses rather earlier in their technical development, when they covered the entire eyeball and gave those who could tolerate them a permanently startled expression. Sheila had not been one of those who could tolerate them for more than a few minutes at a time, but now that lenses had shrunk to a corneal discreetness she was more successful.

The decision to have an operation on her long-hated nose was mildly unusual in her social circle at that time. But then her motives too were unusual. She wasn't trying to make herself attractive to a new audience, or even an old one. The decision hardly involved other people at all, but it wasn't slackly narcissistic. Sheila was engaged on a rather effective exercise in what would now be called something like self-esteem management.

She rid herself of neurosis about her body the way squirrels rid themselves of ticks.

Squirrels, supposedly, pull out a tuft of fur and hold it above their heads while they wade happily into a river. It may help to imagine them holding their noses with the other little hand, as the water rises round their heads. Understandably the ticks swarm upwards on to the decoy tuft. The submerged squirrel then simply flings away the tuft, and regains the safety of the bank. The infestation is over.

Sheila focused her self-hatred on her nose and then flung it away. Her new nose wasn't even quite what she had specified, which had been something jauntily snubby (*tip-tilted* was the word she used), but she had no regrets. The new nose was *not* her nose. That was its virtue and justification. Passing a mirror, she could meet her eyes without rancour.

In May 1973, leaving Moorfields Eye Hospital at the foot of Shaftesbury Avenue where she had been doing voluntary work, Sheila made a small dent in a Ford Transit van. The van made a much larger dent in her.

It was a rainy day with a wind, and Sheila may have held her umbrella in such a way that she could not see the approach of the van, released from the traffic lights nearby and bounding towards her. She was certainly much preoccupied at that time with the fate of her best friend Cynthia, who was suffering from a bone disease. These contributory factors have to be reconstituted artificially, since she had no memory of being struck. Like her despair at sea, these were some of the many moments that go missing from a life; missing but immense, the amnesias of ecstasy and accident.

An ambulance was called to take her to the Middlesex Hospital not far off. Sheila was alert enough to give a name when asked for one, but not quite alert enough to give the right one. The name she gave seems to have belonged to the last person she talked to, during her morning stint of wheeling round the trolley of cassette players and books on tape.

At the hospital, she was booked in under the name she had given and was X-rayed. No one, however, looked with any attention at the resulting plates, so it was not noticed that she had suffered a comminuted fracture at the base of the skull.

Comminuted is posh for *like a little jigsaw*. There was only one superficial injury to the scalp, so they sewed that shut. In the process they sewed hair into the wound, which subsequently became infected.

Of all the professionals through whose hands she passed that afternoon, it is only the ambulance men who emerge with any credit as diagnosticians. They at least realized that this was a woman who wouldn't be in good shape any time soon, and wouldn't be asking any awkward questions about the disappearance of her earrings.

Sheila's medical problems didn't end with the little jigsaw of skull fractures. There was also the question of the contrecoup injury. The brain suffers when a sharp blow causes it to strike the side of the skull away from the impact. The brain suffers.

Sheila's first bit of good luck that day was that an acquaintance, who had also done some voluntary work at Moorfields, was told by the staff there that her friend had been knocked down and was now in the Middlesex. Someone therefore turned up at the hospital who was able to clear up the question of the name, and also to sit with Sheila long enough to realize that she wasn't merely shocked and confused but seriously ill. The pressure of blood in the brain was building up to a dangerous extent. She was beginning to have small stroke-like seizures on one side of her body.

From this point on her luck changed abruptly. At last the X-rays were looked at properly, and John Firth, a brain surgeon with an experimental technique, was alerted for duty. Messages could finally be sent to Bill in court in Cardiff, and relayed by him to the sons at their various educational establishments.

John Firth operated for five hours. He was a good surgeon, so good in fact that he dreamed of something better. Subsequently he stood as Parliamentary candidate for the constituency of Orkney.

He had already started operating by the time any family member was able to attend. The technique he used involved removing an area of bone and refrigerating it for later reinsertion. In the meantime the brain would be able to expand after its trauma, and if there was a complication there would be no need to cut healing bone all over again. From the point of view of an era of keyhole surgery, this seems more like barn-door surgery, but it was state-of-the-art in its day. One of the first things that Bill was told by John Firth, when he arrived, was that this was a good time to have a neglected comminuted fracture of the skull and consequent subdural haemorrhage. A few years ago there would have been no hope, and he had used a new ventilation technique which allowed him to operate for longer, and so be more thorough.

Even so, he wasn't exactly optimistic—to the extent that anyone wearing rubber gloves stained with the blood of a man's wife can communicate optimism to him. Sheila might recover physical mobility and mental power; she might lose either, or both.

In fact her recovery was good. Sheila's first gesture on regaining consciousness, even before she had taken in what exactly had happened to her, was to reach a hand up to her nose. It was safe, it was still there; the new improved nose, the nose she could live with. Only then did her hand go further up, to explore the alien headdress of the plaster cast that now protected her head.

The trapdoor of bone from her head was kept in a fridge for six weeks, then reinserted. In a separate operation, the little area of bone that had gone septic after hair was sewn into her wound was cut out.

In a way, when she reached her hand up that first waking day in hospital and met the firm reassuring prow of her chosen nose, what she felt was a mirage. In a manner of speaking, her nose was missing and didn't come back. Sometimes it seemed that doctors could do anything these days, that they could open an inspection hatch in the brain and knot the dangling wires together, but they couldn't bring her nose back. They couldn't do that. Her nose was dead, or at best in a coma.

Whether because the sensing fibres had been flattened by the van's impact, or because the area of the brain that interpreted their signals had been closed down while the blood pressure built up unnoticed, Sheila never smelt anything again, not fresh bread nor burning hair. The technical term for this is anosmia. Strange: loss of sight or hearing are privileged with an Anglo-Saxon term, while loss of smell remains in Greek, as if this was a rather fancy deprivation. Never mind that smell is the most basic sense, the one that crouches lowest in the brain.

Her sense of smell was the only absolute loss from the

accident, and a good bargain by any standards, compared with how her prospects were announced on the night of the operation. She had sustained damage to the trigeminal nerve that runs down the side of the face, and it was a long time before the neural frazzling settled down, giving her relief from adjacent areas of numbness and a tingly distorted sensitivity.

Her hair grew back from its pre-operative shearing, though less curly than before and perhaps less full—but then few women of fifty (an age she reached a few months after the accident) are natural casting for Rapunzel. She had kept the shape of her chosen nose, losing only its function. Yet loss of nasal function is not nothing.

The structural logic of perception dictates that if you are nose-blind, nose-deaf, then you are palate-impaired, 'hard of tasting' as people are said to be hard of hearing. You may sense only the basic categories of taste as they are exemplified by what is actually in your mouth. What happens on your palate is no longer vivid dinner, but your taste buds attempting a slightly muzzy after-dinner game, a round of charades. Spice or condiment, two syllables, let's see, garlic? Ginger?

This was a period in which brain surgeons were just beginning, while talking to relatives of those on whom they had operated, tentatively to invoke comparisons with computers. In 1973 when even a major hospital such as the Middlesex had no great investment in hardware, and private individuals were even less familiar with the subject, to say that a brain was like a computer was to make a rather abstract statement, but at least it might convey the information that an injured brain heals differently from a broken leg. Bill was told that with luck Sheila, though technically brain-damaged, would retain her skills and her memories. Important 'files' of memory in damaged tissue would somehow be transcribed, in the weeks to come, on to fresh pages of the mind. The word 'file' sounded old-fashioned, even bureaucratic; it had yet to take on a modern overtone. It suggested tall cabinets of olive-green metal.

It was likely that Sheila's short-term memory would be impaired—the idea seemed to be that it would get squeezed out by the demands of all that transcription—though the prognosis overall was remarkably good.

Sheila gingerly took the morning sunlight in the little hidden garden of the hospital. During those early days and early nights, dozing or solidly asleep, Sheila was visited by marvellously humdrum dreams. She dreamed entire days of inconsequence, from morning tea to evening toothbrush, while her brain absorbed the fact of damage.

The transcription was certainly accomplished, but there were perhaps hidden costs. Sheila was bound to feel more anxious about her mental quickness. No one to whom the label of brain damage has been attached will venture into conversation without subliminal hesitation: am I talking sense, am I even using language? Perhaps I'm talking in numbers, and people are only pretending to understand out of politeness, or for their own reasons.

After 1973 Sheila would become unduly anxious about the pronunciation of disputed words, words like *controversy*, *decade* or indeed *dispute*. At moments of trivial stress she would run out of words altogether and resort to a small handful of coinages, so that *I've spilt a bit of wine on the carpet* came out *I've spoobed a bit on the doo-dah-day*.

She had never had much taste for the sort of film or play that keeps you guessing, for suspense of any ambitious kind, but after 1973 indifference turned to positive aversion. All it took was one plot twist or unexplained development, and she would defensively withdraw her attention, convinced that in her stupidity she had missed something vital which would make the entire plot clear to everyone else in the world.

She found it harder to make decisions, particularly about trivial questions. She would spend what felt like absurd amounts of time deadlocked about stupid things, like what to prepare for dinner, as if a marble in her mind was going round and round, never able to settle in the slot marked Chop or Fish.

The experience of denting a van, and being dented in her turn, wrenched Sheila out of her generation. It foreshortened her sense of priorities, so that she found anything short of physical trauma relatively hard to get worked up about. For this reason she became a more indulgent parent. Let them smoke, let them fool around, so long as they look both ways before they cross the road: that was more or less her attitude. Yet survival also made her feel worthless.

Cynthia's illness didn't let up. She and her husband and son came to stay in Anglesey during the summer after the accident. Sheila insisted on being ready for this, but it couldn't be anything but a strain on her, even before Cynthia walked unseeing into a sliding glass door and broke one of the glass bones in her arm. She was taken to the Caernarvon and Anglesey Hospital, the C and A, known locally (alas) as the Cremations and Amputations, where the bell pull by her bed intended to summon the nurses made no sound.

Later that summer Sheila, out walking with Bill in Rhosneigr village and despairing of expressing her feelings of inadequacy, knowing that it was terrible ingratitude for recipients of miraculous reprieves from death or brain-death not to love their lives, broke away from him and tried to throw herself in front of a car. She discovered that road accidents don't always come when they're called, any more than children do. The car was going at no great pace and swerved without even coming close. Sheila ran down to the beach, but Bill followed her, and in due course they returned together to the house.

It was medically suggested that what Sheila's brain needed, to shake it out of the depression that seemed to have followed from so much transcription, was a course of electric-shock treatment. Obediently she paid weekly visits to Queen Square, where the attempt was made to expel her low feelings with high voltage. The theory of ECT is easily stated: there isn't one. It is simply a practice, one devised to capitalize on a discovery made in the 1940s, that epileptics don't get depressed. Depressives, therefore, should be enabled to reap the benefits of epilepsy. Counterfeit fits were provoked originally by means of saline injections, before the superiority of electricity was established.

Sheila would come to herself piecemeal, in fuzzy instalments, and would make efforts to leave without an escort, though Bill or a son was invariably on the way to pick her up. Having her brain struck by tame lightning had the temporary effect of simplifying her mental operations, so that she had no idea, when she came round, that she was the sort of person that people looked after and cared for.

On the other hand her mind, even at its most smooth-running, had trouble entertaining such a cosy idea. This was in fact precisely the state of affairs that electro-convulsive therapy was in some way supposed to remedy.

ECT was a mixed success at best. Since it further scrambled Sheila's short-term memory over the period of the treatment, she could never know whether to believe Bill's assurances that she was getting better week by week, shock by shock. She didn't have much to go on. She knew her husband well enough to understand that he liked problems that could be solved quickly, and depressives who could be cheered up with a single dose of his energy. He didn't enjoy being patient except for short bursts. Her misery would end up undermining and exasperating him.

Cynthia Terry died in 1974, and in so doing fixed the certainty in Sheila's mind that the wrong woman had survived. Hadn't Cynthia loved life, as Sheila never quite managed to do? Sheila spent increasing amounts of mental time in a sort of agonizing parallel universe, in which Cynthia stoutly recovered, while Bill in due time put aside his bereavement and married a Nice Ordinary Woman, who was good to Sheila's sons.

Thinking about the world better off without her, following through into the future her fantasy of family life soothed by her death, was both a temptation and a torture, an addiction. A perversion.

Only someone with a strong streak of self-abasement, a chronically lowered sense of self, could have wished on her children that thing from which she had so much suffered, a stepmother.

It was during this period that Sheila remarked to her least effusive son that she was glad he at least wasn't a sentimentalist, and would turn off her life-support without a second thought. She was quite taken aback when he reacted with dismay. There was no irony intended: she had meant it as a compliment.

If this was a time of interior collapse, it was also somehow a time of self-reconstruction. Sheila put into action a plan that predated her accident, and applied to be the chairman of a rent-assessment panel. Her legal background qualified her for the job, which would be part-time—two days a week, say, plus the appropriate preparation. It was also a whole new area of work, with every possibility of the slowness and confusion she found in herself, her general inadequacy confirmed by the accident, being shown up. Perhaps it was best to know for sure, one way or the other.

In fact she was a quietly spectacular success in the role. Her legal qualifications were indispensable, but what the job chiefly called for was patience and tact. The diffidence of Sheila's authority was underpinned by the fact that, after the accident, she was never altogether convinced of the accuracy of her arithmetic or her reading of the law. She was always open to correction or second thoughts.

The offices of the Assessment were in Newlands House, just across Mortimer Street, as it happens, from the Middlesex Hospital. The recovery that had got under way at the Middlesex, after its false start, was furthered by the bureaucracy on the other side of the street.

She enjoyed the work, with its starchy camaraderie: the duties expected of the chairman included buying drinks for the other panel members in a pub at lunchtime. The real rare pleasure of the job was being allowed into people's homes and being warmly invited to inspect them. Having people point out defects or improvements with a touching frankness and deference.

Every now and then a rent-assessment panel was called upon to inspect premises occupied by someone self-neglecting or demented. On those occasions Sheila's mild poise was much remarked on by her fellow members. No degree of disarray in living quarters shook her. No stench seemed able to make an impact. They complimented her on the seamlessness of her self-control, while she permitted herself a faint anosmic smile.

In the private life of her anosmia, Sheila didn't give up the use of perfume. She was unwilling to do without the rituals of fragrance, reassurance that goes beyond the sensual. She successfully controlled the impulse to anoint herself more freely—the delusion that an extinct faculty might somehow be triggered by sheer excess of stimulus.

Still she had a sense of frustration whenever a new perfume was launched. She didn't want to be trapped in the past by the subtle feminine carbon dating of scent, stubbornly attached to her old faithfuls, Balmain's *Vent Vert*, Guerlain's *Chant d'Arôme*, when everyone else had moved on. A new advertising campaign would quicken her mental nostrils and make her curious, unless it was for an obviously inappropriate scent, something sultry or saccharine.

Sometimes she would buy the smallest possible bottle of something announced as fresh or citric, dab a tiny bit on, and then do what women without daughters or female intimates must do. Ask a man.

The men in her family would try with their snuffling male noses and their small vocabularies of sensation to inform her. Bill would say she smelt wonderful, but then he always said that, and his marriage-long inability to spot a new item of clothing unless it was pulled out of a smart carrier bag made him a suspect witness. Her boys were little better, struggling to be honest, but baffled by even elementary principles of perfumery: that essences smell differently on different skins, that treble notes evanesce and bass ones linger.

The boys were more reliable when she held a vest or a pair of Bill's socks under their noses and asked whether these items needed washing. The doggy binary of fresh against stinky: that they could manage.

So why did she never have second thoughts about the son-heaviness of her family? The sonniness of Bill's temperament at least has a story to back it up—the fable of the four happy farming brothers. Sheila's falling in with the fable has no story of its own. And wouldn't it have been nice for her, if not at first then later, to have a gender ally in the home?

The only obvious possibility—and it is thoroughly obvious, as flat and pat as a newspaper think piece—is that historically it was women who had damaged Sheila: Gladys by desertion, Lilian by imposition. It was men, historically, who had rescued her: Xavier Cremades (toast him in sherry), John Firth (toast him in Scotch). Even, somehow, the toastmaster himself. Even Bill.

Bill was proud of Sheila's recovery and liked to invite her down to Judges' Lodgings to show her off. Sheila didn't mind too much, except when she cancelled an evening class, took a train down to Bodmin or Norwich or Carlisle and then had to sit at the dinner table and listen to Bill saying how wonderfully clever she was, how she was always studying something arty, linguistic or musical, if not all three.

Sheila received a lot of complimentary attention at these dinners, as on most formal occasions, but she had long since learned to neutralize it mentally. She reasoned that in an Ancient and Honourable Society like Gray's Inn, so closely tied to a hierarchical profession, deference was poured so freely over a High Court judge that some of it slopped on to his lady wife—just as tea sometimes spills from teacup to saucer. Bill lapped it up, but she felt she knew better. Nothing she heard was actually about her.

As a wife she realized that she had an obligation to be a good sport on these occasions and didn't mind putting on the glad rags once in a while. She would even have her hair done, something she hated, before she left London. She was convinced that she had virtually no hair left, just as anorexic teenagers imagine themselves saddled with jodhpurs of cellulite. Sheila was a trichological anorexic, a trichorexic. She couldn't bear to see her hair in the mirror.

There weren't all that many consolations of later life, or so Sheila found, but one unexpected one was that you could dress entirely for your own pleasure, now that nobody minded one way or the other. She liked the style of dress required by her work, which she interpreted as being *crisp* but not *cold.* It was no great effort to combine black and white, clean lines and the occasional flirty detail, so as to end up with ensembles that were professional, but not unfriendly.

Even when she wasn't working she gravitated towards a style of dress that was somewhere between formal and informal. She favoured some third state between rigour and casualness, something neither chilly nor gushy. She had never suited either flatties or stilettos—for her it must always be a medium heel. Her clothes were never meant to intimidate anyone, but they played their part in helping her to stay in control of herself, whatever she felt like really.

Sheila was brave enough to resume working for Moorfields on Monday mornings, despite the painful associations with her past, her personal Accident Black Spot invisibly marked on the road metal. In the late seventies the Shaftesbury Avenue branch of the hospital closed down, and Sheila volunteered at Old Street instead.

Indefatigably she pushed the trolley of talking books, trying to wean people off trash, in an interlude of blindness that might even be merciful in this respect, without directly refusing them what they wanted. So if someone asked for a romance, Sheila would think, well, quite a lot of books are romances when you think about it. Surely listening to *Rebecca* had to be more enjoyable than the tired old clip-clop of something from the Cartland stable?

Her slimness, and the vigour with which she pushed the trolley, deceived some of the patients into thinking they were being served by a much younger woman. Sensing a lithe displacement of air, men would inhale appreciatively and be greeted by a fresh and citric scent, difficult to place.

Sheila's flexibility and energy were notable—but then her Aunt Dot, at that time in her nineties, was proud of her sit-ups. Aunt Dot had been a dance teacher; she couldn't walk, but she could do sit-ups. Sheila went ice-skating regularly, at Queens Club in Queensway, at long last conquering her instinctive fear of going backwards on the ice. On summer holidays in Anglesey, she remained the family's water-skiing star, even getting the knack of the mono ski.

She could have gone on water-skiing for hours, if it wasn't for the numbness in her fingers. All her life her extremities had been susceptible to cold, so that her fingers went white when she so much as washed a summer salad. Her system had no sense of proportion. It would interpret a sinkful of lettuce and tomatoes as the leading edge of an arctic tempest, requiring emergency measures, the hoarding of blood near the heart.

The principal indignity of the menopause, from her point of view, was having hot flushes that did nothing to warm her fingers and toes. At work when there were inspections to be done in weather that was less than balmy, she learned to use a little hand-warmer bought from a camping and survival shop. A tablet ignited at the beginning of the working day and laid carefully inside the little case would keep her hands functioning for hours. If the tablet ran out, on the other hand, she would have to spend ages bringing her fingers agonizingly back to life in warm water.

Eventually the tendency to numbness was diagnosed as Raynaud's Phenomenon, giving Sheila another support-group publication to subscribe to, along with the anguished bulletins from Compassion in World Farming and the encouraging updates in her psoriasis newsletter. Psoriasis was beginning to yield to science over this period, first to PUVA, a combination of sensitizing pill and sun-ray lamp, and finally to the drug methotrexate, despite its whispered carcinogenic reputation. Sheila could adjust the dosage to keep lesions at bay.

Science was slower in getting to grips with depression. Whatever medication she was taking during these years, there was a part of Sheila that permanently identified with the abused calves shown in the Compassion in World Farming literature. Seeing herself as veal, atrociously blanched and tender.

While Bill lived in the present, almost to a fault, supremely confident that he was making provision for the years ahead, Sheila lived in the most dismal of futures, imagining eventualities that she felt she could do nothing to prevent. More than ever she felt there was a stroke in her head, waiting to pounce, and knowing her luck, she'd hang on for years unable to speak, trying to close her lopsided mouth round a soup spoon.

At the same time her mind ran obsessively over the past, telling her that she had started with a good hand of cards but had somehow thrown them all away, letting all her advantages come to nothing. The fault was not in the deal, but in the play. If she could only think her way back to the exact point where she had gone wrong, she could . . . what? She would know, that was all, and perhaps she'd be able to live with the knowledge. She reached back mentally into the past, beyond the accident, as far as Lilian, but she could never quite fix the moment of failure.

The house in Anglesey, associated though it was with the heyday of motherhood, was becoming a problem and a burden. Sheila's sons gave no hint of reproductive ambition, and it wasn't that she was in any hurry to be a grandmother. But the logic of a holiday home by the sea fell down if there wasn't a breeding population of Mars-Joneses, a supply of small people to furnish the place appropriately with laughter and abandoned sandy swimsuits. She was afraid of the White House becoming a white elephant.

Already there were times when she and Bill were there alone, and she looked with a sinking feeling from the chop on her dinner plate to the chop on his. How was it possible to have a sinking feeling when your feelings were a sink in the first place? She felt she was getting, not a holiday, but a prophecy of retirement. She noticed that sons didn't visit casually, spontaneously, but in pairs. Their visits had become dutiful, and perhaps there was even a system in operation, of coordinating phone calls to make sure that no son was ever there on his own with those uninteresting people, parents.

She told Bill that she didn't want to retire to Anglesey. He didn't disagree—out of season the island could be bleak—but Sheila wasn't able to make any positive suggestion about the years to come. It was retirement itself she dreaded, the dreary horror of her future.

In 1981 the decision was made to sell the White House, though to the extent that the debate over the house had been a debate about how to handle retirement, no progress had been made. Still, holidays for Sheila (on cruise ships to warm places with ruins and lectures) were now authentic exemptions from running a house, and that was certainly an improvement.

Bill invested the proceeds of the sale in stocks and shares, but in captivity the money could not be persuaded to breed and slowly pined away. The market collapse in 1987 was only the clincher, after which the money lay on its back in the cage, stiff paws in the air.

A curious feature of Sheila's depression had always been that it contained no element of lethargy. She had plenty of energy, but it brought her no satisfaction. She was very struck by the term 'anhedonia', meaning the inability to experience pleasure, when she read that this had been the original title of the film *Annie Hall*, and determined to memorize it. From the time that she had been told that the learning of new words was the hardest task she could impose on a traumatized brain, she had become something of a bulimic of vocabulary.

How to combat anhedonia? One idea was to go to a therapist, specifically a Jungian, since this school of psychology seemed less obsessed with damage than most. She was estranged from her own vitality, that was what was the matter with her, and being united with your own vitality sounded like an orthodox

Jungian goal. In practice, though, the sessions yielded little, and if her therapist was at one with his vitality he did a good job of concealing it.

Perhaps the mind and spirit could be reached through the body? She enrolled in a yoga class, feeling that she should take advantage of a flexibility unusual in a sixty-year-old. She had no difficulty with the exercises, but found the experience anything but transcendent. One particular thing she found unable to transcend was the fear that the individual mats used in the class, sometimes warm and damp from a previous session, were actively smelly. Not being able to verify her suspicions directly and having an anosmic's natural horror of the undetectably unclean, she felt more than ever entrapped in her body and her negative emotions.

Early in 1985 Sheila realized that she had unaccountably fallen behind in her programme of screening for breast cancer. She was months late. When she duly arranged an appointment, a lump was announced. She agreed to surgery, which revealed that the lump had indeed been a novice malignancy.

The men around her, simple souls, argued that if she really wanted to be dead she would hardly have taken measures, however belated, to preserve herself. But Sheila was not so easily to be tricked into manifesting a life wish. She knew perfectly well she would survive, worse luck, she just didn't want to be any more maimed than could be helped. Health was a lottery, and she was only interested in the jackpot. Nothing else would do.

Her life was no more than an old plate for her, but if she was going to be denied the satisfaction of going properly smash, she would choose to have the smallest possible number of cracks.

The surgery was successful and the disfigurement insignificant. She found she didn't think about it. Again, she had a short-term preoccupation, as she had in the Middlesex in 1973 when she had reached for her hard-won nose. Would she be able to continue taking methotrexate, or would psoriasis start to win all over again? That was what she wanted to know.

In the event there was no objection, as long as she continued with regular liver biopsies. She was punctilious with these appointments, at least, and never missed one.

If Sheila had few expectations of motherhood, she had none of grandmotherhood. It was only another form of retirement, really, a genetic redundancy notice. Yet when it came, she took a pleasure in it that became in time intense. At last the family's notional Welshness came in handy: Sheila would be called *Nain* (pronounced Nine), Bill *Taid* (Tide), and these toddler-friendly monosyllables would give them an automatic advantage over Grandmothers and Grandfathers. Gray's Inn Walks proved an undiminished asset, and the playground in Coram's Fields re-emerged as a resource after thirty years. There was even some new equipment.

When she retired from the Rent Assessment, after twenty years, she was given a party—something that even Sheila couldn't quite dismiss as an empty gesture, since no retiring chairman in her time had been honoured in this way.

Bill had retired in 1990, with an agenda of virtually torrential self-expression: he would perfect his neglected guitar-playing. Memoirs and plays would pour from him. He had the titles ready. When a couple of years down the line Sheila shyly enquired what had become of all the creativity, he replied that he was catching up on a backlog that had built up during those long and stressful years at the Bar and on the bench. This as he explained it was a backlog of idleness, and would take an indefinite time to clear up.

He had remained in harness as long as he could, which means seventy-five in the case of High Court judges, so perhaps he too was dreading retirement, though he was not a man who could be made to own up to dreading anything, on either side of the grave.

Husband and wife had in common a religious background, but Bill was the one with the religious conviction, though he called it, unembarrassed, blind faith. He never seemed to pray and was less than fanatical about church attendance.

Sheila had more doubts than convictions, religiously, but could not go to bed without spending time on her knees praying. She was unable to pray in any other position. But then it was the same with teeth: Bill rarely brushed but expected dental salvation, while Sheila wrestled nightly with cutting-edge floss technology, international products available only from John Bell and Croyden in Wigmore Street, since her teeth were too closely set to allow proper access to standard equipment. And still she lived in fear of the hell of dentures.

There was no retirement age for helpers at Moorfields, thank God, and there was also the possibility of new voluntary work. Sheila offered her services (and the benefit of her legal training) to a charitable organization called Access to Justice, conveniently located in High Holborn. Which got her out of the house another half-day a week.

Over the years, Sheila's discreet death wish held out against a whole series of medication regimes. When her GP asked her how she was, she would find herself saying she was all right. It saved trouble, and one of the words she had committed to memory after the accident—*endogenous*, as applied to her type of depression—made her think that medication wasn't really going to make a difference. She took the pills obediently, though sometimes when she felt woolly she would taper down the doses, until she reached the point of wanting nothing better than to feel woolly again.

She wasn't melodramatic about wanting to be dead and she normally knew better than to blurt it out. Whenever she particularly liked a piece of music, she would say that she wanted it played at her funeral, but that was as far as it went, and she smiled when it was pointed out to her that her funeral was turning into a music festival lasting many days.

Still, in the early nineties, when she was explaining why she had an irrational resistance to selling the car, she let something slip. Bill's decreasing mobility made taxis much more practical, after all. She could see the logic. Finally she admitted the basis of her affection for the vehicle. She had made the decision to keep Bill company while he was alive, but after that she was a free woman, and she was reasonably sure she could do the job with the car. She had no faith in pills, one way or the other.

The moment she had spoken she regretted the bafflement and pain she had caused, and guilt made her agree to see the doctor again. She managed to seem reasonably enthusiastic, even, doing her mime of hope, and this time, out of family loyalty, she didn't say she felt all right when the doctor asked how she was.

She had slim hopes of predeceasing Bill. The closest thing she had to true self-destructive behaviour was her continuing cigarette habit, but her consumption of tobacco had risen and fallen in a bell curve across the decades, since the days when smoking had been an aromatic declaration of independence. After her accident might have been a sensible time to stop, except that those who lose their sense of smell forfeit one of the positive motivations for kicking the habit. Carrying on with her smoking was one of the few faintly defiant aspects of her recovery.

By the early nineties she was down to three Silk Cut Extra Mild a day. It was less of a crime against herself than a homeopathic tincture of nicotine. Sons would tease her by telling her not to forget to smoke. Saying goodnight, they would remind her that she still had one cigarette to get through before bedtime, to be sure not to skip it.

When she gave up at last, she was spared from the dismal fate of being a person without vices by a sudden passion for plain chocolate digestive biscuits. Her most recent anti-depressant medication increased her appetite, but this was different. It was the first time she had actively craved something sweet since her childhood love affair with treacle tart. She described her taste for the odd chocky bicky in terms of compulsive behaviour, as if she'd be throwing herself down the staircase of Kensington Palace next.

If this was a binge, it was a binge in extreme slow motion, impossible to spot amid the entrenched moderation of her habits. She showed no signs of swelling back up from her wiry size eight (six or even smaller in the puzzlingly inflated American sizing) to the buxom size twelve she had been the day she married.

This after all was a woman with a passion for strong Cheddar who for years restricted herself to the placebo cheese Edam, and that in small quantities, for fear of elevating her level of cholesterol. Perhaps the austere binge on biscuits was only a letting up of anhedonia in one particular area, a reacquaintance with the basics of pleasure as pleasure-lovers experience it.

Sheila's vision had clouded over during the eighties, to the point where actors were fuzzy angels even from the front stalls of a theatre. She was told that she could have her cataracts removed more or less when she wanted, but she chose to wait until after retirement. She couldn't bear to give up even a day of work while she was still entitled to it. That way too she could have one thing to look forward to after being put out to grass. She would be able to see in full, crisp detail the dreary paddock of her life.

There was a bad moment, during one operation, when she felt a flat click inside her head and heard the laser operator swear quietly to himself. He'd cracked the new lens that he was meant to be bonding into place. In the end, though, her vision settled down without any more surgery. She now had one eye calibrated for vision at a distance, the other one for close work, a bizarre-sounding arrangement when first it was put to her, but perfectly practicable. For the first time since she was a child she was wearing neither glasses nor contacts, and she could not only watch the play, but read the programme. It wasn't the perfect sight without glasses promised so long ago by that charlatan Bates, but it was good enough.

Difficult to pass up such an image of bifocal awareness, vision not perfect but adequate for objects both near and far. To take stock: Sheila in her seventies is a woman defined as depressive, but tirelessly energetic. Only now has she given in to the practicality of a shopping trolley on her daily trips to Leather Lane. At last she makes that concession to the iconography of mumsiness as she trots on narrow feet to the shops, to buy the robust cheese she now allows herself, the Mocha Italia coffee from the Continental Stores that reliably stings her palate.

If depressives were electronically tagged like criminals so that their doctors could better monitor their progress, it would seem to the tracking team that Sheila had mischievously passed off her tag to some very purposeful little person, someone who surged indomitably to the theatre, to Moorfields, to the Royal Academy or the Tate, to Coram's Fields, to Access to Justice. Depression in her case seems to be more a matter of energy frustrated than killed, energy ingrown like a toenail.

Playing with her grandchildren, a group in which the girls now outnumber the boys without any slackening in her interest, she seems absurdly spry. Uncoiling from a long-maintained crouch in the wardrobe where a four-year-old has failed to find her, she mimes a wince at the crepitus of her knees, and seems more than ever like a mediocre actress remembering she has been cast as an old woman. Indulging in a little stage business. It is a poor impersonation of a London senior citizen in the twentieth century.

Sheila has her hair tinted out of a sense of aesthetic preference rather than vanity, if that distinction is tenable, saying she'd be happy to go white but can't abide dirty grey. She sits by the telephone in the sitting room of 3 Gray's Inn Square reading a novel boldly by daylight, but jumps infallibly whenever it rings (the phone, not the novel). From the fierceness of her reaction you would think that Alexander Graham Bell had only just invented the instrument. That he had installed the prototype in Sheila's sitting room, so as to start it up every now and then to see if it worked.

Sheila's life has been rich as well as, for long periods, almost continuously unhappy, although the richness of it is not apparent to her. She has felt trapped, first by other people's choices and then by her own. Like any animal in a trap, she has gnawed at her own leg to get free—it's just that sometimes she has gnawed the wrong leg.

Every so often her life has run into a wall, the wall of a separation (from a mother, a father, a floating husband, a nose, a job) or a collision (with a stepmother or a Ford transit). Is it surprising that when a life runs into a wall it is changed? Not surprising. The surprising thing is actually the reverse: how much people bring, stuffed into their pockets, clenched between their teeth, over the wall and into the lived after life.

When Sheila married, she knew that sooner or later, Bill's nature being what it was, she would have to cough up children. That was always the phrasing she used, to 'cough them up'. She gave birth to Tim in 1953, Adam in 1954 and Matthew in 1957. I am the middle cough of her womb's coughing fit from the 1950s. I love my life, which isn't quite the same as saying that I expect happiness from it. One of Sheila's virtues as a mother was to have stopped telling us, quite early on, that everything was going to be all right. □

GRANTA

JAYNE ANNE PHILLIPS
MOTHER CARE

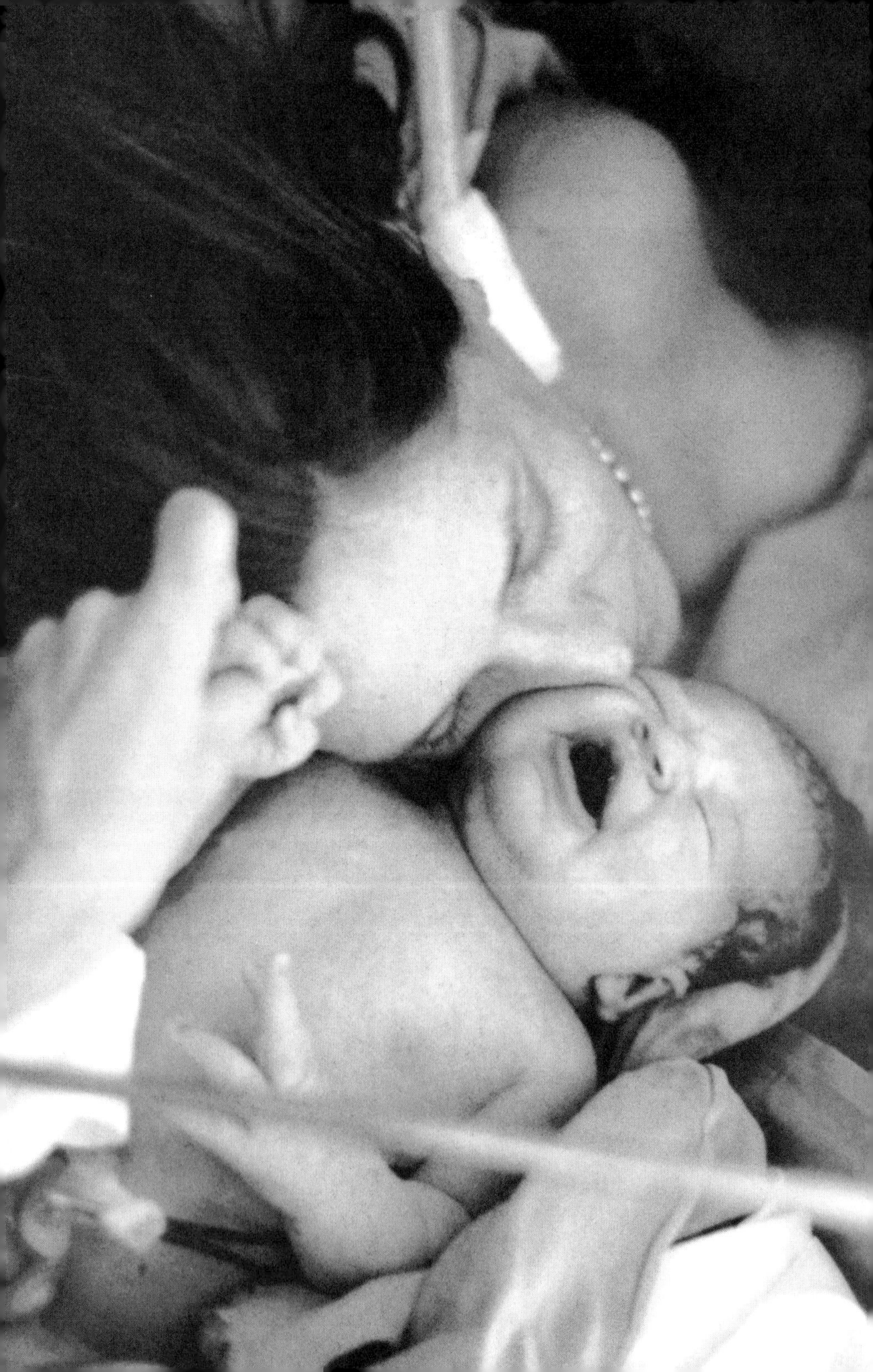

After the birth and the overnight in the hospital she didn't go downstairs for a week. She'd lost some blood and she felt flattened, nearly dizzy, from the labour and then the general anaesthetic. She wept frequently, with incredible ease, and entertained the illusion that she now knew more than she'd ever questioned or known before. The illusion pursued her into sleep itself, into jagged pieces of sleep. She slept and woke, naked except for underpants, sanitary napkins, chemical ice packs. The ice packs, shaped to her crotch, were meant to reduce swelling and numb the stitches; the instructions directed her to bend the cotton to activate the solution; inside, the thick pads cracked like sticks. This bathroom looks like a MASH unit, Matt would say. But it's not your unit that's mashed, Kate would think. In fact, her vagina was an open wound. Her vagina was out of the picture. She couldn't believe she'd ever done anything with it, or felt anything through it.

She couldn't use tampons; there were boxes of big napkins, like bandages, piles of blue underliners—plastic on one side, gauze on the other—to protect the sheets, haemorrhoid suppositories, antibiotic salve, mentholated anaesthetic gel, tubes of lanolin, plastic cups and plastic pitchers. She drank and drank: water, cider, juices. The baby slept in a bassinet right beside her bed but her arms ached from picking him up, holding him, putting him down. On the third day her milk came in, and by then her nipples were already cracked and bleeding. The baby was nursing colostrum every hour but he was sucking for comfort, losing a few more ounces each day. His mouth was puckered, and a large clear blister had formed on his upper lip; he was thirsty, so thirsty; finally Kate gave him water, though the nurses had said not to. *He needs to nurse, to pull the milk in.* That night she woke in the dark, on her back, her engorged breasts sitting on her chest, warm to the touch, gravid, hard and swollen. She woke the baby to feed him. He began to cry, but she held him away until she could sit and prop her arms with pillows, pour a glass of water for the thirst that would assail her. In the beginning she'd moaned as he sucked; then, to move through the initial latching on, she did the same breathing she'd used throughout labour. She breathed evenly, silenced vocalizations cutting in like whispers at the end of each exhalation. The pain cracked through her like a thread of lightning and gradually eased, rippling like something that might wake up and get her.

She called LaLeche League every couple of days for new suggestions. Kate's favourite counsellor was in Medford, a working-class part of Boston Kate didn't remember ever having seen. But the woman had no accent; she was someone else far from home. You'll battle through this, she would say. Be stubborn and hang on. Women are made to nurse, she'd declare in each conversation; any woman can nurse. And then she'd say, in a softer tone, that people forgot how hard it was to get established the first time. 'Don't let the pain defeat you,' were her exact words. 'The uterine pain actually helps you heal, and your nipples will toughen.'

'What about stress?' Kate asked once. 'Will I have enough milk—'

'Stress?' was the response, 'are you kidding? Any woman with a new baby is stressed to the max. She doesn't sleep, she's bleeding, she's sore, she might have other kids or a job she'll go back to. The baby is sucking for life. As long as you eat and drink—drink constantly—your body responds. You don't need unbroken sleep. You don't need a perfect situation. Refugees nurse their babies, and war victims; theirs are the children more likely to survive, even in the worst of times.'

I understand, Kate wanted to say. I understand all about you, and I understand everything.

'Have your husband buy you a manual breast pump at the hospital infirmary,' the counsellor had said, 'and a roll of disposable plastic bottles. The pump is a clear plastic tube, marked in ounces. Use it each time your breasts aren't completely emptied by the baby. Increase production; you can't have too much milk. Freeze all you express. That's how some women work full-time and still nurse their babies. I'll send you some information in the mail. And if you feel discouraged, call back.'

I just want to hear your voice, Kate wanted to say. We're in a tunnel flooded with light.

But she spoke an accepted language, words like air-dry, lanolin, breast rotation, demand schedule. And there was light all around her, great patches angling through the naked windows, glancing off snow piled and fallen and drifted, hard snow, frozen, crusted with ice, each radiant crystal reflecting light. Kate had brought her son home in the last week of December, and the temperature was sixty degrees, sun like spring; her neighbour Carmela had festooned the fence with blue balloons. Kate and Alexander posed for photographs, then she took him in the house, shutting the front door behind them. Immediately the cold came back, and the snows began. At night Kate was awake, nursing, burping the baby, changing odourless cloth diapers, changing his gown, nursing, nursing him to sleep; all the while, snow fell in swathes past the windows, certain and constant, drifting windblown through the street lamp's bell of light. Each day Kate stayed upstairs, and her mother padded back and forth along the hallway connecting their rooms. Just before Christmas she'd finished a full round of chemo, and the tumours in her lungs had shrunk; she had a few weeks of respite now before the next group of treatments and she came to Kate's room to keep her company, to hold the baby while Kate slept, to pour the glasses of juice.

'Are you awake, Katie?' She sat in an upholstered chair that had once graced her own living room; Kate had moved that couch and chair to Boston and covered them in a vibrant 1920s print, navy blue with blowzy, oversized ivory flowers.

'I'm always awake, more or less,' Kate said. 'How was your night?'

'No complaints,' her mother said. 'No nausea.'

'Good.' Kate smiled. 'It's nice to see you sitting in that chair. I always see it in photographs, in one of its guises. In the old house.'

'Yes,' Kate's mother said. 'By the time we moved into town, this chair was in the basement.'

'Now you might admit I was right to drag it to Boston. The cushions may be shot, but at least you have a comfortable place to sit.' Watching her mother, Kate realized the print she'd chosen for the chair, dark blue with white, was nearly the reverse of her mother's choice. 'Remember the fabric of your slip covers, what you used on that chair? What did you always call that print?'

'It was a blue onion print, white with blue vines—'

'Thistle-like flowers,' Kate interrupted, 'like fans, with viney runners—'

'Yes,' her mother continued patiently, 'wild onions, hence the name.'

'And you had those glass pots with lids in the same print on the coffee table. I remember. There they sit, in all the Easter pictures. When we're wearing our good clothes. You always matched things. But before, there was that dark living room.'

'Dark?'

'The walls were dark green, and the drapes on the picture windows were dark green with gold, and the furniture in its original upholstery, dark beige with a raised texture.'

'Well, when kids are young, you want things that are dark and tough, to last. When you were older, we had the white fibreglass drapes and the lighter slip covers. That first upholstery was chosen to last through climbing and sliding and whatever—your brothers gave it a workout.'

'It did last,' Kate said, 'it was what I covered up. It seems ageless.'

'Yes,' her mother agreed, 'but it darkened. This was your father's chair, and the fabric darkened just in the shape of him.'

'Really?' Kate asked. 'You mean, as though his shadow sank into it?'

Her mother frowned, exasperated. 'No, I mean it was worn. Worn from use. Am I speaking English?'

Kate laughed. 'Your energy level is better, isn't it? You're your old feisty self, and I'm just lying here.'

Her mother peered over at the bassinet. 'I thought I might hold Alexander for you, but he's sleeping so beautifully. I've been downstairs already, to let that little girl in, the Mother Care worker. It's been wonderful to have her for a week. She came this morning with her arms full of groceries. She's just putting things away and then she'll be up to see what you want her to do.'

'It was so nice of you to buy help for me, Mom, such a great present.'

'Well, I'd be doing all the cooking myself, if I were able. But I must say, your requirements are pretty daunting.'

Kate smiled. She'd asked for someone versed in preparing

natural foods. No additives, no preservatives. No meat with hormones. 'Your colour is good today, Mom,' she said. 'You're sitting right there in the sun and you look all lit up.'

'I'm sure I do. It's so bright in this room. Why do you paint everything white? And not a thing on the windows, not even shades to pull down.'

'The walls are linen white,' Kate said, 'and the trim is white. And I don't need shades; I'm not worried about snipers.'

'Snipers?'

'My LaLeche League lady,' Kate said. 'She was telling me how war victims can go right on nursing their babies, even in foxholes.'

Her mother frowned. 'Some of these people are way out there. What do war victims have to do with you? You're not in a foxhole.'

'Not yet,' Kate said. 'But really, if you want shades on your windows, I'll get some. You should have told me sooner.'

Her mother waved away the suggestion. 'I don't care. That big tree is in front of one of the windows, and the other faces Carmela's house. I certainly don't care if she sees me, not that there's much to see at this point.'

'But there's always Derek,' Kate said slyly, referring to their neighbour's live-in boyfriend. 'What about him?'

'Derek is occupied in greener pastures. I hope not too occupied. If he lives with Carmela, I don't know why he has to have his own place downtown. And his own crystal and china. And his own art collection.'

Kate shrugged. 'He's a lawyer. Maybe he needs a place downtown. Anyway, he's cute. I remember how they charged over here the first day we moved in, on their way to some swank thing, and there's Carmela, nearly six feet tall, in one of those long satin capes her daughter made her, and all her Navajo jewellery, with a huge tray of assorted handmade cookies and a raspberry pie.'

'Carmela is wonderful. Mark my words, though, Derek is not in it for the long haul.'

'Not everyone is into hauling,' Kate said. 'She's been divorced twice; he's been divorced once; maybe they're better off just relaxing.'

Her mother shook her head impatiently, signalling her

annoyance with a click of the tongue. 'She's certainly suggested he give up the apartment. Carmela loves taking care of people; she'd like to be married. But he is not the right fellow.'

'Gotcha,' Kate said. She realized she often knew in advance her mother's response to a given topic, but she elicited the responses anyway, sometimes to her annoyance, more often for pleasure. She so valued her mother's sheer dependability, the slight cynicism of the old wives' tales she favoured, her bedrock common sense, even the rigid provincial innocence with which she approached discussions of what Kate referred to as 'modern life'. There were so many topics on which her mother held strong opinions based on scant experience. Like serial monogamy and live-in arrangements. Interracial relationships. Homosexuality. Literature. Film. When I go to a movie, she liked to say, I want to be *entertained*, not upset.

Kate leaned back on her pillows. She didn't want to be entertained; entertainment was far too demanding and gave so little in return. Kate wanted someone to read stories to her or speak intensely about a private matter. She wanted to be fed. The Mother Care worker brought Kate lunch on a tray, numerous plates of soft, warm tastes, samples of the various entrées she'd made to freeze, and sliced vegetables so cold and crisp they wore ice fragments. Her name was Moira, but Kate liked to think of her only as Mother Care; Mother Care put a flower on the tray, the head of a hothouse daisy or rose, never in a bud vase—too likely to topple in the journey upstairs, perhaps—but floating, the first day, in a cup. Then the flower always appeared in an antique shot glass. It was so pretty to see a flower, yet Kate felt that the daisy and its lissom petals seemed sacrificial. The soft sphere of the scarlet rose sank inward, pulled from its stem. Kate touched the flowers, their surfaces, as though they were already gone. 'It may be January in New England,' Moira had said, 'but it's still important to see something blooming. And don't worry, I work with unprocessed foods. I'm a vegetarian though I don't mind cooking meat if that's what you want. My objections are strictly personal.' Kate heard her now, her tread on the stairs and the subtle shifting of cutlery. The smell of food came closer and set up a dull fear in Kate, like nervousness or excitement.

'Here we are,' Moira said. 'And I brought the mail up too.' She placed the bed tray squarely before Kate and pulled her pillows back. 'Might want to sit up a bit more. There's a tomato–arugula salad and French bread, and I made you a really hearty vegetable soup with barley. I froze five pints.'

'Great,' Kate said. 'We'll be thinking of you into next month, blessing the fact of your existence.'

Moira nodded. She was so efficient, Kate thought, and she had a quiet, non-intrusive presence, but she seemed a bit humourless. Now she smiled her quick, disappearing smile. Perhaps she was only shy.

'This is my last day with you,' she said, 'so maybe we should come up with a plan. I know you want to do everything with the baby yourself, but the freezer is almost full of food. There's just room for a few pans of lasagne, which I'll make this afternoon. I'll do all the laundry again, but don't forget I could also give you a massage or a manicure.'

'Or you could read to me,' said Kate.

'Don't waste the time you have left,' her mother said. 'I could read to you.'

'How about a massage?' Moira asked.

Kate felt so sore, so weak, the thought of anyone touching her was alarming. But she thought Moira had a dreamy voice, soft, a bit insubstantial; Moira's voice would carry words and disappear in them. 'A massage, maybe,' Kate said, 'and then a story.'

'Sure.' She nodded and took the mail from the tray. 'There's a little package for you and some cards. I left the bills downstairs. Now I'll go and get another lunch, so the two of you can eat together.'

Kate's mother nodded in her direction. 'No, I'll eat later, I'm coming down soon. You go ahead, Katie, before he wakes up, and your arms are full.'

'I'm coming down later too,' Kate announced. 'I hope you both realize that I'm dressed today. It's a nursing gown, but still—'

'You're right,' Moira said. 'I didn't even notice. There you sit, clothed to the elbows.'

'Well, I've always been clothed below the waist, in my various bandages.'

'Exactly.' Moira busied herself straightening the covers of the bed. 'And when you're nursing every hour and you're so sore, it hardly seems worth it to take clothes on and off, or lift them up and down.'

'It's amazing how the two of you think alike,' Kate's mother said wryly. 'Anyway, I wasn't going to say anything. You've been mostly covered with sheets and blankets, and I figured you'd get your clothes on by spring.'

'I have my gown on.' Kate picked up her spoon. 'That's all I'll commit to.'

'And you do feel warm,' Moira said, 'when you're making milk. But I know you don't have a temperature, because I've taken it every day.'

'You certainly have,' Kate's mother said. 'You've taken good care of her.'

'Why don't we plan on the massage then?' Moira gathered used cups from the bedside table. 'You eat all that, then he'll wake, and you'll nurse, and by the time he goes down again, I'll be ready. I'll bring up my oils and a tape to play. All right?'

'You're in charge,' Kate's mother said.

When Kate woke, the bed tray was gone. Her mother was gone too, and the house was perfectly quiet. She remembered finishing the food and leaning back in bed, and then she'd fallen asleep, dreamlessly, as though she had only to close her eyes to move away, weightless and pure, skimming the reflective surface of something deep.

She heard a small sound. Alexander lay in the bassinet, his eyes open, looking at her. His swaddling blankets had come loose. Propped on his side by pillows, he raised one arm and moved his hand delicately. Kate sat up to lean near him and touched her forefinger to his palm; immediately he grasped on hard, and his gaze widened. 'They're your fingers,' she told him. 'You don't know them yet, but I do.' Everyone had told her to leave him be when he was happy, she'd be holding him and caring for him so ceaselessly, but she took him in her arms, propped up the pillows and put him in her lap. He kicked excitedly and frowned. She bent her knees to bring him closer and regarded him as he lay on her raised thighs; the frown disappeared. 'You're like me,' Kate said softly. 'You frown when you think. By the time you're twenty-five, you'll have two little lines between your eyes. Such a serious guy.' He raised his downy brows. He had a watchful, observing look and a more excited look; he'd open his eyes wider, compress his lips, strain with his limbs as though he were concentrating on moving, on touching or grasping. He could feel his body but he couldn't command it to move or do; his focus was entirely in his eyes. And he did focus; Kate was sure he saw her. He wasn't a newborn any longer; today he was one week old. Perhaps his vision was still blurry, and that was why he peered at her so intently. His eyes were big and dark blue, like those of a baby seal. One eye was always moist and teary; his tear duct was blocked, they'd said at the hospital; it would clear up.

Now Kate wiped his cheek carefully with the edge of a cloth diaper, then drew her finger across his forehead, along his jaw, across his flattened, broad little nose. 'Mister man,' she whispered, 'mighty mouse, here's your face. Here are your nose, your ears, your widow's peak. Old widower, here are your bones . . . ' She touched his collarbones and the line along his shoulder under his gown. His skin was like warm silk. She cleaned him with warm water, not alcohol wipes, and powdered him with a product that contained no talc. The powder was fine as rice flour and smelt as Kate thought rice fields might smell in the sun, when the plants bloomed. Like clean food, pure as flowers.

Across the world and in the South, those young shoots grew and moved in the breeze like grass. 'Rice fields are like grass in water,' she said to Alexander. 'We haven't seen them yet. Even in India I didn't see them.' Outside the wind moved along the house; Kate heard it circling and testing. Suddenly a gust slammed against the windows, and Alexander, startled, looked towards the sound. 'You can't see the wind,' Kate murmured, 'just what it moves.' The wind would bring snow again, Kate knew; already, she heard snow approach, like a whining in the wind. Absently she traced the baby's lips, and he yawned and began to whimper. You're hungry? Kate thought, and he moved his arms as though to gather her closer. Her milk let down with a flush and surge, and she held a clean diaper to one breast as she put him to the other. Now she breathed, exhaling slowly. The intense pain began to ebb; he drank the cells of her blood, Kate knew, and the crust that formed on her nipples where the cuts were deepest. He was her blood. When she held him, he was inside her; always he was near her, like an atmosphere, in his sleep, in his being. She would not be alone again for many years, even if she wanted to be, even if she tried. In her deepest thoughts she would approach him, move around and through him, make room for him. In nursing there would be a still, spiral peace, an energy in which she felt herself, the debris of her needs and wants, slough away. It seemed less important to talk or think; like a nesting animal, she took on camouflage, layers of protective awareness that were almost spatial in dimension, like sonar. The awareness had dark edges, shadows that rose and fell; Kate imagined terrible things. That he might stop breathing. That she dropped him, or someone had. That someone or something took him from her. That she forgot about him or misplaced him. There were no words; the thoughts occurred to her in starkly precise images, like the unmistakable images of dreams, as though her waking and sleeping lives had met in him. Truly, she was sleeping; the days and nights were fluid, beautiful and discoloured; everything in her was available to her, as though she'd become someone else, someone with a similar past history in whom that history was acknowledged rather than felt, someone who didn't need to make amends or understand, someone beyond language. She was shattered. Something new would come of her. Moments in which she crossed from consciousness to sleep, from sleep to awareness, there was a lag of an instant in which she couldn't remember her name, and she didn't care. She remembered him. Now his gaze met hers, and his eyelids fluttered; she could see him falling away, back into his infant swoon. His sleep closed around him like an ocean shell and rocked him within it. In this they were alike, Kate thought, though he had no name known to him, no name to forget. He was pure awareness and need. She took him from the breast and held him to her shoulder, patting and rubbing him, softly, a caress and a heartbeat.

Moira came into the room so quietly that Kate was unaware of her until she reached the foot of the bed. She carried blankets, a tape recorder, plastic bottles of oils, a small cardboard box.

Depositing her burdens on the floor, she mouthed, 'Shall I take him?' And Kate gestured, no, not yet. She whispered, 'I'll set up,' and disappeared from view. Kate smelt the sulphur of lit matches and then citrus and gardenia, Moira's scented votives. Kate put Alexander carefully into the bassinet and looked through the books stacked beside her table. She chose one. Which passage? The beginning would do.

'I'm going to put the tape on very low. As he sleeps more deeply, I'll turn it up just a bit.' Moira was beside her. 'Is that the book you want?' She smiled and took it, then indicated the rug at the foot of the bed. 'I've made a space. It's better to have a firm surface.'

'A space,' Kate said. She stood and saw that Moira had made an alternative bed, blankets precisely folded, a pallet covered with terry towels. Sheets and more blankets were arranged over it, neatly turned down. Six votives were lit in a row of little flames at the head. 'This looks quite ritualistic,' Kate said. 'Do I need a chaperone?'

'I don't believe so.' Moira turned the tape on. 'But I won't lie, it is a ritual. I'm sorry I can't lower the light. Evening is a better time, but I don't work nights.'

'It doesn't need to be dark,' Kate said. 'Look how the sun falls across. I love the sun.'

'Yes, you'll feel it. Can you lie on your front comfortably? I'll go out while you get ready.'

'No need.'

'No, I will. And take everything off. I'll bring the warm oils from the kitchen.'

Kate watched her go and sighed. What a lot of work this was. She walked past the pallet into the bathroom, pulling the door to. There, the water running, getting warm. She took off her gown and pants, folded the pads and wrapped them in paper, threw them away. Slowly, she began to wash, water cooling on her legs in rivulets. They'd told her not to bathe yet; she stood like this, cloths and soap, carefully. At first, when she stood or walked, she'd felt as though she were moving on the deck of a ship, as though some rhythm pulsed in the ground, the floor. Rooms subtly shifted. The effects of the general, Matt said, but Kate could see the movement even from her bed, from her window. The way the angles of the ceiling met the walls, how the floor slid to its four corners. How the earth turned. This is the way it's always been, Kate thought; she hadn't known. Now she did. She rocked the baby in the rocking chair and imagined sailing through the window, rocking, with no interruption, into the cold, the air billowing around them. You OK? Matt would ask. I'm fine, Kate would answer. As a child, an adolescent, an adult, she had almost never cried. Now she could. She didn't feel depressed, she felt amazed and moved and out of sync. Or she was in sync, but she couldn't explain how. She left her gown where it fell, dried herself and opened the door.

The music was a little more noticeable now, classical music, strings. A shaft of sunlight poured across the rug, and motes of dust swam in the light. Moira knelt by the empty fireplace, waiting for her. 'Sorry,' Kate said, 'I wanted to get clean.' Moira nodded and pulled back the sheets of the pallet for Kate to slip inside. Slowly, Kate was on her knees, and then prone.

'We won't wake him?' she said, before turning over.

'You wouldn't be comfortable away from him,' Moira answered. 'We won't disturb him.'

Then the sheets and blankets were a silky covering. Moira moved her hands along Kate's form as though to gain some innate sense of her, pausing, exerting a gentle pressure. It's a New-Age thing, Kate thought, and it's from the oldest days, when floors were swept earth. Behind the music she heard Moira breathing, exhaling in time to the movement of her hands, as though she were draining Kate of fatigue or discomfort, releasing it through herself. Surely that was the idea. 'So, Moira,' Kate said softly, 'what are your personal objections?'

The hands never slowed. 'To what?'

'Meat. To meat.'

'Oh. Health, basically, at first, theories about nutrition. But after I stopped eating meat, the smell of my body changed, and the taste in my mouth. I don't mind handling meat—I cook and do catering, and sometimes it's part of my job—but I don't want it inside me. And I didn't want my daughter growing up on a meat diet.'

'You have a daughter?'

'Yes. She's three. I'm a single mom.'

So she works days, Kate thought. Nights at home with her daughter. 'You seem so content and organized,' she said aloud. 'Were you always single?'

'Yes, pretty much. It was a bit difficult at first, but for now, we're content. We do very well.'

'Little women,' Kate said. 'But in those mother–daughter stories, there's always a virtuous hero offstage, the father off at war, or the rich neighbour.'

'And so there may be,' Moira said. 'But I'll do whatever's best for my child. I don't need to be saved.'

'What a relief,' Kate said.

'Yes.' Moira laughed softly.

'But we do have to save ourselves, don't we,' Kate murmured. 'Such a project.'

'You're stronger each day,' Moira said. 'And you're doing exactly what you should be doing with this baby. It's so important to nurse and to have him constantly with you.'

Now the light of the sun had shifted; it seemed winter light again, flattened and diffuse, and the flames of the votives burned higher. Moira's hands were at Kate's hips, lifting her from behind, tilting heat into her abdomen; she moved up along Kate's spine with her fists, a hard and soft pressure, repetitive, patterned with heat Kate felt in her forearms, in her thighs. She felt herself knit together, handled like something wounded; she realized how far she was from herself, and how she might begin to live here again, in her body. Slowly it would happen. She might call and call now for her own return, but she only floated, inhabiting so many former selves with more conviction: just now she saw the backs and jostling shoulders of her hometown girlfriends, all bundled in their coats and descending into snow down dormitory stairs; they still looked like high-school blondes and brunettes in fur hats and boots, bright twine in their hair, but they were getting off on mescalin, falling into the first tinges of visuals, and someone was crooning, *Pleased as punch, pleased as punch.* In India, on the vast terrace of the Taj Mahal, boys had approached Kate with open arms. *Sell blue jeans? Buy hashish? Extreme hashish. You sell blue jeans?* The young men, the slim ones, looked like boys, smooth skinned and lithe. The middle-aged men on the train to Agra were toadish and portly in their tailored clothes; they seldom looked up from their newspapers. Mist rose from the steaming fields as though daybreak would go on for weeks, and Kate saw silhouettes of movement, squatting forms, their morning toilette a slow, dark ballet. An old man, skeletal in white, hunkered by the tracks, brushing his teeth with a twig. On the tortuous mountain track to Chitwan, the Nepalese bus had stopped in a town; farmers disembarked with their caged chickens, and the women with their saronged babies; the Gurkha soldiers piled out with their guns. The women merely lifted their layered, intricately sewn skirts to relieve themselves, standing to straddle the sewage ditch that ran along one side of the only road. Water rattled in it, and the men walked further up, discreetly, but Kate wandered behind the shack-like kiosks to pick her way down a rocky bank to the river. Ropes of faeces blackened among the stones. The riverbank flattened in a broad sweeping curve, and the water was low; outcroppings strewn with boulders rose in crescents from glistened sweeps too still and silver to seem fluid. Kate dropped her loose cloth trousers to her knees and crouched, urinating; to her left, two men appeared at the bend of the river, balancing on their shoulders a long pole bent with the weight of a body. The body swung in delicate motion, bound to the pole at wrists and ankles, the swathed, faceless head flung back.

Kate wanted to look away but could not. Moira's voice came from above her. 'It's time for me to go now,' she said.

'Yes, I know.' Kate turned and lay on her back. Behind her eyes she saw a darkness reddened by light. 'Goodbye, Moira.'

Moira touched Kate's forehead with her fingertips. Her touch lingered deliberately, a firm little bruise specific as a kiss. Kate lay still and felt Moira close to her, just over her, her clove-scented breath, the oil of her dark hair. Perhaps she always ended her massages this way. Perhaps she thought Kate ridiculous, a privileged woman not yet alone with her child. Kate raised her gaze to Moira's. 'You look so grave,' Kate said. 'But then, goodbye is a grave word.'

'It's just a wish,' Moira said and moved away. Her hands pressed in a careful pattern above the tucked blankets, finishing evenly. 'He's sleeping,' she said softly. 'You sleep too, if you like, but here's your story.'

Kate heard a ruffling of pages.

'*Chapter one*,' came a voice. '*I am born . . . To begin my life with the beginning of my life, I record that I was born (as I have been informed and believe) on a Friday, at twelve o'clock at night . . .*' Kate closed her eyes. The river was a high rattling murmur, and the barefoot men moved ceaselessly forward in the islanded riverbed. The men never looked at her. They were there still, Kate thought, making progress down the Narayani to the mouth of the Bagmati, two days' trek. The cremation sites, in view of the blue-eyed stupas and their gold spires, were raised earth bound by stones, and the flaming pyres were set afloat, heaped with burning flowers. Kate smelt that scent, like blackened oranges, sticky and boiled, so close she was enveloped. *It was remarked that the clock began to strike . . . and I began to cry, simultaneously . . .* She knew she must stand up now and walk, or the bus would ascend into the mountains without her.

Kate sat at the kitchen table, dressed in her clothes. Mother Care was finished; Kate herself was Mother Care. The downstairs of her own house looked strange to her, larger, more impersonal, as though she were a visitor with some dimly realized connection to this place. She lay other mail aside and opened only the little package from LaLeche League, postmarked Medford.

Sealed into a white envelope were two small plastic objects and a handwritten instruction sheet: *How to Use Nursing Shields*. The shields were gently conical and extremely simple. Kate considered regarding them as unpretentious S&M aids or punk-rock falsies, but in fact they were objects seemingly more conducive to plastic food storage than to anything used for enhancement, protection or pleasure. Kate got the impression they'd been passed on to her from other women, other breasts. Circular plastic discs that snapped apart, they had a hole in the inner disc where the nipples fit through. They were meant to keep the nipple erect and dry, so it healed, and they had the added benefit of collecting the flow of milk that seeped into one's clothes before the baby could latch on. Milk seeped into Kate's clothes;

milk sweetened and soured her chest and the cleft between her breasts every time she heard the baby cry, as soon as he cried. Milk wet her shirt when she sat down alone near her bedroom window and saw the exposed brown grass in the yard, rents in the snow; when she read some item in the newspaper about a child falling out a window; or when she saw a commercial for long-distance dialling on television. Sixty seconds of manipulative human-interest images, and her eyes were wet, and she didn't bother wiping her face. Her breasts let down, and her uterus cramped sharply, turning like a small animal inside her, contracting in its nest. When her eyes got wet, her breasts performed, as though she wept milk. She could cry and she could nurse, or when she nursed, she didn't have to cry; her body wept. She wept food, and he grew on sorrow.

'What are those things?' Kate's mother stood behind her, peering over her shoulder.

'They're nursing shields. Look, they're like something out of *Barbarella*.'

'What's *Barbarella*?'

'You know, that Jane Fonda movie where she's a blonde space bimbo and she wears pointy warrior shields over her breasts, and silver gladiator boots and tights, and she gets picked up by an eagle—'

'An eagle?'

'Yes. She wakes up in this huge bird's nest looking—soporific . . . anyway, the LaLeche woman sent these things to me for my breasts. They go inside a nursing bra, now that I'm wearing a bra, to keep the cloth from sticking and making everything worse.'

'What else did she tell you to do?'

'Well, there's the wet method and the dry method. One school of thought is to feed through the pain and keep the cuts moist with lanolin, because otherwise the baby breaks them open anyway every time he nurses. But then nothing ever really heals. Or, you hope you heal, but it might take a long time. The other is to stop nursing, go naked and air-dry, express into a pump to feed the baby, but then the baby might refuse the breast when you start up again, or the nipples heal and just crack repeatedly—'

'What do these things have to do with it all?'

'They keep you dry and pull your nipples out if they're inverted, so the baby latches on better. And I guess they beat going topless. I mean, suppose I want to answer the doorbell or leave the house someday.' Kate put one of the plastic shields inside her shirt, in her bra, over the sorest breast.

'Of course you'll leave the house again. My God, after what you went through, you needed to stay in bed for a week. You had a general anaesthetic after that long labour. And then all this with the nursing.' Kate's mother sighed and sat down in the chair opposite. 'It's amazing how nature slaps women with everything at once—you take care of a new baby twenty-four hours a day, just when you're most exhausted.'

Kate gazed at her mother's face and felt her wholly familiar presence. In this place, this house where they'd all lived less than three months, her mother was so real, so connected to all they'd come from, to everything Kate had taken with her, the burden and the weight and the furious beauty she kept trying to turn around and see. She wondered if she would see anything of that first world anymore, when her mother was gone. 'Yes,' she said aloud, her voice faltering, 'it's so unrelieved. You never really wake up or sleep. Time stands still.'

'And later,' her mother went on, 'you forget. You don't think you will, but you do. I must have gone through all this with nursing, but I don't remember. I do remember the time your brother bit me.'

'Which brother?' Kate put her forefinger into the hole of the other nursing shield and began to spin it slowly on the table top directly in front of her. It made an unsatisfying, lopsided axis.

'I'll never forget that,' her mother said. 'He took a bite right out of me. He came away with blood all over his little face.'

Kate looked up. 'But I thought I was the only one you nursed.'

Her mother frowned. 'You're right. It must have been you.'

'It had to be me.' Kate laughed.

'What's so funny?'

'I'm thinking about the song. You look confused. Never mind.'

'Oh,' her mother said. 'That song. That's "It Had To Be

You". No, I'm just surprised. Aunt Maud, who was the closest I had to a mother-in-law, told me I'd never be able to nurse because I was a smoker, though I stopped each time I was pregnant. So I didn't try with your older brother but I was determined to nurse you. I drank beer and milkshakes by the hour and I had plenty of milk. You were so fat your boobs hung to your waist.'

'That was fleeting,' Kate said, 'until now.'

'You'll get back into shape. Actually, nursing takes the weight faster—it all goes to the baby. But with my third, I was too tired. I had three kids under four. Think about it.'

'I can't,' Kate said. 'But I think bottle-feeding would be so much more trouble, all those bottles to wash and sterilize, and have you ever tasted formula? It's just chemicals and water. I think babies only drink it because they're starved to it.'

'Maybe. Mine sure sucked it down.' She paused. 'They were skinnier babies, much skinnier.'

'No one would ever advise you to drink beer to nurse now. You must have been slightly looped all the time. Think of all the IQ points I lost. No wonder I bit you.'

Kate's mother gave her an exasperated look. 'I don't think it hurt you any.'

Kate smiled. 'By the way, how old was I when you gave me that IQ test? Fourth or fifth grade, I believe. Just think, if not for all that beer, I might have scored solidly in the genius category.'

'I didn't tell you what your score was,' her mother said, abashed.

'No, but you told me approximately what it was, within precise parameters. I'm sure you remember. I lost out by a few points, and see, it was all your fault.'

'Fine, fine,' her mother said. 'In any case, you're smart enough. If you were any smarter, you'd have been unbearable. I couldn't have coped.'

'I'm not feeling smart,' Kate said. 'I feel as though half my brain is missing.' She positioned the other nursing shield in her bra. The top of her breast felt hot. Under her palm, her fingers, she felt a hard spot, like a knot. What was that?

'You look a little flushed,' her mother said. 'Your cheeks are red. Maybe you'd better go lie down.' She reached out to touch

Kate's wrist. 'Just rest. Soon you'll be yourself again.'

'No,' Kate said, 'I won't. And why should I?'

She had mastitis. Desperately she wanted to walk outside into the cold, up and down the snow-bound streets. Antibiotics, her doctor said. Hot compresses and bedrest, fluids, said her LaLeche League counsellor. Give it a day. Antibiotics are a last resort; no one can really know how they'll affect the baby. Nurse even more frequently and pump and change compresses as soon as they begin to cool. If the fever reaches 102, take Tylenol. Is there someone to help you?

'Mom, please,' Kate said, 'open the window.'

'Don't be ridiculous. You're feverish and you have an infant here. Lie back and cover up. The water is good and hot. I just don't want to burn you.' She came to Kate's bed with an aluminium basin in her arms, and Kate looked dully inside it at the steaming cloths. 'Let me change the compress again,' her mother said. 'How long would you say the heat really lasts?'

'Oh, a hundred years or so.'

'I know you're restless. Could you read?' her mother said. 'Shall I turn on the TV?'

'No,' Kate said and threw off the coverlet. 'You're terribly efficient, Mom, but I don't see how we can go on like this all day. Weren't you just here three minutes ago?'

'Matt will take a shift when he comes home.' She removed the cooling cloth and lay the hot one delicately across Kate's breast. 'Should we see if Moira could come back?'

'That's not necessary.' Kate held her hand above the steaming cloth and imagined the heat on her breast increased. 'We can't afford another week of Mother Care. And this is not rocket science, it's hot washcloths.'

'We have to keep them this hot,' her mother said. 'The more constant we keep the heat, the more likely you are to get results. You've worked so hard at this, I don't want you to have to stop nursing.'

'I'm not stopping,' Kate said, incredulous. 'Who said anything about stopping?'

'Well, no one,' her mother said worriedly. 'You would only

stop if your health were at stake.' She put down the basin and took up the edge of the wrinkled duvet, smoothing the white flannel.

Kate sighed. 'I see you've got the coverlet in your hand. Don't come at me with it. Unless someone has chills, you really don't bundle up a person with a fever. You only make them hotter. Where did you go to medical school, anyway? Mastitis is not serious; it's almost de rigueur. Nursing mothers who don't get it are really not even respectable veterans.'

'I wouldn't be concerned about your status. With all you've got on your plate, you'll surely come out of this a veteran of something. Is that cloth cool yet?'

'Mom, you'll make yourself tired. Please, sit down. If you want to distract me, read to me from something panoramic. There, read from what Moira started. Not the first lines, I don't want to hear them again, but start anywhere on the first page.'

Kate watched as her mother pulled the rocking chair close to the bed and felt for the book behind her on the seat, where Moira had left it. '*I was born with a caul . . .* ' she began uncertainly.

'No, no,' Kate said. 'Let's skip the whole beginning. I heard it earlier today and came down with a fever. Go near to the end, when it's all coming right. Didn't you ever read this book? Doesn't everyone have to read it in high school?'

'Good heavens, I don't remember what I read in high school. Do you want the very last pages?'

'No, a little earlier. Do the reunion scene; you'll like it.' She took the book from her mother's outstretched hand and turned it to the right page. 'Start with, *Agnes, shall I tell you what about? I came to tell you.* Right here.'

'This print is so small. I feel as though I need my glasses changed.' Her mother leaned back slightly and peered at the page through her bifocals. ' . . . *do you doubt my being true to you . . . what I always have been to you . . .* that part?'

'Right. *You have a secret, said I. Let me share it, Agnes.*'

'Now, if you know it from memory, why do you want me to read it to you?'

'Because I *love* it, of course. And who wouldn't? *Said I. Let me share it.* And the way he keeps repeating her name. My God, why don't people speak to one another that way every day, every hour?'

'People don't necessarily want to share secrets,' her mother said. 'And maybe I should read something else. The point of this was not for you to get upset.'

'I'm not upset!' Kate leaned back on the pillows, took a breath and lowered her voice to a near whisper. 'Just read, please. I beg of you.'

'*Said I*,' her mother intoned. 'All right. I'll start at the top of this next page.'

She began to read, and Kate trained her eyes on a middle distance, a space informed by winter light. It was the space behind her mother's chair, a shape consisting of bare floor and air just in front of the window. When Kate peered into that space correctly, the snowy view of descending streets and drifted roofs lost specificity and interest. Her eyes rested in emptiness that held nothing but a particular light of day and time. The space seemed concave, difficult to hold or see if one tried, but effortlessly present within a certain focus. The mode of the listener was that focus, and Kate let herself enter it, drifting and aware. Like active dreaming, infant dreams, dreams in which the body subtly flexes while the mind moves into other stories. Dickens's language was a story Kate knew, shadowed, burnished and detailed, even the descriptions of filth and ruin rendered in a language so controlled and rich, so confident that stories exist and listeners hear. Dickens's listeners were gone now; gone, all those living souls who'd paid to hear him speak in lecture halls, on stages, who'd stood within reach of his voice, all companions to a homeless boy, travellers to the death house, the poor house, all of them moving along streets made of stones, the horse-drawn wagons creaking, the clotted mud on flanks and boots. It was always winter in Dickens's London boyhood, always cold and foggy, and the bridges so long one couldn't see to the other side through wet, cloying mist. Everyone's hands looked chapped and old; so Western, Kate thought, that white, mottled skin, like the faintly mauve hands of kids from the coal towns, kids with old eyes. They knew how to say goodbye, those children, lined up in school hallways in their wrinkled coats, their chafed wrists delicate and dirty, the lines and whorls of their skin etched with old dirt. They were children from her mother's classrooms, children her mother had taught to read and write, children she'd clothed with whatever her own kids had outgrown. They boarded school buses at day's end and never waved, only looked, sideways glances through the rectangular windows. Kate had thought no one kissed them; she'd thought they'd be cold forever. Now in her mind's eye they cast their clear gaze through Dickens's unfurled words . . . *toiling on, I saw a ragged way-worn boy, forsaken and neglected . . .*

In Sri Lanka, in India, babies burnt with cholera or malaria. Moist skin, dark, lustrous hair. And ripe, endless gardens, fertile riots, fecund with colour and smell. Those babies could drown in dense scent, even through the membranes of their mother's bodies, through the protective caul of Dickens's story, any story. Kate watched her mother's mouth, a mouth not so generous as Kate's, a rosebud mouth perfectly suited to the bright red lipstick she'd worn all the years Kate had stood near her, looking up, the daughter so small in stature; or followed her, skipping to keep pace, her mother's black coat disappearing along grocery aisles, corridors, slushy streets. Dimly she heard the words her mother read: *Long miles of road then opened out before my mind . . .* Goodbye was not so simple as a kiss. Goodbye went on and on.

'Mom, wait,' Kate said softly.

Her mother stopped speaking and raised her eyes, startled.

'I'm sorry,' Kate said. 'I wasn't concentrating and I missed the part I really wanted to hear. Can you go back a bit and read the underlined paragraph?'

She glanced at the book and moved her chair closer to the bed, then half stood, remembering the compress, reaching to touch the cooled cloth that lay across Kate's breast. But Kate gestured to leave it be and nodded, encouraging her to go on.

'*I went away, dear Agnes,*' her mother read, '*loving you. I stayed away, loving you. I returned home, loving you. And now, I tried to tell her of the struggle I had had, and the conclusion I had come to. I tried to lay my mind before her, truly, and entirely.*'

There was a hush in the room. Kate's mother looked back at the lines once. Then she leaned forward and touched her open palm to Kate's face. Kate touched her own hand to her mother's wrist and inclined her head as her mother stood to embrace her. Listening, she heard the beating of her mother's heart as snow brushed the windows in sweeps of wind. □

GRANTA

DAVID MAMET
SOUL MURDER

The child sat with his head in his hands, rocking back and forth. ' . . . and if you did not *want* it, you should not have asked for it,' the woman said, 'for you do not know what it means to *deserve* something, for you do not know what it is to *work* for something.' She paused. '*Do* you?'

The boy did not look up. And it seemed the woman did not require him to. She rubbed one eye for a moment, and while she rubbed it, her mouth went slack. The boy continued rocking.

'Now,' she said, 'when we get home, do you know what I'm going to do? I'm going to rake your *toys* and *box* them. And I'm going to ship them away. Do you think I'm fooling?'

The two other children, the man thought, now, they would be his brother and sister. They looked on, not dispassionately, but at a remove.

Well certainly, the man thought. If they were to intervene, what would they say?

The boy stopped rocking and rose from the bench and began to walk, stiff-legged, looking down.

'Where are you going?' the woman said.

He raised his head, cow-eyed, to indicate his destination—a men's room sign across the waiting room.

' . . . then why do you walk like that?' the woman said. 'I'm talking to you. Why do you *walk* like that, for God's sake?'

His mouth moved like a fish's for a moment.

'You sit down,' she said, 'and I'll *tell* you when I want you to go somewhere.'

He waited a moment and then sank down on the bench. His mouth was open, and his hands were pressed over his ears. He put his head down, just above his knees, and began rocking again.

The woman addressed herself to the other two. She drew them close around the pile of baggage and spoke softly to them.

Yes, that's right, the man thought. Yes, that's right.

She gestured to the baggage and pointed at them, and they nodded; and she gestured at the washroom and she nodded and then she, and then they, looked over at the other boy. She got up quickly and gathered herself together and walked crisply off.

The other children looked guiltily at the boy and then they determinedly busied themselves with their books.

Well, now's the time, the man thought and he had this fantasy: he would walk over to the boy and sit beside him.

'Do you know who I am?' he would say. The boy would look up. 'I am your guardian angel. I have been sent to tell you this: you are not bad, but good. Do you understand? You are not bad, but good. I only have a moment, but you are to keep this,' he would say.

Oh, what would I give him? he thought and he inventoried his pockets.

'You are to keep this,' he would say. 'It is a magic quarter. Every time you see it, every time you touch it, you will magically remember that you are not bad, but good. You are good. Do you understand?'

'Now, listen to me—one day you will *lose* the quarter. This is part of the plan. When this occurs, it means that each time you see *any* coin then you will remember that you are good.'

In the fantasy the man pressed the coin into the boy's hand and quickly stood and walked away into the terminal.

As he finished the fantasy he saw the woman walking out of the washroom and saw her return to the two good children and saw the three of them smile and rise and organize themselves around their bags and lift them and start off. As they left, she looked at the boy on the bench and glared at him to say, ' . . . well?' And the boy rose and followed them. □

GRANTA

BLAKE MORRISON

DOCTORS AND NURSES

It's early evening in the bedroom, the heat of honeysuckled July, a sweet breeze through the sash. Skirtless, jumperless, she lies on the floor, her hair settling about her like a silky parachute. She turns away and laughs, stretching her left arm to a book behind her, just beyond reach, stretching further to slide it from the shelf. I unbuckle her shoes and pluck them in turn from each heel: they brush her soles as they pass, tickling, it seems, for she turns her head away from the book and giggles. The tights next. Tights on such a day! It must have been cold this morning when that decision was made. Practised, instinctive, not stirring from her page, she lifts her bum to let the seat of the tights pass under, and then I roll them down over her moley thighs and gleaming calves. The tights furl and thicken as they go, closing in on themselves then dropping from her ankles in a figure of eight. I hold her foot in my hand and run a finger along its length, from the heel, over the film of sweat beads on her arch (like the moist underside of canal bridges), to the caterpillar softness at the back of each toe. I wiggle my fingers, as if to tickle her, an intzy-wintzy spider, moving up from toe to neck. It drives her mad, most nights, but tonight she's too preoccupied to notice, growing into her book, maybe, or growing out of me. How often in the past she's sat in my lap, drumming those legs against my legs, my face behind her neck, as she sings a jingle to me or I recount some well-worn story from my paltry canon. It can't last, I know, the way she hangs on to my words as I hang on to her, the transfixion, the big-eyed trust and reverence. It can't last, her sense of me as someone who can do no wrong, or at least no wrong by her. I want to savour it while I can: the luck, the idolatry, the responsibility it bestows.

The blouse now, penultimate: I unbutton it from the top. It snags here and there where thread has loosened in the buttonholes, down to the last button, which as it comes away brings with it the right side of her blouse, exposing her right nipple, shallow navel and the rose-pink butterfly hovering on the waistband of her white pants. She sits up now, languorous from evening sun and carpet pile, still no words between us, though she's quietly humming to herself as I slip the right sleeve of her blouse off, then peel the last of it away from her left. I expect her to stand now so I can kneel in front of her (as is our custom) and slide her knickers over her knees and let her, step by step, walk free of them. But she's frolicsome on the shagpile and lies back again, waving her legs in the air as she dips back in her book and waits for me to do it all for her. Between finger and thumb, I take hold of the waistband by her little hip-juts and pull the knickers off—upwards, not downwards, for her legs are still pointing at the ceiling. Finally naked now, she pedals her feet and skirls with laughter, though whether at the book or at her nudity it's hard to say. I want to move her to the bed for the rest of our nightly ritual, but no, she says, no, she's staying as she is, digging her spine into the pile, leaving me impatient but marvelling at her body—tilty nose, avalanche of hair, pale nipples, soft stomach, candid slit—and pondering my part in it. I think of tickling and pinching her to transcendent helplessness. I think of hoisting her on top of me, to ride and jockey me, another of our games. I think of lifting her by the feet and dangling her upside down, like those abandoned children in medieval paintings, tied by the ankles from the branches of trees to save them from wild animals. But her languor wins me over: all right, she can have it her way. I lift the pillow on her bed and from under it her nightie, which I carry to where she lies. Time's running out. I hear a shout from below.

'Ready yet?'

'Nearly,' I call.

'Shall I come up and do her?'

'No, it's OK, my turn.'

Then, quieter, just to her, I say: 'Story now?' At once she's on her feet, arms raised as the nightie collapses over her head, washing herself at the basin with her green hippo sponge, taking from me the yellow toothbrush with its twirl of Macleans Milkteeth, hopping as she does. A gleamy, gappy grin, a last little spitout of pink and then she hurls herself into the gap between the pillows and the duvet, the runkled hollow where half her life is spent. I serve her with a last kiss. I stare down into the lair of her infancy. I stand and wait as my wife comes in with *Alice in Wonderland* and milk.

Is a father allowed to miss his children physically? Should I feel guilty that I do? Tactility, skin-joy. A baby's hand around my little finger. The silver seal of a milk blister on an upper lip—a suck-bruise, a transparent chancre. The rolling Rubens thighs, and yet the legs so pliable that babies can suck their own ankles. The pink implosion of a birthmark. The downy downs of shoulder, back and bum. The damp patch on my cotton T-shirt where a mouth's been nuzzling at my heart. Or whiter, frothier tidemarks—the sick-up from a drained breast. Unbroken threads and plumb lines of drool. Those reflex smiles and whimperings in sleep, exactly as you see in dreaming dogs. Banana goo darkening in a dish with Peter Rabbits on the rim.

The economy of language when they're babies—no wasted words, no words at all, just these hums and purrs and back-of-the-throat pleasure sounds. Your own inarticulacy, matching theirs—the silly names you use. The untroubled brow a tabula rasa. The puggy plughole of a nostril, struggling to take it all in. The black eyes you can see yourself come and go in. For six months even their shit smells beautiful—soft fudge and caramel.

A child in my lap, being read to, and I find myself erect. Love of children. It's not supposed to be to do with sex. It isn't to do with sex. I have no desire to have sex with my child, with any child, but this feeling is something like desire. It would horrify me for this child to touch my erection, or even know I had one, yet it is there. Love of children. No mother would have to defend herself. For fathers it's more difficult. No one trusts a man now with small kids. The anger I felt when that woman in the babysitting circle explained with some embarrassment she could not let me sit for her, nothing personal I must understand, but she would not leave her three girls in the custody of a male. No point being angry. We're liabilities. Too many other men have queered the pitch. And how to explain that erection if you had to? Not desire but love's ecstasy, suffusion, bliss, warmth in your lap, the rub of a little bum on a prick. A child makes you feel alive, yourself a child. Newness amid so much age and death.

And yet their life eats into yours, takes it away. Newborn, they bring you closer to mortality. Their cries are like little ropes, tying you down—Gulliver among the Lilliputians. Children: a vexation to our youth, what's left of it, and no comfort to old age. That great need for them to sleep—for their own good, for ours too, whose dream is to rest in peace. All those opiates—poppy syrup, quietness, Mother Siegel's Soothing Syrup, Calpol—to get them off and out of the way. All that cradle-rocking, the gentle push of exasperation.

I have another memory from a holiday in North Wales: moon, midnight, the knife beam of the lighthouse. She has been crying for two hours, inconsolably, from an angry red mouth. I've walked up and down and back and forth with her, feeling the anger rising in me too. But now she's silent at last, rocked asleep on my shoulder, her body against my chest, my right hand cupping the back of her head, my left arm tucked beneath her bum. Slowly, still rocking, I move towards the object of desire. A barred chamber of rest, the cot glows under its night light like a prison camp. I bend my knees so that I'm poised above it. The white sheet shines from the compound. She stirs, my prisoner stirs. She is now inside the cot, but poised nine inches above the mattress, at arm's length, suspended in flight. Slowly I pilot her to the sheet and lay her down, a landing so soft the passengers are cheering in my head. One of my hands is still trapped beneath her, the other pressed soothingly above. Rocking with my knee against the bars, I have to slide the lower hand free without disturbing her. Before I withdraw the upper hand I slide the duvet over and up to her chin. I raise myself to upright, the pain in my back making me catch my breath (shhhh). Gently, silently, I walk backwards from the room, remembering to miss the creaky board. Once I'm in the hall, I leap two feet and punch the air. I feel a touch of contempt for her now—that she hadn't seen through my little trick. But my triumph is short-lived. Two minutes later I hear her cries. Livid, I go back into the room with clenched fists, ready to kill her.

I don't, of course, but not for the first time it strikes me that the term employed for getting babies into their cots and asleep—'putting them down'—is also what we call the mercy killing of sick or injured animals. The need for silence and end to pain. Most people with children understand that momentary desire. Family life contains such extremes: loving your children and hurting them, dreading them dying and wanting them never to stir.

Is sex abuse part of most people's histories? Is it part of mine? Neither my parents nor other adults abused me. We were warned of strange men with sweets, whose cars we were not to get into, but no such temptations came our way. So we abused each other instead. 'Sexually explored each other.' Played Doctors and Nurses.

Whose idea was it? Who suggested it first? It could have been any of us. It could have been all of us. It is like trying to discover who moved the glass on the ouija board. 'Mummies and Daddies' was another name, but for my sister and me, our parents being doctors, that came to the same thing. We played it with friends. Keeping it in the family, we played it with our cousins. Most incestuous of all, we played it by ourselves. 'Oh, please let us,' we pleaded with our parents, 'We won't make any noise. We won't make any mess.' Not knowing what went on, or knowing but believing it educational, they lent us the necessary equipment: plastic medicine spoons, swabs, cotton wool, bandages, a metal kidney dish, safety pins, a stethoscope, a flick-open metal blood-pressure box, syringes with the needles removed, a thermometer in a silver case like a propelling pencil. Not necessary, really: you could play without props. The main point was taking your clothes off.

To be a doctor you had to be a boy, put a stethoscope round your neck, sit down at the table beside the bed, pretend to be writing a prescription and ask, 'What seems to be the matter?' To be a nurse you had to be a girl, fetch patients for doctor, hand him his knives and scalpels and change bandages. To be a patient you had to lie down, open your mouth, say aaah, breathe deeply, sit up, breathe deeply, take your top off, breathe deeply, turn over and lie down, breathe deeply, undo your zip, pull your pants or skirt down, breathe deeply, take the rest of your clothes off, please, the knickers and vest, lie down again, breathe deeply, keep still while we just check your body over, stop wriggling please, the stethoscope may be cold, the thermometer may tickle, but how do you expect to get better if you wriggle about like that? Breathe deeply, lift your arm, lift the other arm, your left leg, your right leg, could you spread your legs a little? Breathe deeply, a little wider with the legs please, wider and lift a bit, ah nurse, I think we have located the problem, it will be necessary to do some probing about here, a wooden scalpel, please, and then—this may hurt a bit—the injection, a few moments and you'll be feeling better, is that better? Better now? Good, take this prescription, these pills, and come back and visit me in a month.

The rules were very simple and everywhere the same. Once a friend called Emma came and played Doctors and Nurses with me in the stables, just the two of us. It was hot and prickly with the straw, and I'd forgotten what girls looked like. It was funny how I always forgot and needed to see again, even though each time I saw, I thought: Now I know, that'll do me. Showing yourself wasn't wrong at Emma's age (five, was she? six?) when you didn't know what it was for. But I was ten now (or eleven, was it? twelve?) and sensed there was something illicit about it, and knowing this when Emma didn't know but still making her do it felt (or afterwards felt) wrong.

There had been another incident, Irving's idea, not mine. We'd made this deal with my sister, Gillian: she could have a sherbet fountain if she and Christine Rawlinson came into her bedroom and undressed. Irving and I would be hiding under the beds but we'd not say anything, and Christine would never know. Gillian wasn't keen: it took the sherbet fountain we had and the promise of a Mars bar. We lay in the dust with the bedspread hanging down, where things had slipped down from behind the pillow, pencils, dolls' clothes, a glass rabbit, a book of pony stories. The girls came in, and Gill said, How about being dancers? And they got down to their knickers and vests. We saw this through the purple tassels of the bedspread, where we were trying to keep still but had to shuffle a bit so both of us had a view. We didn't think Christine would take the rest off, but, no arguing, she did. They were doing high scissor kicks, and I could see the scissor snip between their legs. Irving and I were snorting by then, with dust and the giggling out of hand, and the girls stooped and lifted the bedspread and we crawled out. They got back in their knickers and said it wasn't fair, that we must do the same, show them our willies. No chance, I said, we're off now, but Irving thought we ought to, fair's fair, just for a tick, not as long as they'd done, but so they could see, three seconds, that was our final offer. OK, so we dropped our shorts and then our white underpants, and our things stuck up at the same angle, the angle of the pole outside the barber's. Could they touch them for a moment? they asked, just to feel what they felt like? No. Please. Well, all right.

Only Auntie Sheila seemed suspicious about our Doctors and Nurses.

'Again? You're always playing that.'

'Oh, please.'

'Where's the harm, Sheila, love?' my father said. 'It's natural at their age.'

'I know what they do, that's all.'

'Of course that's what they do. But it could be worse, love: it'll be Postman's Knock in a year or two, snogging in cupboards.'

'Please.'

'All right. But not too much taking clothes off.'

That day we took Gillian's clothes off once, and Edgar's twice, and Jean's (she being the youngest) three times. We were getting bored when Auntie Sheila called 'Is there a doctor in the house?' and in she walked without knocking. We were not used to grown-ups in the surgery, and it was a bit of a mess with the wooden tonsil-prodder things scattered everywhere and a roll of bandage which we'd used to tie Gillian to the chair with, and Jean naked on her back on the bed, and Edgar pumping himself up with the blood-pressure gauge, and Robert and me fighting inside the pillowcase. Auntie Sheila looked slitty-eyed cross and said she would speak to my father. I was afraid. Maybe we'd gone too far—like the time I lost the cricket ball at Uncle Gordon's caravan and hacked his gorse bush to bits trying to find it. There was a right way to behave, and most kids knew it, but sometimes you got carried away and could forget. Anxious, we tidied up with extra-special care and then ran out to play tennis on the back lawn, over a strawberry net strung between two poles.

There can't have been much trouble, because we continued playing Doctors and Nurses for some years after. How many years? Till I was eleven, twelve, thirteen? Did that, does that, make me an abuser? Of my sister, as well as cousins and friends? Ugly to admit to myself, hard to face. Merely to touch a boy's penis, or girl's vagina, is not abuse, or wasn't once thought so, even when adults are doing the touching: those mothers and nannies who used to stroke their babies' sexual parts (still do) to soothe them off to sleep. And aren't children naturally immodest, before they're anything else? Which means when they abuse each other, it's consensual, not a matter for censure. All the same . . . It's hard to know what innocence is and what's left of it when consciousness enters and if shame is a condition only of being adult. Doctors and Nurses: it was a harmless game and it was not. □

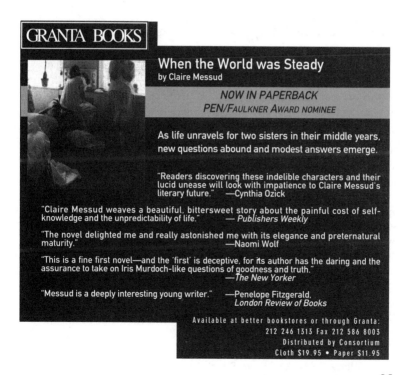

GRANTA

BRIAN HALL
I AM HERE

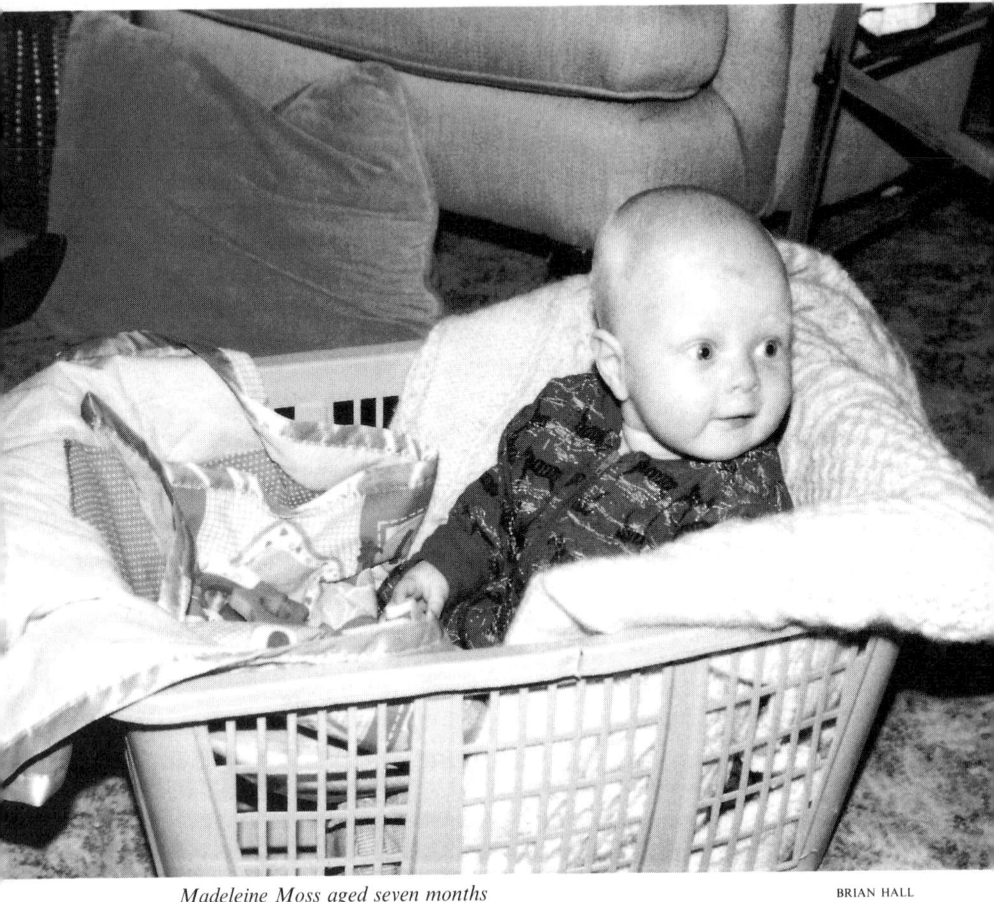

Madeleine Moss aged seven months BRIAN HALL

We knew almost nothing about her before she was born, not even her sex, so we must have referred to her as 'it', although I can't imagine that now.

She was quiet when Pamela moved and active when Pamela was still, particularly after we had crawled into bed. Perhaps the motion comforted her, as Pamela's rocking or my pacing would later, and her kicks and somersaults as we lay in bed were protests. Or perhaps the motion cowed her, and our bedtime was a chance to be bold. She would also stir, sometimes violently, when I played the piano, or sang with my lips pressed against Pamela's stomach. The same doubt assailed us here: was this pleasure or indignation? Or was there no more feeling involved than when a pupil constricts at a bright light?

Foetuses often suck their thumbs, or even their whole hands, sometimes so hard they raise a blister. Is this because they need comforting? (Do they suck their thumbs when their fathers sing to them?) If so, why do they seek it in this way, when the primeval comforter surely is food, and nourishment has always come to them through their navels? Or are they merely practising, strengthening the sucking action for the day when they will need it?

Do foetuses dream? If not, why do they exhibit rapid eye-movement during sleep? If so, what could they be dreaming of? Their thumbs, perhaps, the perfect shape of them. Or the rhythmic boom of the cosmos, the first music of this first sphere. Or a muffled dog's bark and the mother's adrenalin that jolted them, too, something to fear already, something to make them suck their thumbs while they dream.

On a September evening two days after Pamela's due date, I was picking vegetables in the garden and as I walked back toward the house I saw a fat moon rising over the sugar maples. I remembered having read somewhere—in the *New England Journal of Medicine*? the *National Enquirer*?—that once a month, at the full moon, there is a spike in births. Early the next morning Pamela's water broke. She laboured lightly through the day and night and on through the following morning until, at mid-afternoon on the day of the full moon, it got serious. Since we had planned a home birth we didn't have to compete for a birthing room in the presumably swamped hospital, but had midwives with us in the dining room, where Pamela rocked in a rocking chair, lowing, hour after hour. She has a high tolerance for pain and she didn't much need me, but I sat next to her, stroking her hard, squared-off stomach with a circular motion she said was comforting, and though I am not a mystical sort, I thought of the pregnant moon, pregnant Pamela, the chair rocking back and forth like the ebb and flow of tides, the tides of her contractions, the tide of sea-watery amniotic fluid, the high tides far away along seashores on this full-moon night.

Madeleine was born just past midnight. The room had been heated to eighty degrees, so it would not have felt cold, but what a chilling void it must have seemed. Perhaps it felt like free fall, to have the hugging walls slide back and her arms and legs spring out, jerking like antennae searching for a surface. But free fall is weightless, and she would have felt instead a new heaviness, a lost buoyancy, as though for nine months she had been falling, falling, and now she had landed.

Laid on Pamela's stomach, she churned her arms and legs, and slid on her grease toward the breast. She gave a predator's glittering one-eyed squint up at her mother's exhausted face and chomped down on the nipple. Now, at last, she could vent this primal urge on the organ for which it was designed, the Platonic ideal of her thumbs. Nothing came out. But perhaps she didn't know anything was supposed to come out, she knew only that she must suck. She presumably did not know that the immediate purpose of this first, dry chewing was to make the uterus throw off the placenta and clamp shut over its massive wound before the mother bled to death.

What could she hear? Water remains in the newborn's ear, easing the transition to the sharper sounds outside the womb. She could probably already recognize Pamela's voice and perhaps mine, but the midwives' steadily rising argument—Pamela was bleeding too much, this was frightening, the uterus would not shut down because the bladder was full, but Pamela was too numb to urinate, they should call the doctor, no they shouldn't—probably didn't even register as background noise.

How well could she see? Not across the room, not to the door through which one of the midwives was hurrying toward the telephone. A newborn can focus between eight and ten inches, the distance from breast to face. Adrenalin grants her an hour or so of alertness and calm, a heightened awareness that will not return for days, and this is the window celebrated in recent years as an opportunity to bond with the maternal face, the one clear image in the little circle beyond which vague shapes flutter and murmur. But the maternal face was replaced by a bearded one, as Pamela was coaxed into the shower, where warm water on the abdomen would supposedly help her urinate. Madeleine didn't seem to care. She stared into my eyes. Her face was squashed, her eyes Uralic, her skin pink and blemishless. Perhaps she concentrated. I could not. I listened to the shower, and fatigue and the sight of so much blood made me feel faint, and I was distracted by fierce admonitions to myself to bond! bond!, since bonding would be especially important if—as at that moment seemed possible—I ended up raising this baby on my own.

From the shower, gasps of relief. It had taken an hour. A few minutes later the steady bleeding stopped.

The new family got into a fresh bed. Midwives and relatives faded away. It was three a.m. The only sound in the room was one Madeleine had surely never heard before: her own gummy snorting, as loud as a warthog.

Tiny nibs of white-blonde hair marked out a hurricane whorl on her red scalp, and her irises were storm clouds of dark blue-grey. Her pupils were enormous. As windows to the soul, they were thrown wide open, drawing me toward them for a look, a trip, a fall through. I am not being fanciful. Since your pupils dilate when you see something you like, and since we all love to be liked, this is probably the genes' way of seducing the parents, of preventing them from abandoning this alarming burden somewhere in the forest.

As for Madeleine's attitude, one can only guess, in the first weeks, at the mix of volition and reflex. Placed on her stomach, she 'swam', kicking her legs and flailing her arms. Attagirl! I might think, or I might hurry to relieve her of what could be distress. But all newborns do this automatically, like wind-up toys.

Is it a dying remnant of life in the womb? Or a much deeper genetic signpost, pointing back to our primeval aquatic existence?

In the so-called Moro reflex, a newborn who thinks she is falling will shoot out both hands, spreading fingers to clutch at the air, and then pull her arms tight against her chest. An idea almost inevitably intrudes: branches! The hairy, pea-brained pre-australopithecine babe is falling out of the tree and it spastically spreadeagles to catch branches in its strong grip. If a human baby, in falling, happens to be holding a pencil in one hand, only her other hand will shoot out. Evidently, she thinks the pencil is a branch. But if the baby is holding her thumbs, this satisfies her as well as the pencil does, and neither hand reaches out. Newborns frequently hold their thumbs. You could argue this supports the theory. If the hands are reaching for branches, then branch-like objects are comforting, and babies hold their thumbs all day for the feeling of security it gives them. You could equally argue it undermines the theory. I see primeval babies plummeting down through the understorey, blissfully holding their thumbs.

The swimming reflex, the Moro—these are remnants, somewhat mysterious, of larger urges and larger questions, spanning aeons and species, out of which the baby sails. They disappear before our eyes as she individualizes, as she slowly coalesces out of Life into her own life.

At twelve and a half weeks, when it is less than two inches long, a human foetus will turn its head to the right if its right palm is touched, or to the left for its left palm, open its tiny translucent mouth and suck. When I held Madeleine to my shoulder for a burp in the dim pre-dawn of the first and many subsequent mornings, she would work her way from my neck to my cheek to my chin, a mountain climber rounding the corner of a cliff face, her eyes closed, chuffing all the way, leaving a trail of incipient hickeys. Like the true mountain climber, she had no choice: I was there.

Later, when I watched her grip the air and bring two fists to her open mouth, the word 'mammatropic' would come to mind: she was perfectly capable of distinguishing a face from a foot and a breast from a brick, and yet when she got hungry she did not look around for Pamela or the breast, she simply tried to stuff whatever was near into her mouth—my shirt, the table edge, empty air—and kept doing it until the breast came within reach. Like the hands grabbing for the invisible branches in the Moro reflex, this rooting seemed blindly opportunistic and dubiously suggestive of some deep past when each mother (of whatever species we were back then) had thousands of babies, paying attention to none of them, and they all grasped blindly; if one happened to find a breast, it survived.

And yet it was in the nursing that Pamela and I got our earliest sense of Madeleine as an individual, something more than a mere bundle of irrepressible urges. When we compared her with the babies of our friends (all of whom seemed to be having babies at the same time we did; or did we just lose our other friends?), she seemed by far the most avid nurser. She had an idiosyncratic way of attaching. She would dart her head forward and fasten on the nipple with a sudden bite, vigorously shaking her head. Later, when the rooting reflex abated, and she was capable of turning away from the nipple after a couple of sucks to see what else was going on, she seemed partly to do this so often because it allowed her to start again, with another attacking bite and shake. She already had amusements.

All newborns seem pre-programmed to be attracted to the human face, but only some of them will respond to your stuck-out tongue by sticking out their own tongues. At my repeated attempts, Madeleine only furrowed her brow and slightly tucked her chin. Puzzlement and mild concern? Actually, books say newborns focus on the human face, but whenever I held Madeleine she would usually stare, if she looked at me at all, at the top of my head, or over my shoulder. Developmentalists coolly explain that babies like edges. New Agers have their own positively Wordsworthian interpretation: babies can see auras.

Like many parents, I found it almost impossible not to imitate her expressions back to her. This seems an odd instinct, since surely Madeleine was supposed to be learning from me. As long as she was smiling, everything was fine. She was happy, I was happy she was happy, and either she was happy I was happy she was happy, or more likely, she was confirmed in her original happiness by the fact that I was happy she was happy. Either way, it was a closed circuit of intense satisfaction to me, and enough to her so that she would stick with it for a minute or more. Unfortunately, along with smiling back at her, or crossing my eyes back at her, I would unthinkingly look startled back at her. This particular feedback loop would immediately spiral into a screech. She would startle at something trivial, say my bumping a drawer on the changing table, and on seeing my cartoonish wide-eyed 'Oh!' would infer that her worst fears were true (that she was hurt? that I was hurt? was there yet any distinction between 'she' and 'I'?) and would instantly break into wailing.

She stared intently at round things, presumably because they looked like breasts. Or perhaps because they looked like faces. I had never realized how many round objects there are in our lives: doorknobs, watches, plates, saucers, tops of glasses, bottoms of glasses, crackers, cookies, cucumber slices, deodorant roll-balls, light bulbs. I could stand anywhere, and after a second or two she would focus on something round, lean toward it, lock on. Someone gave us a padded-disc squeeze toy with concentric circles and a bull's-eye, black on white. She adored it. Perhaps the central black spot was an eye, with concentric eyebrows. Or perhaps it was a nipple, creating its own magnetic field, an emanation of 'suck here' lines. The globe on our piano was either a winningly friendly fat-head or the gloriously over-swollen breast of her dreams. Above her changing pad, a mobile of black-and-white patterned discs (our impression that black-and-white objects were part of an educational craze for newborns was confirmed by this gift's brand name: Stim-Mobile) made a whole crowd of faces, jostling for an admiring view, or perhaps it was a happy return to the days when the baby had eight teats to choose from.

Madeleine also stared up a lot. One of the midwives said she looked at the ceiling because its blankness provided relief from over-stimulation. (I suppose I could have solved that problem by getting rid of the mobile.) But I wasn't convinced. I suspected the smoke alarms, which were round with nipple-like test buttons, or the circular plates holding up the ceiling lights. We eventually discovered that she loved to hold yogurt lids, and it occurred to me that they were both round and blank. Like me with my brandied evening coffee, did she prefer her stimulants soothing?

But there was more to her looking up than the ceiling. She also looked 'up', when lying down. That is, she arched her back to look along the bed, away from her feet. She apparently just liked to arch her back. Often when we held her, she pushed the back of her head hard against our palms until she ended up prone in our lowered arms, her head hanging upside down. Interestingly, Pamela had done the same thing when she was a baby. Perhaps the point is to strengthen the back and neck muscles, since the first physical achievements will be to sit up unaided and to roll (which is accomplished by arching the back).

Whatever the reason, as I paced with her, or carried her around doing chores, she was always twisted in my arms, looking backward. In her wide-eyed, solemn gaze I imagined I saw sadness, but with a mature resignation. I seemed always to be carrying her away from the object of her greatest desire.

The sound of conversation was comforting. Both Pamela and I talk a lot, but since I could hold Madeleine indefinitely without getting tired, she would usually be in my arms, and she would never lie quieter, she would never slip more easily into sleep than when she was leaning back against my chest while I droned on and on. Once asleep, nothing conversational—crosstalk conducted at a roar, barked agreements, finger-jabbing pontificating—would rouse her, or even cause her to stir. In marked contrast, there were two soft sounds that invariably made her jump and whimper in her sleep. One of them was clearing my throat. The other was any kind of rustling. Balling a plastic bag next to her crib would disturb her more than dropping a pot lid.

I happily settled on a theory: to Madeleine, the conversational roar was the sound of the tribe, filling the void, keeping the predator at bay with noise around the fire. The rustling—so quiet, so stealthy—was the predator itself, creeping up over dead leaves and twigs. And my throat-clearing was the very growl of the beast. Men tend to talk in high voices to their babies. As a fake tenor in pick-up choirs, I had a well-developed falsetto anyway, and I derived a (perhaps significantly) deep satisfaction from wa-wawing old songs to Madeleine an octave above where they belonged. One theory I've read holds that men do this instinctively in order to sound more like the mother, who is, after all, the vital parent at this stage. But perhaps we do it in order to sound less like a sabre-toothed tiger.

Once you settle on the primate-memory model—the idea that while parents are driving to the doctor or the supermarket, honking at other members of the herd, their baby in the back seat is crossing the veldt, fearing carnivores and lethal weather—you can amuse yourself devising reasons for all sorts of things. The most terrified we ever saw Madeleine in her first three months was when I put her in her car seat on the morning of the first snowfall and unthinkingly set about scraping ice off the windshield. The black scraper blade was a paw, clawing at the fragile saplings hiding the mouth to her cave. My allergic sneezing was so common she eventually got used to it, but to my blowing my nose, never. The white tissue was some small but insanely aggressive animal, a proto-wolverine, which with greedy snorts was devouring my face.

For these fears, or the pain of gas, or the obscure misery of fatigue, she could be soothed by pacing. The rocking chair worked well enough, but walking worked better. From the kitchen through the dining room to the living room was about thirty feet. Refrigerator to piano, back to refrigerator. I walked to California on that quarterdeck in Madeleine's first year. She would almost immediately quiet down and look up and watch the smoke alarm sail to the rear, then the round plate of the ceiling light. Then the plate would come back, then the smoke alarm, then the smoke alarm again, then the plate. (I'm tempted to see in these comforting discs passing overhead a root of the popular passion for flying saucers, filled with aliens who are almost all face, and knowledgeable beyond our understanding.)

Parents tend to pace or rock their babies at the heart's rate of seventy per minute. Although I am left-handed, I always carried Madeleine in my left arm, thus forcing myself to do chores with my clumsy right hand, and I have since learned that both right- and left-handed people usually carry their babies on their left sides, where the heartbeat is loudest. So surely pacing calms because it's a return to womb rhythms, physically and aurally. But I am reluctant to abandon my model. When the primate family set out on a journey it was at its most vulnerable, in the open, in the unknown. Babies who cried when their parents walked out into the world betrayed their location to sabre-toothed tigers and proto-wolverines.

When I first held Madeleine up to a mirror, she ignored her own reflection and stared at mine. I tried to direct her attention to her image, but she merely glanced at my pointing finger and back at me. At this stage she took in everything with the same wide, bright-blank eyes, all reception and no transmission, so interest could be gauged only by the length of time she stared at an object. My face was noteworthy, and hers was not, which suggested to me that she could already recognize my face, and in the confused swirl of her world settled on it as a familiar island. Perhaps she also knew that engagement with this face brought results, like getting picked up and carried to the breast.

The third or fourth time we stood in front of the mirror, she made a discovery: me, my reflection, me, my reflection. Two of me! I imagined surprise. But why should she have been surprised? Why not ten of me? Why not two faces for all the people in the world, one with breasts and the other with arms to carry her to them?

One might wonder why babies would be surprised by anything. But some expectations do seem to be hard-wired. Newborns turn their eyes in the direction of a sound. Apparently, they have an *a priori* expectation that aural and visual clues will match. Perhaps Madeleine was not surprised by there being two of me, but by the fact that the mouth in front of her moved, whereas the voice—'Look! Two of me!'—came from off to one side.

After six weeks of loving parental beams evoking blank stares, Madeleine's first real smile was bestowed on her Uncle Jon. The smile may originate as an appeasement gesture, and Jon, strange-looking anyway, was grotesquely flapping his tongue and rolling his eyes at the time. An alternative theory hit upon by the wounded parents was that Jon's bald pate made him look especially like a big breast.

Around two months, she began to prefer her own reflection in the mirror to mine. Perhaps she had now grown familiar with her own face and liked its simpler, more ideal features, its exaggerated eyes. Or perhaps it was still less familiar to her than my face, but as the world around her grew less intimidating, she was beginning to prefer novelty. Certainly her interests were expanding beyond mere faces (love me!) and breasts (feed me!), as she perhaps began to assume the bare fact of her survival and wonder what else there might be.

For example, colour. The black-and-white Stim-Mobile and bull's-eye squeak toy were appropriate to those first weeks when her eyes would float in opposite directions—her hands flapping in panic as the already bewildering world doubled on her—and she needed a sufficiently stark edge over which to throw an ocular grappling hook. But at two months, Madeleine could track a moving object. She no longer cared about people's auras. Among her earliest possessions was a small yellow terry-cloth duck with a printed wing of blazing red. That wing fascinated her. It was so bright it seemed to float off the body of the duck. She would arch her back in the fold-up travel bassinet that was her bed for the first four months and stare up at the red wing in the corner.

One morning I was peering in at that avid stare. Something momentous was happening. Her right arm was twitching. It jigged her hand up and flapped it down again. The hand fluttered at the end of the questing arm like a fish on a line, struggling, but unable to control where it would be yanked next. It fetched up against the cloth side of the bassinet and stuck there. The autonomous wrist joined the fray, and commenced wiping the hand up and down the wall in an attempt to drag it free. When it succeeded, the force of the effort shot the arm above the head again. Madeleine arched her back farther, focused on the wing. The arm jerked. The hand whipsawed. At last it glanced off the duck, nudging it out of reach. The arm lay still, and the hand softly flexed and unflexed, as though gasping for breath.

Interaction! Agency! Surely our hands are our most important discovery before speech. Madeleine was no longer a passive viewer, a mere receptacle. The world was different for her being in it. She had moved the red wing. And a more profound discovery was now possible. She and the world were distinct from each other. Her hands—these fascinating wiggly objects that floated into her field of vision even more often than the face with the breasts and the other one with the arms—could be commanded. They, like the two obedient faces, apparently belonged to her. The red wing did not. It would not move until the hand touched it. And when the hand did touch it, Madeleine could see the boundary of self: Madeleine touched not-Madeleine.

When the pacifier was brought close, she would make a clumsy grab for it to stuff it in her mouth, usually forcing it sideways so that the nipple lay along her cheek. Holding it firmly there, she would turn her head to get her mouth on the right part, but since the whole thing turned with her, she would keep turning until the twist of her neck stopped her, and she would drop it over her shoulder. Plugged in at last, her eyes taking on a sated, distant look, she would keep a finger on it to prevent its escape, and soon learned to loop the finger through a hole in its plastic shield for added security. Then she would forget the arrangement and, reaching for something else, she would inadvertently pop the pacifier out of her mouth and fling it away.

Glitches aside, that was clearly the point of hands, to stuff things into the mouth. Now when Madeleine was held up to the mirror, she not only beamed at her reflection, she reached out to enfold it and drag it in for a few good hard sucks. It is said that babies put things in their mouths in order to explore them, that mouths are more sensitive determiners of shape and texture than fingers are, and I have seen babies for which this seems to be true. It was not true for Madeleine. She did not put things in her mouth to explore them, but to eat them.

Here was her first great frustration, her first sense of the inherent insufficiency of existence. Here was the universal human desire, in its unsublimated infancy, to consume whatever appealed to her, to erase the subject–object division that these same hands had taught her only weeks before. Madeleine's pleasure in a discovered object was literally visceral. Even before she got it in her mouth, one could sense in her arm-pumping excitement—want! want!—an edge of desperation. And then the thing itself: hard, tasteless, milkless. She took it out and shouted objections.

Eventually she gave up trying, and by four months was never putting anything in her mouth except the breast, the pacifier and her own fist, which presumably did not highlight so painfully the subject–object division. If her hands could not be the means of returning her to the paradisiacal days before she fell out of the surrounding world, then she had to accept and refine their real function, that of emphasizing the distinction between herself and the world.

A pointed finger became a concrete manifestation of the attention Madeleine could focus on not-Madeleine. Bending low over the tray of her high chair, she would fix her gaze on a stray droplet of juice and lower the index finger on to it with excruciating care. She would not so much probe the drop as hold it down. Looking at us, she would solemnly raise that finger and guide it into the line between her eyes and ours, as though commanding us, too, to stay where we were.

Fingers tested existence. Meal after meal, puzzled anew, they tried to pick up the pictures on her high-chair tray of babies like little princes riding planetary rattles, arguing that her eyes had been fooled. They could annihilate: a single sweep of her hand across the rimless tray and all her lunch ceased to exist. They could transform: they enlarged the white roll by the toilet a hundredfold, then made it smaller than ever, and multiple.

The most rewarding transformations of all—so complete, so unpredictable—could be accomplished with a simple turn of the wrist. Flaps! In *Pat the Bunny*, the blue scrap of cloth is poked up, and Paul's face appears. In *Where's Spot?* a piano becomes an alligator, a grandfather clock becomes a snake, and (to the accompaniment of triumphant parental cries of woof-woof-woof) the basket becomes Spot himself. Create and destroy, create and destroy, a power beyond anything else in her experience. In a sense all books are flap books, because pages themselves are flaps, and Madeleine loved those biscuit-like board books from the moment she could grapple with them, certainly not for any story, nor for mere mechanical progression through the pages, but for any one of the hinged boards, tilting back and forth to change its face.

Globes and circles retained their importance, but now a whole new class of objects in the house called to her. Drawer handles that flipped up and fell back down. Pot lids that turned over with a cowbell clank. And best of all, doors! To a baby not yet strong enough to lift an orange these were an amazement, as a single swipe transformed a whole wall.

Along the way she had learned to use both hands together, to pick up an object too big for one alone. Then she discovered she could shift a smaller object from hand to hand. Next, with what I thought was amazing speed, she learned how to use this technique to hold on to an object while a shirt was being put on or taken off, casually shifting it between sleeves.

From here it was a short step to handing objects to us. Partly, this was imitative, since as far as she could tell the point of our existence was mainly to hand objects to her. Partly, it was reassuring, like peek-a-boo, which appeared at around this time (six months). In peek-a-boo, the parental face does the worst thing it can do: it disappears; but a few seconds later it pops back, and relief bubbles up in a giggle. When Madeleine raised her dress above her head and waited for us to sing out, 'Where's Madeleine?', precipitating a downward fling on 'There she is!', it was not she who was hiding, but the whole world, and what reassurances later in life could match that budding realization that the cosmos did not need her constant vigilance to continue existing? (Perhaps this early scepticism is also at the root of infants' distress at something so natural as falling asleep. How can they be sure that their eyelids descending are not curtains coming down on the last act?)

Handing objects to us provided a pale echo of this reassurance. Madeleine would hold up a cracker and stare, mesmerized, as my hand approached and latched on to the far side. She would release, and the object would float away. In control, out of control. But not like the red wing in the bassinet, which was beyond all control. Part of her fascination in our exchange perhaps came from the realization that my hand was a large version of her hand, that the cracker was moving from her control to my control. But she taught us early that this could not be the end of it. No, the point of this experiment (none of these was a game) was to provide proof through induction that the object would return to her. This was more a social reassurance than the ontological one of peek-a-boo. Although, as it had turned out, we were not part of her, we would not take her things away.

The handing back and forth of an object served another

social function. We were communicating. Since Madeleine could not yet talk, her way to get me on to the subject of her cracker was to hand it to me. The culmination of this hand-centred sociability was the wave. As I held Madeleine up and chirped, 'Wave! Wave!', and Pamela or some stranger flapped her hands, perhaps it seemed to Madeleine like some sort of handing-off at a distance, a conversational lobbing of invisible greetings at each other. Only God knew what bye and hi meant, but that didn't matter; what mattered was that a wave established that she and we were thinking of bye or hi at the same time. Carrying such a freight of potential reassurance, the wave was a serious matter. Out of the corner of my eye I would glimpse a pale flutter across the room and turn to see Madeleine's hands, both held high and opening–closing (like the giving and taking of a cracker), and Madeleine staring at me as gravely as though the continuation of time and the cosmos depended on my response. I would of course wave back, and there we would be, stock-still at opposite ends of the room, waving solemnly at each other.

And if waving meant communing, and was therefore her first lesson in sublimating the desire to consume, perhaps it was no surprise that it also appeared when she ate. As I guided the spoon toward her mouth, was she waving to me to signal that yes, we were in agreement, I had understood what she wanted? Or was she waving to the food itself, out of some inarticulate need to pay tribute, the unburied seed of a culture's prayers to the corn god, or the saying of grace?

Falling asleep, she would have one hand on the pacifier in her mouth, the index finger looped through its side hole. The other arm would lie behind and stretched up along the head, the index finger inscribing slow circles in the short nap of hair. Those hands formed a cradle, an impenetrable barrier, and they had the entire universe covered, front and back. The index fingers pointed inward from either side, suggesting I Am Here. The two curtains would come down on this act, but the two hands would preserve a space for her until morning, and the two fingers would hold her in it.

I am here! Long before Madeleine acquired words she shouted it, her face purpling, in burr-edged annhs! achieved by clenching her diaphragm and forcing the last teaspoon of air from her body. The shouts reverberated through the house. She would pause for a moment to listen to that glow, pleased to have echo-located herself, before howling again, louder.

For Madeleine, immersion in language began in rituals of rhythm and song and only later calmed into utilitarian prose, a progression reflected in the maturation of national literatures. Don't all parents sing to their babies? Pamela rocked Madeleine to sleep with lullabies: 'I Gave My Love a Cherry', 'Hush Little Baby', 'Shenandoah'. I preferred pacing to rocking, and ballads to lullabies: 'Barbara Allen', 'The Demon Lover', 'Henry Martin'.

But songs were only a fraction of it. Virtually every time I spoke to Madeleine I used the sing-song voice that seems to come unbidden to parents, a rhythmic, rhyming chant, as though I were summoning her spirit, or coaxing a new one out of myself. The altered cadence must be useful to the infant, a signal that these words, hopping and bopping out of the background chatter, are meant especially for her. I found myself speculating about this one day after I had spent five minutes bouncing Madeleine in my arms and asking her, in a dotted eighth and sixteenth rhythm arranged in bars of 2/4: 'Who's this little | ba-by with the | stuffed-up | nose?' The theory, anyway, lent some dignity to the endearments for Madeleine that popped out of my mouth without my ever having consciously formulated them

Pamela relied less on rhythm in speaking to Madeleine, and more on pure ardour. She called her 'sweetest girl', 'love child', 'love bug', 'buglet'. She was counterbalancing my simple-minded doggerel with simple-hearted Homeric epithets. We didn't know it at the time, but we were filling stereotypical complementary roles, since mothers tend to soothe their babies, and fathers tend to stimulate them. The mother strokes, the father pokes. The mother hymns, the father rhymes.

I thought more about this when Madeleine began to speak in clear syllables. All over the world, babies begin with the same basic repertory of utterances. This core vocabulary, reasonably enough, consists of the easiest sounds to produce: the vowel sound 'ah'; the labial consonants p, b, and m; and the tongue taps t and d. It is no coincidence that the fundamental family words, 'mama', 'baba', 'papa', 'dada' and 'tata', which occur throughout the world, are constructed out of these sounds. But individual babies vary as to which of these sounds they use most, and Madeleine's preference was unequivocal: da!

She would say it upon spotting an object, a terse, tense sound, as though exclaiming, 'There!' Once we had handed the object to her, she would emit a 'da da da da', a ripple of satisfaction, descending like a sigh. As she lay in her crib, happily awake from a nap, she would say, 'Da da?' with a contemplative upward drift, and it would sound so uncannily as though she were addressing me that I would only half jokingly answer, 'Yes, honey?' and hover for a moment on the edge of a surreal expectation, until she tripped back down the scale: 'Da da da da.'

That point about 'mama', 'papa' and so on being nearly universal words for the core family has been frequently made, but I had never seen anyone go a step further and speculate as to why the 'm' sounds refer in most languages to the mother. (The father is assigned variously among the others, and the word for baby sometimes bears no resemblance to any of them, suggesting that parents don't need so urgently to believe that the baby is talking about itself.) Could this be connected to the observation that mothers tend to comfort their babies, while fathers stimulate them? 'Ma', with its initial phoneme conceivably rising out of a moan, the lips pursed as though around an absent nipple, struck me as a needy sound, whereas 'da' or 'pa'—declarative, plosive—were excited ones. To my admittedly biased eye, Madeleine seemed an exceptionally happy baby when compared with her peers, almost never crying and engaged to an unusual degree with the world around her. It was easy to convince myself that it all made sense. With no need of the solipsistic *ma* (me!), she could confine herself to the stochastic *da*—not only 'there!' in the Germanic languages, but 'yes!' in the Slavonic.

Crypto-sexist speculation aside, the bare fact remained: Madeleine said, 'Da'. And with this first sonic tool she beat out a rhythm, a treble-drum accompaniment to parental song—da! da! da! da!—complete with arms and legs jigging, the very motion that, as soon as she learned to crawl, would result in a back-and-forth, butt-high bounce, and when she learned to walk, would become the true stiff dance that most toddlers break into at the sound of music, the Mexican-bean jumping that dissolves their parents into surprised laughter, even though the kids have been attempting something like it ever since birth.

Madeleine's next step was to discover that vocalization—this stick with which she tapped objects, or beat out a rhythm to beat back not-Madeleine—could also be used to communicate, as her hands, in waving, were learning to do. Perhaps it made sense, then, that her first understanding of the call-and-response possibilities of sound seemed to come in conjunction with the hand. One day Pamela hummed to her while dribbling an index finger over her lips and Madeleine picked it up almost immediately. Now, from across a room, she could make me stop whatever I was doing to wave to her with one hand and dribble my lips with the other.

Once the breakthrough was achieved, her repertory of sounds grew quickly. The hoarse 'I am here!' shout—originally intended for the world at large, a comforting assertion—was redirected at us, and retuned as a complaint: 'I am here (and I'm hungry)!' 'I am here (and you're not paying attention to me)!' She worked up a gravelly weasel noise that was less grating, more neutral. From the complicitous look on her face as she caught our eye, inviting us to join her, it could well have meant 'We are here,' rather than 'I am here.' Then there was a softer sound, a thrummed gurgle in the throat like a dove's call which was affectionate, appreciative: 'You are here.' She could produce this one with her mouth in an open smile, and when I held her, she accompanied it with a lean into my face, hands around my neck, the smile landing on my chin. As a tactic designed to keep us from abandoning her in the forest it was extremely effective.

Soon she learned to form a real kiss, but did not use it to kiss us. Instead, she squeaked her lips in our direction and waited for us to squeak back. But as soon as she learned the Bronx cheer—the punchline to a fart joke of Pamela's that was just about right for a six-month-old—it became her favourite, perhaps because of the spray of spittle that shot out like sound made visible, and the cohering of it in a pendulous drop on her chin that made us hurry toward her with a tissue. This sound, too, was intended to call up the same in us, and we were usually happy as fools to oblige.

To the parents, these are games, but the fact that the baby also laughs does not prove it's a game to her. Surely for the baby it is real language and a whole language, expressive of all the concepts she knows: I am here, I am here (and I'm hungry), I am here (and you're not paying attention to me), we are here, you are here. Her laughter is also language, a response to the parent's call: we are happy to be here, we are relieved to be here. And the intent stare that accompanies the baby's call, the disconcerted look that comes with the failure of response, suggest that this is not merely language, but the word that calls into being the thing it names, the primal chant in which nomen and numen are one. We are here because we say we are.

At eight months, Madeleine loved this: I would touch my head to hers and sing a tone. She, wide-eyed, concentrating, would match it. The tone would vibrate through both our heads. I would nudge my pitch up or down and a pulse would begin, as the two nearly identical sound waves throbbed in and out of phase. Madeleine, imitating me, would adjust her note as well. If we eased the pitches farther apart the pulse quickened into a blur, if we brought them back toward each other it slowed, to a run, a walk, a wary standstill. Everything was combined here: pitch, rhythm, communication, touch. The slow pulse in our heads was like the heartbeat in the womb, that first music of that first sphere, but this was music of two spheres, social instead of solipsistic, the rhythm in each impossible without the other. We were there. □

GRANTA

LEILA BERG
SALFORD, 1924

Leila Berg (front row, holding board), aged five, at nursery school in Salford

Yesterday two boys got hold of me in the playground and banged my head against the wall over and over and said 'Why did you kill Jesus?' I don't know who they thought I was. My head hurts. I am six years old.

I keep thinking about stroking the puppy the wrong way. Actually it's the same way you get the scales off herrings. You take hold of the herring's tail and you take a knife and you push the scales up to the herring's head, and they fly off like sparklers. You have to hold tight because it's slippery. The scales are brilliant silver and they fit together as though a very clever dressmaker had fixed them for a bridesmaid's frock.

The scales fly everywhere when you do it—on your clothes, into your hair, over the pots and pans, everywhere. And the herring's head is bright red scarlet—and it looks very beautiful with the bright silver and scarlet. But I know the scarlet is blood really, and it's because it's dead. Ellie is playing with Sidney. Boys don't have to do herrings.

Wallflowers, wallflowers, growing up so high,
All you pretty flowers will soon have to die.

You sing that in a line, facing the wall. Then you turn round and sing

Excepting somebody, the sweetest of them all.

I don't mean you *say* 'somebody', you say someone's name, and then you turn round and flick your frock up to show your knickers and push out your bottom and wiggle it as if you were hitting someone with it, and then you sing

I'm ashamed, you're ashamed,
Turn your face to the wall again.

It is a very sad song.

There are two kinds of birds, big ones that are pigeons and little ones that are sparrows.

The sparrows eat the straw in the street. Sometimes the straw is horses' mess that has been flattened out by the cartwheels and dried up. The sparrows like it.

I saw one find a bit of bread that someone had dropped. I was very quiet, and its crunching was as loud as shouting. The pigeons are like rainbow puddles.

Big girls often flick their frock up to show their knickers and push their bottom at boys and make an ugly face at them over their shoulder and wiggle their fingers. Then the boys throw stones at them.

Round the corner of Sidney's house, in Hilton Street, where the other sweetshop is that doesn't have Devon Cream toffee and the things grown-ups like but lots of things for a ha'penny, there's a family with ever so many children in it. I don't know their names because they're Irish and they're Christians. There isn't anybody Christian in our street. Except Davidson's. And last night their dad was fighting all the grown-ups in their street. They were all shouting, and some of their faces were bleeding. And their mammy was walking along singing very loudly, and her friend was walking with her, holding her up because she kept falling over, even though the friend was much littler than she was. And her little girl was walking behind, and she was screaming because she was frightened, because her mammy had changed. I can tell her mammy wasn't generally singing and laughing and jolly. And the little girl was very frightened because she had suddenly changed and was jolly.

Clogs are Christian.

A telegram is when someone is dead.

In Great Clowes Street I saw a telegram boy on a bicycle with a message, and I stood quite still. Everything went very far away.

In Lewis's I have seen a lady fold up a piece of paper and put it in a little box. And she puts it on a wire and shoots it along to another lady. And the other lady takes the box off the wire and takes out the paper and opens it and reads it.

I have looked and looked at the telegraph wires in the streets. If I am shopping with Mammy I always watch them as we walk along. When I am by myself I go to the bottom of Fenney Street and put my head right back till my neck hurts and I watch the wires. But I can never catch the boxes rushing along the wires with their messages saying someone is dead.

Do they only go at night-time?

But what about Lewis's?

Do they say someone is dead in Lewis's?

Jam and custard is like the sunset. I draw in it with my spoon, making bars of orange and swirls of purple, and the blackberry pips make deep blue speckles in the gold. The sunset is like jam and custard. It is my favourite, even better than tinned peaches or pineapple. We have it for breakfast on Shabbos morning, because you don't have to cook it and because it's so lovely.

Christians hit everybody. Other men. And women. And children. Jewish people hit only children.

Ellie knows lots of things because he's older than me. But he won't tell me. And when I say, 'Tell me! Tell me!', he laughs and says he doesn't know. But I know he does. He just won't tell me.

Mammy gives me some white net to sew beads round. There are lots of beads, and I can put any colour I like. Then they go over the milk jug or the sugar basin. When I see them on the table I feel I am belonging.

If I made them for everywhere, then we wouldn't have to have the fly-papers. The flies buzz and buzz, until they die. But I would have to make so many, all different sizes, hundreds of them, millions of beads. I don't think I could do that.

Today Sidney let me take his electric game to play with on the sofa. I was playing by myself, and Daddy came downstairs, and I looked at him because I couldn't help it, and he looked back, his black look, at me. He hates me. When he'd gone, Edna was in the room and she said, 'He isn't angry with you, pet. It's because your mammy's just had a baby, and it's been born dead. It's upset him. It was another boy, and he wanted another boy.' I didn't know she was having a baby. Is he very angry with Mammy for killing the baby? I'm sure she didn't mean to.

Edna tells me things, sometimes.

I'm making some mats to stand things on. Like the teapot, or Mammy's scent bottle on the dressing table. It doesn't have scent in but it has a lovely smell. I do blanket stitch all round and in the middle I do yellow daisies. I like choosing the colours better than doing it. In Albert Park, if you look down the hill at all the trees, there are so many colours, but all green. How do people know they are all green when they are all different?

The blood doesn't show very much. It's only specks anyway.

I say 'anyway'. I think you don't say 'any road' if you want a good education.

Sometimes—not often, but at special times—he gets out the magic lantern, moving the slide slowly. He does it for Ellie. He doesn't look at me.

I don't really like reading letters to people. I can read them, but sometimes I don't know what it means, and I don't know if I'm saying it right. Mrs Sugarman sits in her rocking chair and nods her head and says, 'Read that again, chuck,' and I do read it again, but it still doesn't sound right, and I don't know what it is. But Mammy sends me to do it because it's a blessing.

They come from America, the letters. That's farther than London. In London it's Piccadilly, but here it's Piccalilli.

It isn't Haroloid. I thought it was like celluloid. But it's Harold Lloyd. That's his name.

There is a box made of shells that is magic.

And there is a box like a dark red mirror, and inside the lid a little square where it says FIRST PRIZE FOR NEEDLEWORK.

They are Mammy's boxes.

We have an ice-cream bucket, to make ice cream out of Bird's Custard Powder. It's yellow and thick and it makes a sandwich with the wafer biscuits. Daddy does it. He does any special thing.

The Stop Me and Buy One man is at the corner. He sells very special ice cream for the grown-ups. Sometimes grown-ups give you the ice-cream paper to lick, and if you don't, they say you're sulking. I don't like it. It makes me feel sick.

I'm going to get a Snofrute from him with my penny. I squash it on the cardboard and lick it off. It stays on your tongue like a tuning fork.

Mrs Garber sits on the edge of the pavement and plucks hens. There are feathers everywhere, drifting with the grit and blowing in the wind and heaping up in soft, silky, swirly piles—white feathers, brown ones, orange, black. Even red ones.

Today I saw a brown wispy one on her nose. It was curly like the curly horn of Roland in the picture when he raised it to his lips and blew. It *tickled* her, so she flicked it with her hand. Flick! Like that! But there were feathers all over her hand, so now there were *more* feathers on her nose, red and white and brown feathers, curling, and fluffing out, and dripping, as if her nose was running feathers! Then she sneezed. And they flew away.

Felix kept on walking, kept on walking still,
With his hands behind him,
You will always find him,
Blow him up with dynamite but him you couldn't kill,
Right up in the air he flew,
He just murmured Toodle-oo,
Landed down in Timbuktoo,
And he kept on walking still.

They always play that when there's a Felix the Cat picture.

I can't bear the way they wet the corner of their handkerchief on their tongue and rub it on your face because you've got a smut. It smells. It's really horrible. I try to get away, but they always hold you tight.

Edna is going to get married and not be here any more.

They are building the bonfire in the yard. Everyone is dragging bits of wood down the entry and putting them on the pile.

The chair where I sit when Sidney plays is in a soft dark corner. The music is like a summer afternoon, with bare feet on the hot flagstones and water near with a chained cup.

Sidney played it again today. He said it's Spanish. He told me who wrote it. The name is like water in summer too.

Christians beat boys and girls. Jewish people only beat boys. That is because they think only boys are important. But Christians think girls are important enough to beat too.

Today Miss Reilly said, 'All the Jews stand up on the forms.'

We had fireworks in the yard. Not *our* yard. I mean the big yard that's for everyone. There were lots of sparklers that we could hold in our hands, and they fizzed with cold stars. And rockets, shooting like corks out of bottles of med, and exploding in the sky. And Catherine wheels spinning with colours. And then something terrible happened. A banger chased me. Somebody let it off, and I knew at once it would come after me, and it ran at my heels, snapping and barking, and I ran as fast as I could and I ran into our own yard and I ran into our lavatory. I was afraid it would come through the gap under the door and then I would climb on the seat, and if it jumped on the seat, I would have to jump into the lavatory, and if it came after me, then I would die.

But it didn't see where I had gone. I waited a long time. When I came out, all the fireworks were over.

They lit the bonfire. I like the crackling and the flames leaping, curling and twisting in the dark.

Then I saw they had put someone on top of the flames, and they were shouting and laughing. I wanted to scream but I don't know how. Edna looked at me and said, 'It's only a guy. It's made of rags.' But it turned in the breath of the fire and it held out its hand to me, *begging*. Edna said, 'It's made of rags. It's only fun. It's because they burnt a man years ago.' But to do it! To remember and to *do it again*! And to *laugh*!

I don't like On the Floor and a Bit Higher. You tie one end of the rope to the lamp-post, and somebody holds the other end. At first the rope lies on the pavement, and everyone can jump over easily. But it gets higher and higher. Until you fall. That's the only way it can end, when you fall. There isn't any other way.

I play it because everyone plays it. You have to. □

GRANTA

TODD McEWEN
ARITHMETIC TOWN

In September Favourite Teacher handed out workbooks, and said to us, *when you're done with these exercises you can go out on the field and have free play.* Free play is when you have fun instead of playing kickball.

This is easy is a dumb thing to say, you should always be afraid when you hear yourself saying that, it AUTOMATICALLY means that what you're doing is impossible, and you are blowing it, and people are going to ridicule you. And EVERYTHING. I was so messed up, the problems on those three pages looked short. I knew what I was doing, I whipped through them, I couldn't believe it, my heart was singing.

I put my workbook on Her desk. She really had little inkling of the boundless scope of my difficulties as yet, this was still fall. She knew I wasn't great at arithmetic but She didn't know the picture I had of it on my mind dial, the crater of a volcano, confusion, lumps of things, muffled cries from all the people who always told me how to do it. Mom, Dad, Julie, Fard, lost to me. Then sometimes it was the inky blackness of the ocean, where the wreck of my arithmetic lay, a grim reminder there was something wrong with me. But I listened to my heart SING that I could solve these problems, that *understanding had come to me in the night.* Now I was going to be like everybody else.

I went out to the field, which seemed beautiful, great, like a day from a movie. A couple of kids were swinging, and Billy Williamson was playing football with the Czechoslovak kid from the other room, the kid who called everyone FARMERS when he meant FARTERS. Or so we thought. I got on a swing. Man, I thought, all you have to do is fill in those *blanks*, with those little *answers*, now that I understood that, I'd hardly done any thinking, maybe that was the secret. Then you come out here, and things are really neat. I felt like I'd made friends with the world. After a while more people came out, and She came with them, Her hair in the breeze and the pile of workbooks in Her arms. Her eyes like the little flowers that grew next to the crabgrass on the dirt of the field. I was swinging and swinging, talking to Fard now he'd come out, no one had said anything to me, ME, about being one of the first guys out here, I was so stupid I didn't even think about that myself, the IMPOSSIBILITY. She hadn't even given

EVE ARNOLD/MAGNUM

me a look when I put the workbook on Her desk. She called to a couple of people, minor corrections, they stayed with Her for a minute and then went back to their free play, She must have looked at my book already. Then I heard Her sweet voice calling *Joe? Joe Lake? Come over here please*, and there was a new tone to it, PAIN is what it was. Something a little bad started to happen way at the back of my head, it wasn't exactly that arithmetic sickness, but maybe She—

Cripe, here was my workbook open in her flowered lap.

Joe, what were you thinking when you handed these in?

She didn't sound mad, She hardly ever gets mad and when She does it's kind of funny, Her forehead gets larger and it de-powders, and She gets a really weird pink colour as Fard always points out. He makes a science of Her skin. But Her voice was hurt, She couldn't believe I would turn in the wrong answers, not just wrong answers but answers *which revealed* I had not read the directions, that I have understood nothing since 1958. Answers which showed I hadn't listened to a thing She said all day, all week, all month.

All year. I couldn't believe it either, how come these small problems were so difficult, why can't you just answer them the way they look like they OUGHT to be answered, small easy ANSWERS in just a second? Now the crappy feelings started, not only was I really dumb but I'd hurt Her, betrayed Her, She would have to be RESCUED by Fard, from me. Without being mean She told me to get back to work, which I couldn't do, because the way I did the problems was the only way I could do them. And I could only do them once.

What are you supposed to say, I asked Fard on the way home. It doesn't do any good to tell them you wouldn't even be able to get THOSE answers again. How could my brain do this to me, and why?

Last year wasn't good. Fard and I had this really mean teacher, Mrs Plank, and she was *really* mean about arithmetic. She made you stay after school a lot when you messed up but she didn't HELP you, she just sat at her desk doing her own stupid stuff. Once in a while she'd look up and shake her head or say something really mean, *I don't know why some children can't settle down and learn.* Fard and I used to talk about her the whole way home.

Some children, said Fard, I hate it when they say that, it makes me feel like I'm going to have diarrhoea. And she doesn't even tell you what you did wrong.

I know, I said, like if you sit there long enough you'll just start writing the right answers. That's what's wrong with arithmetic, that's why I hate it and it shouldn't exist: there's no why. In history and spelling and all that stuff you can always ask why, WHY did George Washington start fighting England? You ask them, and they tell you.

Yeah, said Fard, 'cause the English guys were being really mean.

Or you ask them, why does it rain?

Because the clouds get full, said Fard.

But in arithmetic, I said, taking in a huge breath, you can't ask why, you just have to believe them when they tell you stuff, they get *mad* when you ask, they're telling you *this is how you add*, and you say well, why is THAT number on the bottom, and then Mrs Plank looks at you like she wants you DEAD, NOW.

Yeah, said Fard. Tears came to his eyes.

And then her mouth gets real sour, and she puts down the chalk and says *I don't know, some boys just don't want to learn.* But you're TRYING to learn—

Damn it, said Fard boldly—

—and you're asking questions about it, isn't that what you're supposed to do? But questions have nothing to DO with arithmetic. And they never even said you're not supposed to ask questions, but they become hysterical when you do.

Yeah! said Fard.

Mrs Plank hates me because I'm not *moving forward* in arithmetic, I said, that's what she said to my own mother. I'm sitting in my seat wondering why why why all the time, I *am.* And there are no answers in arithmetic either, really, in addition to no whys. The only answer they can give you is IT JUST IS, THAT'S WHY, and then they go back to yelling this junk at you *they* can't explain, that's it, I said to Fard, *they* can't explain it so they yell at us.

You know what I'm going to do, said Fard, I'm going to

start saying that when she asks me about my answers. It just is, that's all. You old bag.

We laughed hard and bitterly at this, crossing the Big Street. Fard started talking about how his brother let him drive their pick-up truck back and forth in the alley. Fard was the only kid who was interested in driving, everyone else was still riding bikes, I still had my tractor, my *spazz tractor* as Nunzio called it, thanks a lot, and my Small Wheeled Bike, something Dad embarrassed me by asking for at the hardware store, *we want to get a small-wheeled bike for this boy*. There were some people who had full-sized bikes, they went bobbing up and down, they had bruises and bandages and scabs.

What do you want to drive the truck for? I said, I bet you could get hurt really bad, and it's AGAINST THE LAW.

Fard looked like I'd insulted him for a sec, but then he said, when I can drive I'm going to run over Mrs Plank in the dark.

Great idea, I said. Man, if you ran her down in the inky blackness, you could leave her body there as mute testimony, a grim reminder to other teachers.

Yeah, said Fard.

He was right too, *I'd* like to run her over, she's still alive. Still alive.

Even LINDA JOHNSON couldn't make herself into Plank's pet, which shows you how mean she was.

I wasn't like Simon and the other toy kids, I didn't have to have something right inside my desk to fondle at the first sign of trouble, but Mrs Plank made me feel so bad I decided to bring a special pencil for arithmetic. If I dedicated a pencil I really loved to arithmetic, it would help me. In the inky blackness of arithmetic the pencil would stand as mute testimony to my efforts. I was getting these words from the book I read every night in bed, *The Illustrated Book of the Sea*, which was obviously more about arithmetic than molluscs. And if I died of arithmetic, my special pencil would be a grim reminder to Mrs Plank and Mom and Dad of my wasted life.

One night in Los Angeles we went into Chinatown, and Dad bought me a big jade-green pencil. At the end was a wooden

Chinese guy with a purple tassel instead of a pigtail. I had to choose between the pencil or clam shells that opened up and let out streamers and flags if you put them in water. The Chinese pencil wouldn't fit in my pencil box, so I had to carry it to school in the same hand as my lunch box, FOR ALL TO SEE. It was the kind of thing Gomez would really get you for.

In Mrs Plank's class arithmetic came when lunch seemed even further away than it did when you got to school. Fard used to call that *9,000 o'clock*. But I was less afraid when she said *take out your arithmetic notebooks, children*, I felt a little hopeful because I had my Chinese pencil. She gave us page numbers, and we started to work, they were adding, so I could do some of them. I felt cheerful because the tassel of the Chinese guy's head swung back and forth when I wrote my answers. Also, Chinese guys invented the abacus. I made hatchmarks in the margin just to watch the tassel flip left, right, and then I saw Mrs Plank with her sour mouth, *the world's most curved thing*. She stopped at the top of our row and folded her arms and looked right at the tassel.

You can't use a pencil like that for arithmetic, Joe.

That's all she said, but huge tears leaped out of my face and splashed all over my desk. I wished I could think of Mrs Plank as Teacher, as most people called her, then her name wouldn't have kept me awake at night. I whipped out a yellow pencil, you had to do stuff very fast for Plank. I hated the way it looked, and having to read those dumb words over and over, after every problem, BONDED LEAD, M, CERES BY MUSGRAVE PENCIL CO. SHELBYVILLE, TENN. 909 N° 3. The word *Shelbyville* started to drive me crazy, Shelby, the sound *Shelby*. So Plank was happy now, she hadn't helped me with my arithmetic but she'd told me how I *couldn't* do it, with a CHINESE PENCIL. When she turned away I put my head down on my workbook and cried, utterly silently, maybe I could soak the thing to death. Julius turned around and looked at me.

God, Joe, he said, just because you're lousy at arithmetic.

But Julius didn't care if I got arithmetic or not, he just hated crying, because crying made *him* cry. These surprising big tears were hot and they smelt like chalk, they were just like the tears they had for you up at the blackboard. Mrs Plank made you go up there exactly because she knew you didn't know how to work some kind of problem. She'd let you boil away to almost nothing up there, she did it to Kurt a lot. *Some boys just don't want to learn, I s'pose,* she said, *you can go back to your seat now, I guess.* Did she ever show him how to do it, NO, she got LINDA JOHNSON to do it which meant nobody cared, they'd never do anything *her* way.

While I had my head down on my desk there because everything STANK and there was no way to do arithmetic, they took your very pencil, I uttered my word. I have a word I discovered which I say to myself, violently, when I'm very very angry. I discovered it by its sound, it doesn't mean anything, but it sounds horrifying, and saying it, even silently, calms you by getting rid of crappy feelings AND stirs them up so you can take a bath in them. Sometimes when I was mad at home I wrote it on a piece of paper and then tore it up in a rage and threw it away, that was as exciting as saying it. So I said it there, in Mrs Plank's class, silently and violently. I'd never had to use it in school before.

But I used it a lot in my room, that's where Dad 'helped' me with my arithmetic, by driving himself crazy with my stupidity. Since he made the blackboard in my room he thought that gave him the right to make me do arithmetic at it, which just about wrecked my whole room, like filling it with deadly gas. The feeling of looking at his unendurably precise writing on my blackboard, twenty-five problems, the sound of the door shutting, *call me when you've finished.* I thought about dying, or setting fire to the house. I could take the sponge and erase all the problems, if only I could come up with something to say. *I don't know who that was.* Or, *what problems.* His neat writing on my blackboard made everything less colourful, the world was drab and oppressive, the light in the ceiling glared out, really mean, and I started hating the cowboys on the walls and curtains, watercolour cowboys who roped nothing. Even if I listened as closely as I could, Dad's words didn't make any sense, there were the whys, I wanted to ask at least one why between each one of his words. But why gets you nowhere. I made a stab at the threes and fives, I could do those once in a while, but then he was coming back IN, with these QUESTIONS, *Don't you understand this,* WHY *don't you understand this, what seems to be the problem here, looks like we're going to have to shoot you down on this one.* Then his *OK*, meaning *I'm going to explain to* YOU *everything from the beginning*, starting from the Phoenicians or how you make fire probably.

Whatever they're doing to you, a moment eventually comes when the torture is over, and you're crushed when they leave. Even though Dad sent the armies of arithmetic against me, I was scared and even more alone when it was over. *Well sir, let's call it quits there*, and he went out to tell Mom how dumb I was.

Last month, after that farce of free play, they sent a note home, and we had to go to Los Angeles, to a big book store. Mom and Dad wouldn't talk to us, they huddled in one aisle, while Julie and I roamed around. She required a book about ducks, while I found *Mr Atom*, full of powerful grey pictures of electrons. There were pictures of atomic reactors, atomic power plants, atomic bombs.

What is that about? she said.

Everything atomic is good, I said.

I almost threw up when I saw what Mom and Dad were buying, arithmetic books. One was the same stupid book we had at school, without the decency to look worn out, so that gave me the sickness right there. The other was the most horrible thick-looking stupid workbook, *Arithmetic Town*.

God, I hate the word workbook, said Fard only last week.

The cover was red and black, and there was a picture of one of those towns that have low two-storey schools, parents in cars waving, kids heading into the school looking expectant, not like they're going to get kicked in the ass, a few stylized dogs that wouldn't bite, clean roads, a stop light. The flag. Houses with TREES across the street from the school, everything looked like fall and spring at the same time. These two stupid books cost a lot of money. Dad wasn't too happy about getting the duck book and *Mr Atom* too.

You have to make it a pleasant experience for them, said Mom in the car.

Pfft! The purpose of this trip, said Dad, is arithmetic.

I said, I feel—

Not here!

Now came the end of afternoon as I had known it. I had to leave Fard at my own door every day to spend two hours with, *in*, *Arithmetic Town*. It was enormously, endlessly thick, the pages were so thin you could tear out fistfuls at a time, and it would make no difference.

It's supposed to last your whole life I guess, said Fard. I hope you get better soon.

God, this was bad, and *Arithmetic Town* was going to wreck Saturdays too. At least I would be safe from it early in the morning when I got up to be with my friends Laurel & Hardy, who hated arithmetic. While Mom and Dad slept like beasts in their warm bed they couldn't make you do anything. But Saturday had been OK until this happened, I was allowed to go to the variety store, sometimes I'd take Julie. If I saved my allowance three weeks in a row I could afford to get a model. The models were all the way in the back of the variety store, past the baseball stuff I never looked at, past the games, skates, cowboy hats and past the stupid craft kits, make your own Indian moccasin, well, whoop de do.

That's the kind of thing, I said to Fard, that your *aunt* gives you, if she doesn't send you a dumb book about God.

Mine too, he said eventually, just to be on my side.

I didn't know that Fard knew all about God. But he was way too neat a guy ever to make a craft kit, could you imagine your best friend wearing grey felt with junk glued on it?

The model shelf was pretty big, but who cared about ships or planes or war stuff, what I needed was MONSTERS, their long dirty tongues getting caught up with the gear shifts and brake pedals of their humped-up wild kars. DADDY, the Swinging Suburbanite, mutated Tyrolean hat, blood-stained Glen-plaid suit, green face. Commuting to Hell in a car made from a coffin, the hood ornament a wildly slopping martini. I don't know why Dad didn't hate this junk.

I got each monster as soon as it came out, as soon as I could save up for it. Fard made one and then gave up, I don't know what he played with, Noxzema jars. I had to have these models, they were a SERIES, everything has to be COMPLETE. Doesn't it? I liked having all the boxes, TO HAVE. I was lousy and sloppy at painting, I could only think about three weeks from today when I could buy the next model. You also had to keep buying the little jars of model paint, I could afford one of those a week. You had to have every colour, and you had to buy new ones, FRESH ones, of any colour that might be running out. I only liked the jars when they were full. The way they display EVERYTHING of something in stores drives people crazy.

It's important to get stuff that's on TV. Honking around at recess we went through all the commercials to see what was what. Nunzio and Peter always had the most stuff as seen on TV, but since Nunzio STANK it didn't count as much as if Fard or Kurt got something. We all got jet-fighter helmets, with birthdays and Christmas, some people got Easter presents. Jesus is still alive, here's Robot Commando for you. The helmets were all exactly the same, then Nunzio started saying his was better somehow, it came from a better store so it had *thicker plastic*. I hate Nunzio.

Arithmetic Town loomed over Saturday like a monster, it was grey and DOOM LADEN, but I couldn't wait to get my model home, lay out the newspaper and paints, make it in a sweat, get it out of the way as fast as possible. I couldn't STAND it that it might lie around unmade, yet making it was going to give me no pleasure whatsoever and make me really mad. There was always too much glue, oozing out of the joins and all over your fingers, mixed with dirt and paint, and then the tube of glue didn't look nice any more and you had to worry about getting another one. Nothing looks like it does on the box. I thought of laying out *Arithmetic Town* instead of newspaper, but that wouldn't work.

That Saturday morning Julie and I turned the corner, she was talking about RUBBER ANIMALS. I couldn't tell them apart, they all looked like melted erasers. I told her Captain Nemo ought to take them somewhere in the *Nautilus*. The low fences dividing the front yards one from another on our street are all the same height, even though they're made from different things, redwood rails, flower wire, ivy. Saturdays the dads of every yard walk back and forth, wash their cars, water their lawns, talk to each other, fix and paint their stuff. The way they talk to each other is weird. Neighbour Talk, Julie and I sometimes do it in the back seat of the car on a long trip. *See you've got something eating your geraniums. Heck, yes, got to get down to the nursery, thanks for pointing that out.* Ha ha ha ha ha ha ha!

Down at our house I could see Dad moving backwards and forwards. At first I thought he was mowing the lawn, but as we got closer the humid grey weather pressed down and I started to think it was a kind of maybe NOT OK Saturday. He couldn't be mowing the lawn, he was pacing between the green car and the brown car, puffing on a cigar like a steam train. When we were almost there, I got scared because I saw that the huffing Dad locomotive was chuffing up and down the driveway with *Arithmetic Town* in its hand, held high like a flag. He held it SHOULDER HIGH so I would see it as SOON AS POSSIBLE. Sheesh. What Mr Neighbour, raking right there thought, I couldn't guess.

Uh-oh, I said to Julie, I guess we shouldn't have gone to the variety store, now I'm going to get it.

Which was something we never said, *get it*, that's from cartoons or the Kellys. But I started to get mad, there was no RULE you had to do arithmetic first on Saturday. But there was the Permanent Rule, which I was stupidly ignoring, the rule nobody talks about, FUN LATER.

He looks mad, Julie. I didn't know I had to do arithmetic first.

Julie was always optimistic and encouraging, she wasn't afraid of Dad.

It'll be OK, she said, just say you'll do arithmetic now.

That's the kind of thinking these Julie people do, they don't understand how complicated and *full of crappy feelings* everything is.

I can't do it now, I said, it's almost lunchtime.

So do it after lunch.

But he'll hate me all through lunch for not doing it, I said. If you can't go to the store or do a model before arithmetic, you sure can't have LUNCH before arithmetic, did you hear about that kid on Santa Ysabel who got REAL SICK trying to do homework with NO FOOD?

No, gawked Julie, though maybe it was the idea of HOMEWORK that made her eyes bug out.

Now we were on the driveway. I tried to smile, tried to draw my model out of the bag to show him, distract him, anything . . .

Forgot something, didn't you, he said right away. He was wearing his safety glasses, no doubt he'd been HAMMERING in the garage, and in the cigar smoke his eyes BEAMED OUT like Santa Fe locomotive eyes.

Yes, well, I, I couldn't make myself bring up the RULES, what was the point, you try to say there is no rule, and they shoot you down with one of the YOU KNOW THAT rules, you always finish school work before you buy wax lips—YOU KNOW THAT.

Better get to work, he said.

OK, I said, and saw that the day was so grey that the frontier lamp was on over the kitchen table, where I would shortly be beaten by the police of *Arithmetic Town.* I'd be suffocating in one of those friendly family cars, LINDA JOHNSON's family I bet, all of them with that *fixed smile* of hers, or mauled by one of the schoolyard dogs that smiled like Linda Johnson. Under the frontier-style light at the kitchen table, the harsh light that made every duty sad, every meal angry.

I got rubber animals, Julie said to Dad in the outside world.

Some things work out OK, I thought, not great, but OK, even though this was a cloudy NOT OK Saturday, I could do the model later, and that would FIGHT GLOOM. But the whole family was waiting to eat lunch at the kitchen table where I was doing arithmetic, where the horror light beat down on me every second. That started to scare me because Julie got cranky when she didn't eat and might turn against me. And Dad would have to use his large teeth to tear into his Monterey Jack cheese sandwich after stomping around in his gardening boots. I was getting some problems done but I started to study the nubs of the colonial tablecloth, they were shaped like the problems, I noticed. Dad came in, covered in impatient gardening dirt, then Mom shot in and started rattling pots she had no intention of using, if I have something wrong, I thought, he'll tell her to GET OUT.

I got the multiplication all wrong, I was guessing at the look of the numbers, trying to think how, then *trying to get out of my mind how*, the problems looked like the nubs.

Think you'd better have another stab at these, he chuckled.

Yes sure, now we can laugh, I thought, because LUNCH is on the way.

Why don't you do them this afternoon, he said.

Mr Generous, pushing my model and my little time, my little square of happiness, that's how I thought of it, a warm wood-coloured box with a light in it, WAY to the end of the day, maybe into the night which was all wrong for making a model, it didn't have the right light coming through the windows.

After lunch I sat in my room, sickened by the OVERHEAD LIGHT which Dad put on when he abandoned me, just to make sure I'd probably throw up. Man, you know you're doing arithmetic, or having an operation, if that light is on. I looked down at *Arithmetic Town*, kept turning back and forth between the problems and the cover. The cover *was* the problem, that was EXACTLY the kind of town where Linda Johnson and all the people who can do arithmetic live, I bet that was how Linda Johnson actually thought of our school and our town, even though we had no season like that, whatever the season on the cover was, or TREES. I started to get real mad and I also had to go to the bathroom, but if I opened the door Dad would be on me like a German shepherd, *Are you finished?*, I could just hear it. Say, he'd think, let's just go into the kid's room and see if he's having any fun by mistake, is anything, any TOY out of place?

I always have my table. That's what Fard says too, *neat table*. Everything I've thought about or dreamed up or tried to make, except for my machines, I've done at my table. It's an old table from the garage, painted black, though some of the wood shows through. It has a drawer underneath which smells like pencil shavings and ink. When I'm happy I sit at my table and I don't have to do anything, I share my happiness with my table, and it shares its happiness with me. When I'm sad I *always* sit at it, I can open the drawer and breathe the pencil shavings and ink and I feel better. The way the black paint is worn off the corners and the knob of the drawer.

Fard feels better, he told me, by looking at the brass knob in the middle of his ceiling light. I know exactly how he feels, but no OVERHEAD LIGHT would make me feel any better. I draw monsters at my table, I was sitting at my table when I drew the bad pictures with Gomez, that I completely forgot about, in my drawing pad,

Don't miss out on major issues (or on major savings).

Subscribe for yourself

YES I would like to subscribe:

❑ 1 year (4 issues) at £21.95 *(saving £10)*
❑ 2 years (8 issues) at £41.00 *(saving £22.95)*
❑ 3 years (12 issues) at £57.50 *(saving £38.38)*

(*Granta* sells for £7.99 in bookshops.)

Please start my subscription with issue no: ____________

NAME & ADDRESS *(please complete even if ordering a gift subscription)*

POSTCODE

96J5S55B

Total* £ ________

❑ Cheque (to 'Granta') ❑ Visa, Mastercard/Access, AmEx

Card no:

/__/__/__/__/__/__/__/__/__/__/__/__/__/__/__/__/

Expire date:/__/__/__/__/ Signature: ____________

* POSTAGE: NO ADDITIONAL POSTAGE REQUIRED FOR UK SUBSCRIPTIONS. FOR EUROPE (& REP IRELAND) PLEASE ADD £8 PER YEAR. FOR OVERSEAS SUBSCRIPTIONS, PLEASE ADD £15 PER YEAR.

Please tick this box if you would prefer *not* to receive promotional offers from compatible organizations ❑

or for a friend.

I would like to give a subscription to the following. My name, address and payment details are above.

NAME AND ADDRESS: Mr/Mrs/Ms/Miss

Postcode

NAME AND ADDRESS: Mr/Mrs/Ms/Miss

Postcode

Return, free of charge if posted in the UK, to:
Granta, Freepost,
2-3 Hanover Yard, Noel Road, London N1 8BR

Or use our
CREDIT CARD LINES:
UK (free phone and fax):
FreeCall 0500 004 033
OUTSIDE THE UK:
Tel: 44 171 704 0470
Fax: 44 171 704 0474

GRANTA

the wiener and the bottom. In brown crayon with stuff coming out. When I have my outer-space headphones I stand at my table, at my window, and look out, my window is now the window of Mission Control, I'm looking out at Cape Canaveral, not Mr Postum's yard with his blind dog Ralph yapping and falling off the kitchen steps. I'm glad my window is wide, I can really SURVEY things from here, standing at my table holding the headphones to my head. Nunzio has the same kind of window, sometimes that's Mission Control, Nunzio and Fard and I look out at Nunzio's pool, which Nunzio insists is *more like Cape Canaveral.* Because of the ocean. Nunzio stinks. When they gave us our school picture last year I coloured his teeth in with BLACK CRAYON and then put a big X over his head and wrote with the ballpoint pen that has the school's name on it DO NOT LOOK AT NUNZIO'S PIKTURE, I spelt it that way to *add stupidity to Nunzio.* I've written my word, my secret angry word on pieces of paper at my table. Sometimes I hold the pencil in my fist and push down really hard to write the word, so that it almost tears the paper, that's the best way to write it, though if you push too hard you'll dent the word into the black paint of the table, which wouldn't be good, my word that is only ever said in private or torn up, you don't want your secret word of misery to be found, anywhere.

Just to show myself I was MASTER OF MY OWN ROOM, I very quietly took the model out of its bag and opened it up. It was a monster in an airplane which was supposed to be held up by balloons he'd tied to the wings. There they were, balloons modelled in grey plastic. I thought I'd just take a little break and paint the balloons, then get right back to *Arithmetic Town.* I glued the two halves of each balloon together, really bad, the glue oozed from the joins and got all over my hands, mixed with dirt and paint, wait'll Dad saw. I'm such a crummy model maker that I started putting the paint on right away, maybe it was the wrong kind, Kurt would know, but true to the weather and the overhead light and everything about that Saturday the plastic just *melted,* went soft, and the balloons that were supposed to look buoyant and funny like on the box, looked like grapes somebody'd stepped on at school. Everybody hates fruit. So there was nothing to look forward to, my monster was going to melt, it was going to be a PROBLEM Dad and I would solve under *harsh light*, everything was becoming arithmetic.

I really had to go to the bathroom, but I couldn't go to the real bathroom. If I opened the door Dad would smell the glue. I went to my closet, where I had a round cardboard box. It would be neat to have your own toilet in your closet, I thought, it would be like the TRAIN where everything you don't need folds away and is hidden. I could tell Nunzio I had my own bathroom in my closet. I shut the closet door and in the dark I aimed for the round box, man, was that thrilling, wait till I could tell Fard, who cared that it didn't flush. It would just GO AWAY like most things do. I felt good and mad at the same time. I went out to my table, grabbed *Arithmetic Town*, my wiener was still sticking out, went back in the closet and holding *Arithmetic Town* over my secret toilet, with steamrollers of feeling going up and down me, PISSED UPON IT. □

GRANTA

JUDITH JOY ROSS

HAZLETON PUBLIC SCHOOLS, PENNSYLVANIA

Judith Joy Ross went to school in the small town of Hazleton, Pennsylvania. She was born there in 1946, the daughter of two classical pianists, and after senior high school went to Philadelphia to study art and then Chicago to study photography.

In 1992 she went back to Hazleton to make a series of portraits of the children at her old schools. By then she had an international reputation. Her photographs were collected by the Museum of Modern Art. She was forty-six, the age adulthood strikes home, when there is as much to look back on as to look forward to. She had gone back to Hazleton partly to try to make sense of her own childhood memories, but also because she wanted to express her more general social concerns about the kind of world that would be waiting for the next generation.

She had begun a similar series of pictures ten years earlier, soon after her father died. She went to the park where she and her brothers had played, and photographed children there. She used a large, old-fashioned eight-by-ten-inch view camera on a tripod (which must have solemnized the encounter for the children) and discovered her mature working method. In 1983 she photographed people visiting the newly inaugurated Vietnam War Memorial in Washington. And in 1987 she made portraits of more than a hundred members of the United States Congress, whose faces were familiar from television but rarely available for long-term scrutiny.

All Ross's photographs lack the melodrama we've grown used to in commercial magazine portraits. Her subjects don't mug for the camera or take up poses. She doesn't use tricksy framing or introduce props. She just sets people in the centre of the picture against their ordinary backgrounds and lets us look.

The Hazleton children meet her camera on equal terms, with a level gaze. The less they act up, the more clearly we can see them as individuals. Ross avoids sentimentality without losing any of her subjects' sense of promise, but it is impossible to stare at these children for long before any pleasure in their potential and in the sweetness of personal memory is undermined by the knowledge of how easily things go wrong. And they go wrong early. Eyes harden, mouths tighten, hair is teased and treated, or chopped into a cut with tribal significance. Growing up is learning how to take a stance, before the camera and before the world. LIZ JOBEY

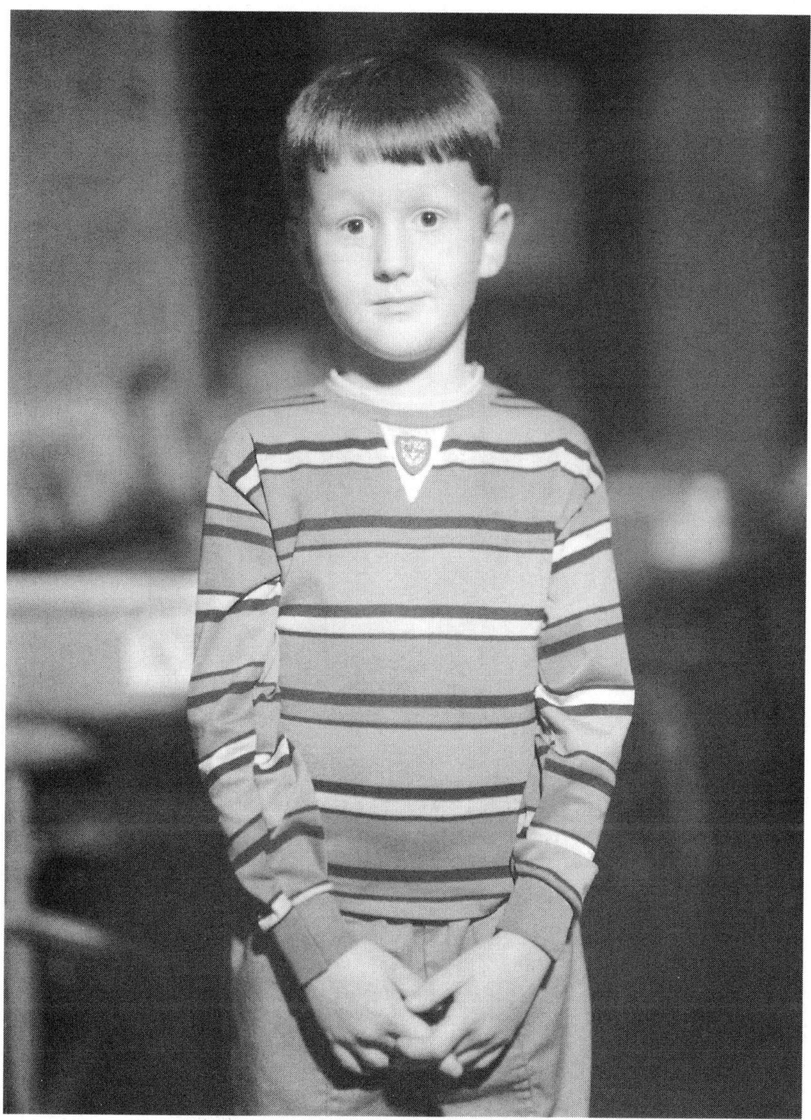

Michael Bodner, first grade, A. D. Thomas Elementary School

Randy Sartori, first grade, A. D. Thomas Elementary School

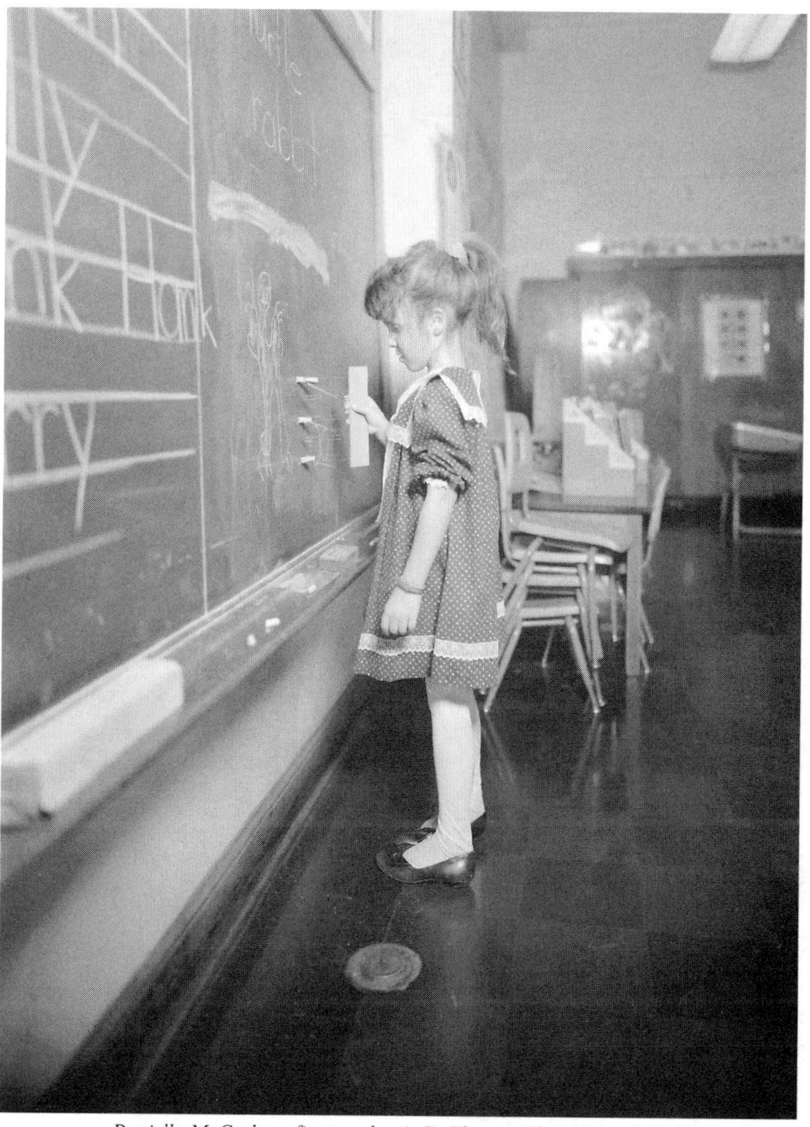

Danielle McGeehan, first grade, A. D. Thomas Elementary School

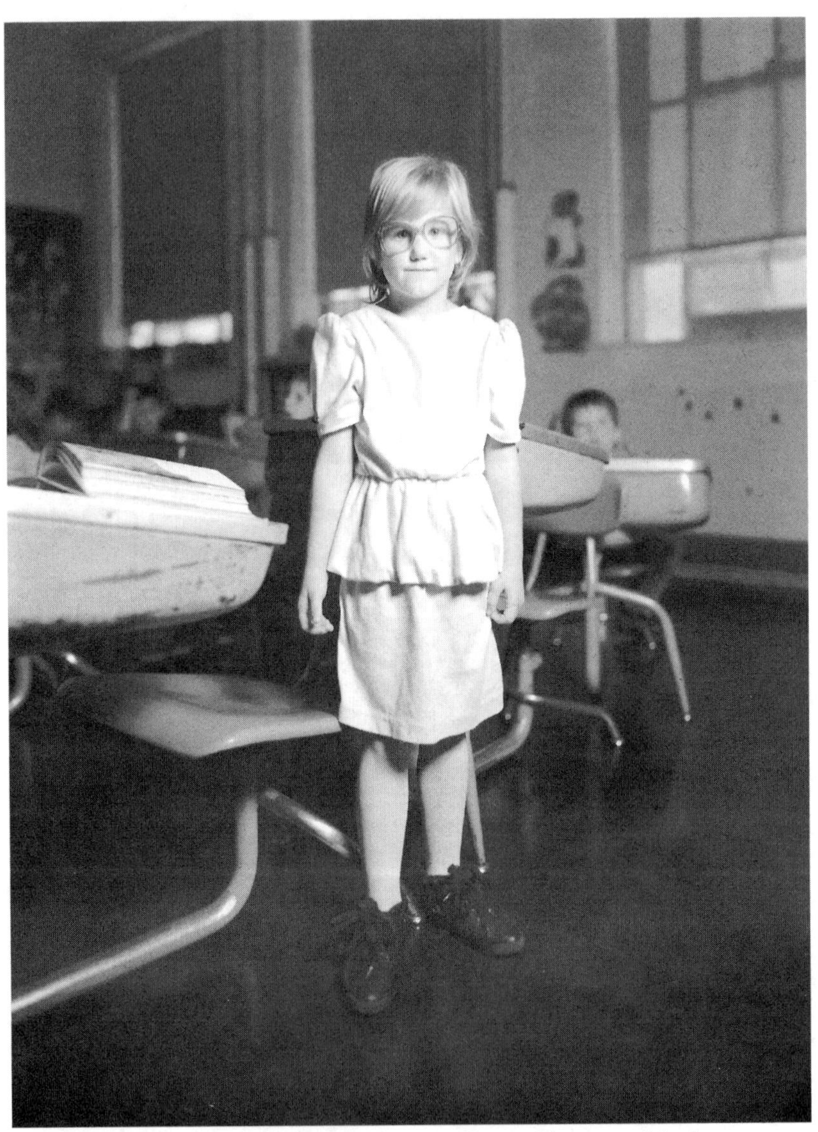

Jackie Cieniawa, second grade, A. D. Thomas Elementary School

The third grade's Christmas play rehearsal, A. D. Thomas Elementary School

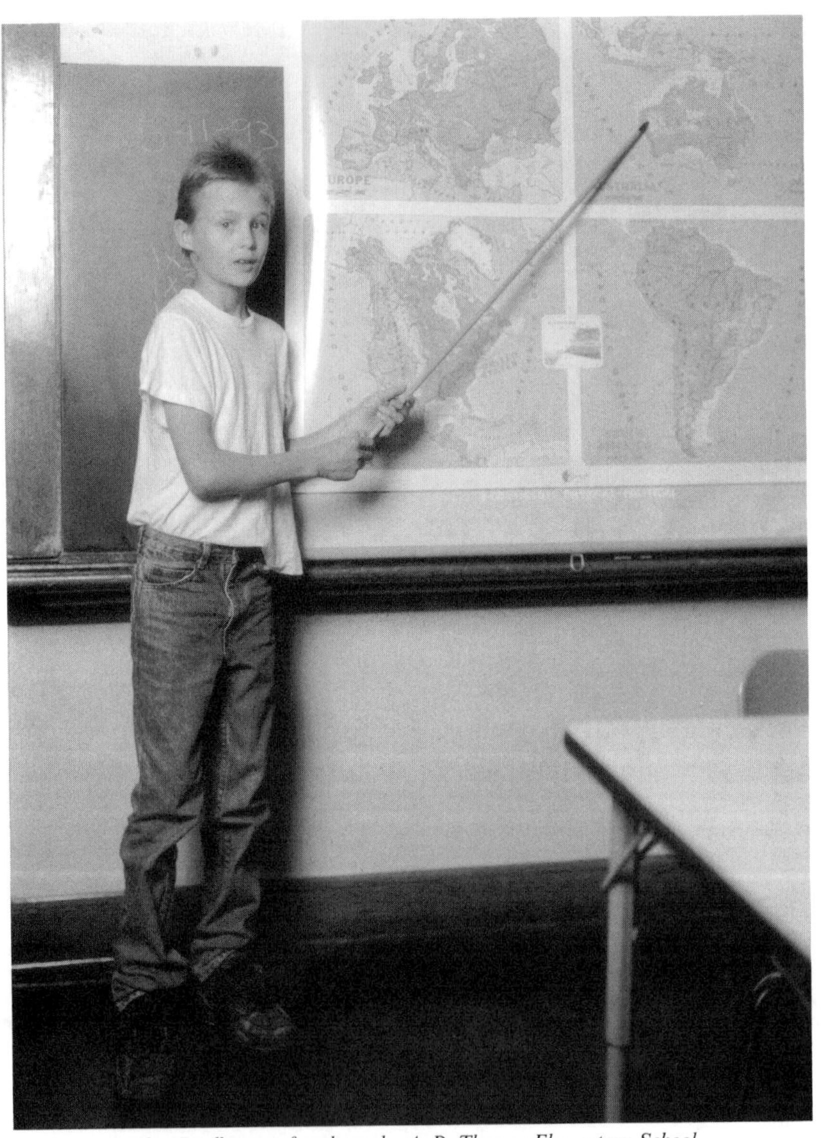

Alan Bredbenner, fourth grade, A. D. Thomas Elementary School

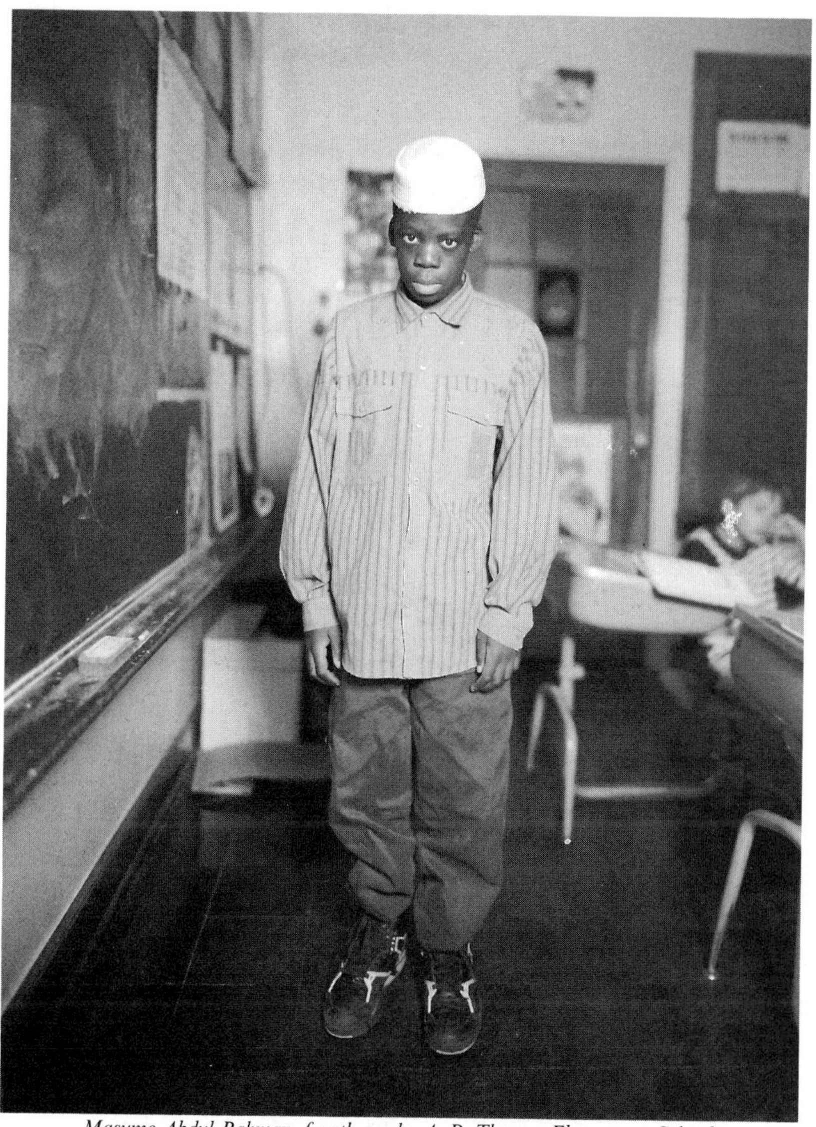

Masume Abdul-Rahman, fourth grade, A. D. Thomas Elementary School

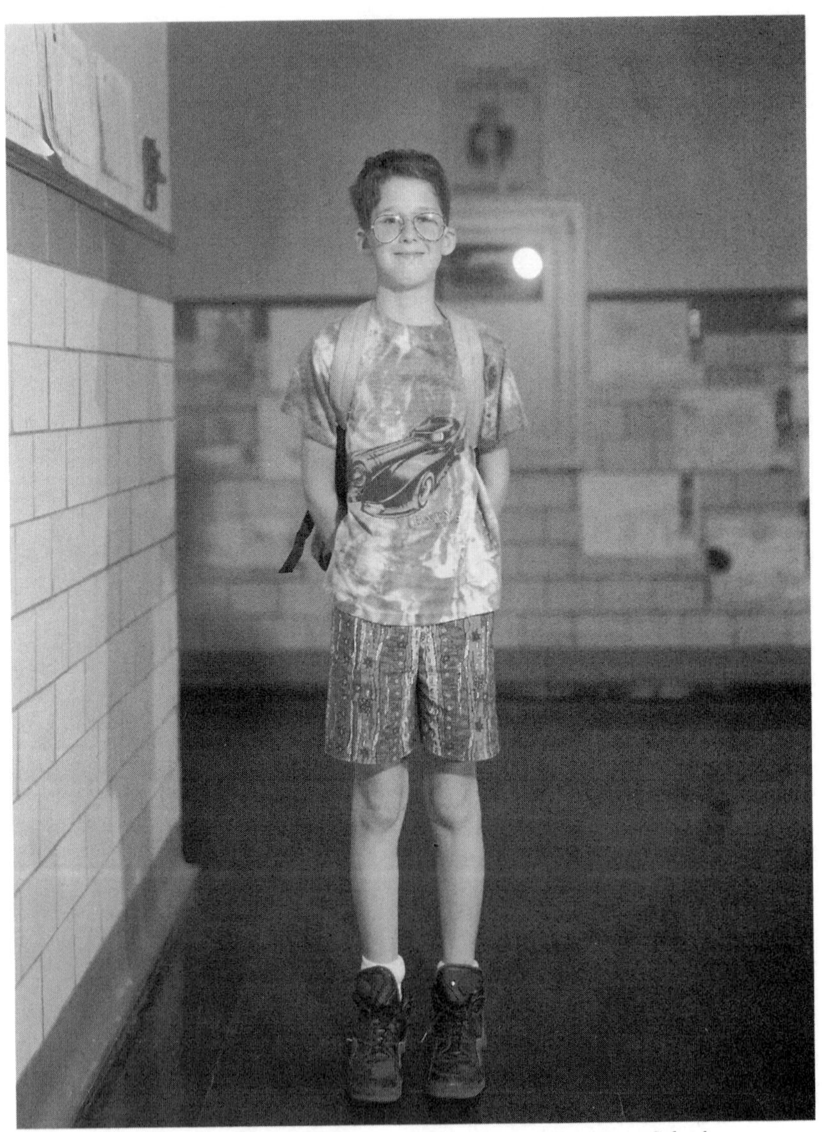

Above: John Carroll, fifth grade, A. D. Thomas Elementary School

Brian Ellis, seventh grade, presents a lecture on the Mafia, H. F. Grebey Junior High

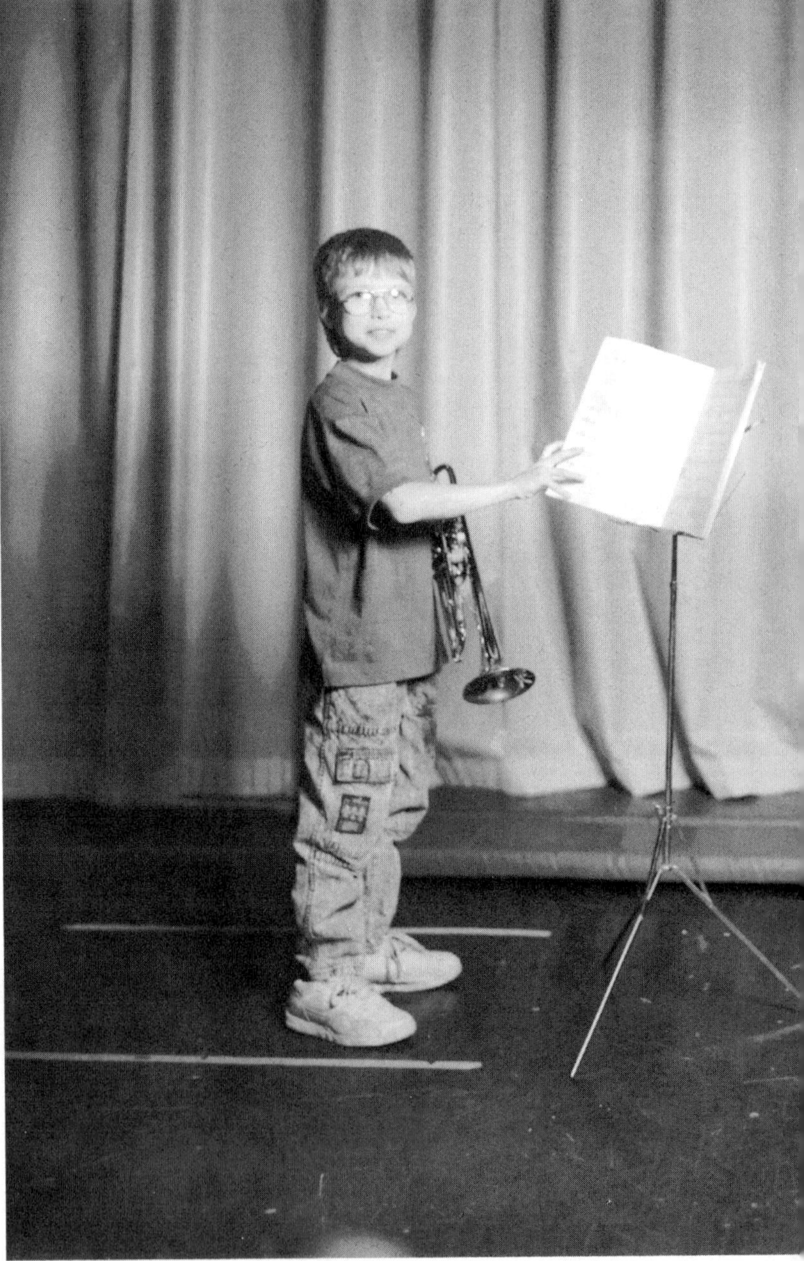

Ryan B. and his music teacher, Mr Brubaker, at A. D. Thomas Elementary School

Pasqualle Castrino, Ronnie Kmetz, Robbie Kozel, English class, Hazleton Area High

'Girl by Locker'

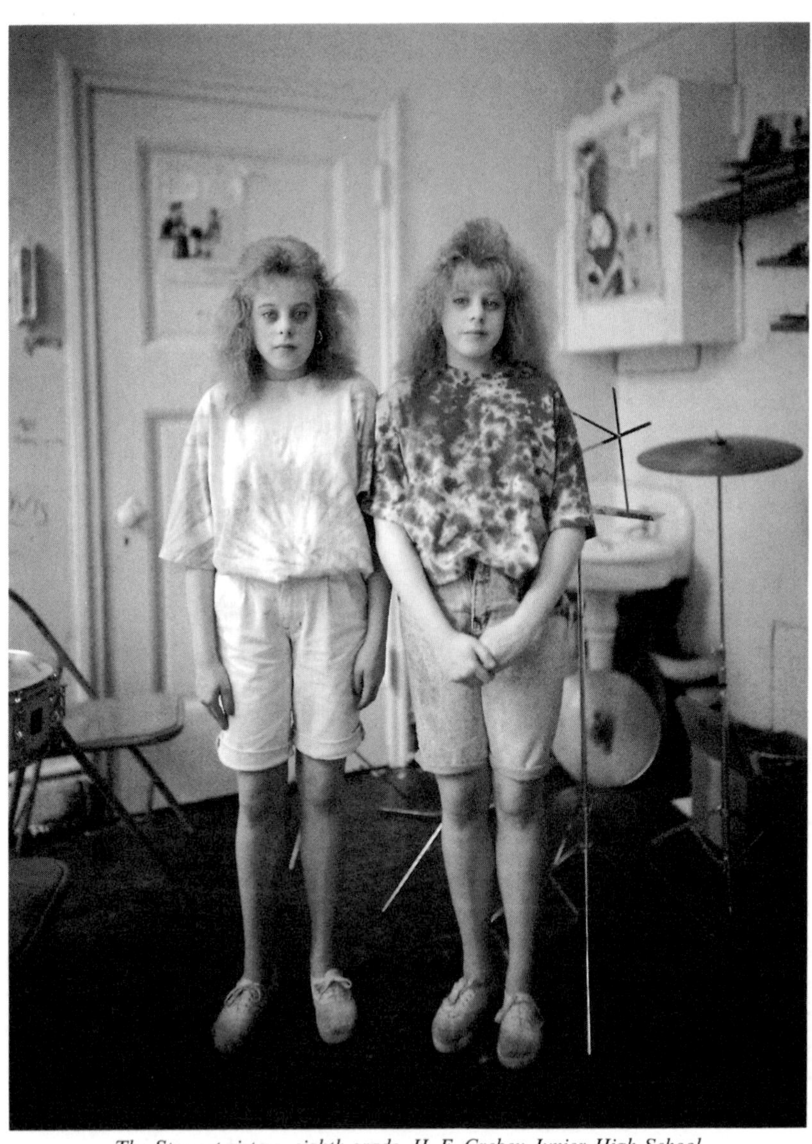

The Stewart sisters, eighth grade, H. F. Grebey Junior High School

John Lonczynski, band class, Hazleton Area High School

Jodie Hoats, home economics class, Hazleton Area High School

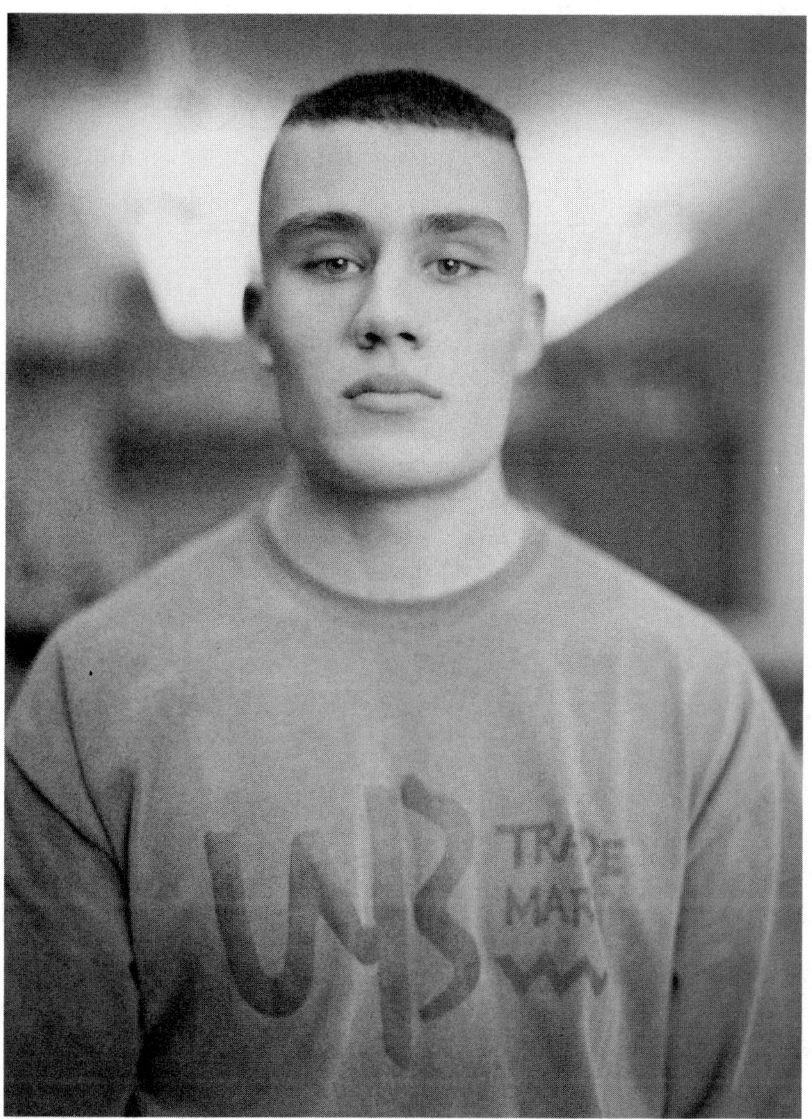

Brian Martonic, art class, Hazleton Area High School

GRANTA

TONY GOULD
BLACKMORE'S TART

Tony Gould

In the early 1950s I spent three years as a boarder at a public school—minor, but venerable—in the West Country. I remember puberty as a time of purgatory.

Towards the end of my first year there, when I was fourteen, I was standing with another very junior boy watching a group of seniors playing 'alley cricket' in the high-walled passage between the playground and the road. We wanted to join in but didn't dare ask. The others ignored us until one of them lofted the tennis ball so high that it cleared the wall on the other side of the road and went into the vicarage garden: six and out. Then a senior called Snape corralled us into helping him find it.

The vicarage garden was out of bounds, but that did not prevent Snape from wandering in, sitting under the vicar's raspberry canes and helping himself to the fruit, while we two juniors rooted around in search of the ball. When he caught my eye he beckoned me over, grabbed my arms and pulled me down on top of him, saying, 'Come on! It's my birthday.' Instinctively I wriggled free. I was relieved to see that the other boy wasn't looking. As we had already found more than one missing tennis ball we returned to the playground.

It was over so quickly, and Snape seemed so unabashed, that I began to wonder if I hadn't dreamed up this brief tussle. I understood that he had been trying to kiss me and, though I knew it was wrong, I found myself wishing I'd let him; I was afraid he might never try again.

I needn't have worried. The next term I had a walk-on part in the school play—Shaw's *Saint Joan*—and, in the theatrically heightened atmosphere, conceived a passion for the boy playing Dunois. Actually I think it was Dunois I fell for, since the passion did not long outlast the production; it was then that Snape, now a prefect, pounced a second time and exacted his kiss. This time he got it without a struggle. But, as with 'Dunois', whom I had jilted in his favour, I soon grew tired of the clandestine meetings in dark corners and oppressed by the lengthy necking sessions in icy fives courts and swimming-pool changing booths. By the end of the spring term I was looking for a way out, and that was when Blackmore intervened.

Friends had warned me against Blackmore. Short but

athletic, with dark good looks and a sallowness that made him seem older than sixteen, he strutted around the place in a cocksure manner. I thought he was loud and vulgar and disliked almost everything about him, from the flashy way he dressed to his passion for golf. I couldn't imagine we would ever be friends. Yet when he began to show an interest in me, to favour me with quizzical looks and smiles, I was flattered.

On the last night of term there was a film show in the gym. I was walking back to the house when Blackmore and his golfing chum Kenwood, whom I liked even less, came up behind me and asked me where I was going. I could hardly say I was on my way to meet Snape. But Blackmore seemed to know that already; he whispered in my ear, 'Tell him you don't want to see him any more. Ken and I will wait in the changing room, and if he turns nasty, we'll deal with him.' He squeezed my arm.

Snape was waiting for me in a dark corner of the showers. My heart started to pound as soon as I saw him. Were Blackmore and Kenwood already in place, straining to catch every word we might say? I stopped just out of arm's reach and blurted out that I didn't want to see him again. At the same time I looked over my shoulder to alert him to the fact that we were not alone; I was still confused as to where my loyalties lay.

At first Snape tried to win me back with a potent mixture of charm and flattery; then he changed tack and warned me loudly against a person, or persons, unknown whose morals were not all they should be; someone beside whom he was an exemplar of virtue. He urged me not to succumb to this person's seductive charms. Because if I did, he counselled earnestly, I would be sure to regret it.

Just at the point when my resolution was beginning to waver, he wished me luck and left. If it hadn't been for the hidden watchers, I might have run after him.

Blackmore and Kenwood emerged from their hiding place, and Kenwood tactfully left the changing room. Blackmore came over to where I was standing, miserable, and said, 'Don't waste your sympathy on that plausible bastard. You know that all the time he has been seeing you, he's been carrying on with Richards, don't you?' Richards was my friend and, though I knew there had been something between them once, Snape had assured me this was over and had anyway never amounted to much. Richards and I did not discuss such matters.

When Blackmore kissed me, not tentatively but with passionate intensity, I hardly knew how to respond; I didn't feel involved in the way he seemed to. But the following morning, when we met behind the cricket pavilion before going our separate ways for the spring holidays, his excitement was palpable, and I felt, for the first time, the fever of desire.

The next term we found ourselves sleeping in the same dormitory along with some twenty other boys. Blackmore suggested we took it in turns to visit each other at night when everyone else was asleep. Our beds were at opposite ends of the room, so there was a long trek across no man's land before we reached the safety of the other's bed. Not that we got into each other's beds: Blackmore knelt beside mine, or I beside his, and we kissed one another, whispering words of love until satiety or fatigue drove us back to our own.

We were in love, or so Blackmore was always telling me, and I believed him. We were convinced that what we felt for one another was unique and spiritual, not common and physical; that such licence as we gave ourselves was an innocent expression of the intensity of our passion. Far from being sensual for its own sake, we were obsessively puritanical and worried that each development might tip the balance of the relationship into carnality. When Blackmore reached under the bedclothes, unbuttoned my pyjama jacket and touched my nipple for the first time, for instance, he wondered anxiously if he hadn't gone too far. Did this mean that we were no different from all the other boys who sought gratification through each other's bodies? Better that we should stop seeing one another than descend to that level of banality.

But though I was troubled over the morality of our relationship, I longed for Blackmore to squeeze my nipple again; he seemed to know so much more about my body than I did. It never occurred to me to question how he'd acquired that knowledge; I believed him when he told me he had never been in love before; that for him, too, it was a process of discovery.

He even persuaded me to go and see the school chaplain. This priest, with his thick-rimmed glasses and blubbery lips, his silver hair yellowed with age and nicotine, laughed wheezily and put a hand on my knee. He told me about several of the boys he had known who had been lovers at school, how they had remained friends for life, even after they'd married and had children of their own. It was perfectly natural that boys should become fond of each other, he said and, to further my education in this direction, he lent me the thinly disguised homoerotic novels of Frederick Rolfe ('Baron Corvo').

One free Sunday Blackmore said he was going to teach me to play golf. We took a packed lunch and bicycled several miles to a golf course so remote that we scarcely saw another soul the entire day. Blackmore coached me all morning, standing behind me, showing me how to grip the club and guiding my backlift and follow-through until he was satisfied that I had got the idea. He proved a dedicated teacher despite my ineptitude. He gave up only when I sliced the ball so badly that it left the fairway and landed in some adjoining woods. While we were searching for it we came upon a secluded, sunny spot where we could have our picnic. Blackmore lectured me on the principles of golf while we ate our cheese sandwiches and then lay back in the sun.

It was a balmy day; we were far away from school and we were quite alone. For once there was no hurry; we lay in each other's arms for a while, and then Blackmore suggested we would be more comfortable it we shed our shirts and vests. Beside his brown and already quite hairy torso, mine seemed too white and naked. He told me not to be embarrassed, I had a nice body, and to prove that he meant it he started to kiss my shoulders, my neck, my chest and my stomach before heaving himself on top of me so that I felt, through two layers of grey flannel, his stiffened prick against mine.

I was thoroughly aroused when he suddenly rolled off me, sat up and reached for his cigarettes (we were both seasoned smokers). He lit two, put one in my mouth and took a long drag on the other.

'We'd better stop now,' he said sternly, 'before we do something we might regret.'

'I suppose so,' I agreed, unable to hide my disappointment. Blackmore was amused.

'Come on, Tony,' he said, 'where's your will-power? We can stop now, can't we?' And he gazed at me challengingly out of narrowed green eyes. 'Can't we?'

'After all,' he continued, his hand resting on my stomach, his fingers probing under the waistband of my trousers, 'we haven't done anything irrevocable, have we?'

I could neither move nor speak.

Blackmore removed his hand and was suddenly brisk. 'What shall we do, then? Play another round of golf or cycle back? You choose.'

'I don't think I'm much good at golf,' I said miserably. 'Besides, we'd have to find the ball first.'

'That's true,' Blackmore said. He stubbed out his cigarette and turned back to me, leaning on one elbow. 'I do believe,' he said thoughtfully, 'you'd rather stay here. Well, wouldn't you?'

He started to kiss and fondle me again but this time, instead of rolling on top of me, he undid my fly and released my hard cock. 'It's big,' he whispered admiringly as he held it. Then he undid his own fly, got out his prick and placed my hand on it. It was fatter than mine, though not quite so stiff, I thought; it was the first erect penis, other than my own, I had ever touched.

We cycled back to the school in a very different mood. Blackmore was quiet but did not seem unduly perturbed; I pedalled along, full of guilt and shame and convinced that nothing would ever be the same again. Previously, when my classmates had referred to someone as 'So-and-so's tart', I had joined in; now I was a tart myself—'Blackmore's tart'. I could already hear them jeering.

The idyll of requited love lasted well into the autumn. Then, for me at least, the physical passion began to wane, and a kind of revulsion set in. I doubt whether this had anything to do with the discovery that I was not the sole recipient of Blackmore's caresses. He was adept at explaining away other encounters: he was merely doing a friend a favour, he would say, for old times' sake. Surely I wasn't jealous, he'd continue, amusement giving way to incredulity. To compare those perfunctory episodes with our abiding love, even to mention them in the same breath, would be sacrilege. Nevertheless Blackmore insisted on absolute fidelity on my side and made me promise to tell him if I so much as masturbated without his knowledge or participation. It was his possessiveness, and my own lack of privacy, of autonomy even, which began to grate on me, so that I looked forward to the day when I would be free of his smothering love.

In the meantime he made me do things I would never otherwise have done: pick fights over trifles, take offence where none was intended. As I slugged it out with some friend who, he claimed, had slighted me, I would catch sight of him skulking in the background, observing the bout as though he were my manager. Even our moments of intimacy, which had so excited me initially, became abhorrent as they developed into a kind of sexual gymnastics, and Blackmore pushed me into performing acts I found repugnant. I was his creature to such an extent that I seemed to have no will of my own; I became abject in my enslavement and—greatest shame of all—even took a masochistic pleasure in it.

The autumn became winter, and winter turned into spring, and still I could not escape. My school reports reflected my misery; over breakfast one morning during the holidays I saw my father studying the latest one with unusual attention and when I finally steeled myself to ask him what it was like, he answered, 'Like the curate's egg: good in parts.' I was relieved that some parts at least were good, but the way my father said it implied he was more concerned with the parts that weren't. He warned me that if my reports did not improve he was no longer going to waste his money on fees, and I'd have to go to the local grammar school—a humiliating prospect.

Our housemaster was reluctant to make Blackmore a prefect but was obliged to do so when he was appointed captain of cricket that summer. Soon after his elevation Blackmore came into the dormitory and caught me smoking. I made no attempt to hide my cigarette and offered him one since normally he would have lit up too. This time, however, he told me to put it out and wait for him there; then he left the room. I was puzzled by this sudden and uncharacteristic pulling of rank; I was astounded when he returned with a cane in his hand and ordered me to bend over the nearest bed. I assumed he was joking until he said, straight-faced, that I could either accept a beating from him or, if I preferred, he would report me to the housemaster: the choice was mine. I bent over, and he laid into me as hard as he could. But after three strokes he flung the cane aside, took me in his arms and kissed me passionately, while I rubbed my stinging behind.

One day I was watching him bat, lying propped on my elbows outside the boundary rope. His parents were also watching; I had greeted them as I went past on my way to join Jackson who, like me, was a member of the second eleven and wasn't playing that day.

'I'm surprised they didn't pick you for this match,' he said.

'Blackmore says I've got to make some runs first.'

'What about him?' Jackson snorted. 'He's not exactly chalking up the centuries, is he?'

'He's doing all right today,' I said.

Jackson smiled but didn't comment. We had been watching the game for a while in companionable silence when I felt his hand slide under my thighs and come to rest between my legs. I was too surprised to say or do anything; there were other spectators on either side of us. So I continued to watch the cricket as if nothing were happening. Later I found myself accompanying Jackson to our dormitory, where we accomplished the age-old rite of mutual masturbation in private. Afterwards we gave the cricket a miss and went for a walk. I was amazed how lighthearted I felt, how natural and uncomplicated our moment of intimacy had seemed beside the tortured intensity of my affair with Blackmore.

Returning from a second-eleven away match a week or two later, Jackson and I repeated the performance in even more outrageous circumstances: on a crowded coach, under cover of an open scorebook. But that was the last time.

A month after that, when I had almost forgotten these incidents, someone passed me a note during prep informing me that Blackmore wished to see me urgently. I wondered what could be so important that it could not wait till after prep, but I was used to Blackmore's dramatic gestures. I went out and found him waiting for me in the shadows; he didn't say a word but punched me in the face, knocking me over.

'What on earth was that for?' I asked in amazement.

'You think about it,' he said, starting to walk away.

I couldn't believe that Jackson had snitched, but I realized that somehow Blackmore had found out about us.

'If it's what I think it is,' I said as I wiped the blood from a cut lip, 'I can explain.' Hadn't Blackmore himself explained many such incidents?

'I'll see you after prep,' he said. 'And it had better be a bloody good explanation.'

But when I thought about it, as I did obsessively till the end of prep, I wondered what explanation could possibly satisfy him.

As soon as prep was over, I made a dash for it. I had no idea where I was going, only that I must get away from Blackmore, the house, the school, life itself—if that were possible. I ran along the road till I was out of sight of the house; then I slackened my pace to a walk. It was a clear, starry night, and for once I was alone; if only I could disappear completely, evaporate, vanish as all those stars would by morning. I went through a gate into a field where I sat in the semi-dark, looking out over the small town below, whose twinkling lights evoked the comforts of home. But for me there was nowhere to go but back to the house where Blackmore, I knew, would be prowling around, awaiting my return.

'Did you think you could run away?' he sneered when he saw me coming. 'I thought you said you could explain it.'

'Well, I can't,' I said.

'Then you'll just have to take your medicine, won't you?' He began to punch me. Though I was taller than him, he was nearly two years older and far stronger. In addition, I was paralysed by guilt and made no attempt to defend myself. This merely enraged him all the more.

'Come on,' he taunted me, 'why don't you stick up for yourself? Are you really such a coward?'

When I tripped and fell, he stood over me until I got up

again. But he suddenly seemed to tire of the game and ordered me to get cleaned up and go to bed.

There was silence when I entered the dormitory; everyone seemed to know what had happened. I walked past Jackson's bed without looking at him, but after lights out he came over and begged me to listen. Blackmore had tricked him into telling, he whispered, by pretending to know already; Jackson had tried to deny it, but Blackmore insisted, telling him 'that you had no secrets between you'. Would I ever forgive him?

'It wasn't your fault,' I told him, wanting only to be left alone.

At least it's over now and I shall be free, I thought as I lay wakefully in the dark. But in the morning Blackmore greeted me as if nothing had happened, remarking only that I looked 'a bit of a mess'. By evening, though, he had worked himself up into another frenzy.

Why, he wanted to know, did I have to cheapen myself with that little tart Jackson of all people? Was I getting my own back for those times when he had seen Green? Hadn't I understood that that had been for Green's sake, that Green had begged him to do it? And he had told me about that, not kept it a dirty little secret. He'd always trusted me, and now this . . . sneaking off for a wank with Jackson. Did I really care for him so little that I could insult not just him but his parents as well?

I thought he was going to attack me again, but instead he punched the door of his study so hard that he split his knuckles as well as the panel and had to go to Matron to have them dressed.

Even now, I realized with a sinking heart, he did not intend to leave me alone.

I was now sixteen, and Blackmore nearly eighteen. The prospect of National Service hung over us both, but we had very different attitudes towards it. Whereas I regarded it as inevitable, even welcome, for the simple and manly contrast it seemed to offer to my present existence, Blackmore was appalled. Despite being a prefect and captain of cricket, he had never been promoted in the Combined Cadet Force and repeatedly failed the elementary military test known as Certificate A. If I showed the remotest inclination to consider the army as a career—and at fourteen my ambition had been to become a field marshal—his response was hysterical.

But at the end of that summer term we both attended corps camp on the Norfolk plains near Thetford. For Blackmore this was merely a pretext for spending more time with me, and after the camp he had arranged for us to spend a few days together in London before separating for the holidays. At the end of a hot and dusty day of military exercises he summoned me to the tent which he shared with his friend Hughes and said, to both Hughes's and my embarrassment, that he knew we had a crush on one another and why didn't we kiss and have done with it?

'Go on,' he said grandly, 'you have my permission.' He was not jealous so long as he was the controlling force, manipulating others to act out his desires.

In London, which I was visiting for the first time, we stayed with his aunt. She lived a long way out of town, in the Kentish suburb of Beckenham. We went to the cinema—for days after seeing Robert Mitchum in *Not as the Stranger* I walked around with my eyes half-closed in imitation of him—and we shared a room in which we got up to things in front of the wardrobe mirror that would surely have shocked his aunt. But this was to be the end of our intimacy. My father, who was finding it increasingly difficult to pay the school fees, gave me the option of leaving now that I had taken my O levels, a suggestion I gratefully accepted.

At last I had escaped. When I wrote to Blackmore (who also promptly left school, though he was halfway through his A-level course) I feigned regret, but my spirits soared, free of the incubus that had blighted my public-school life.

There was a postscript to this affair. Five years later, when I was at home on my father's farm recovering from polio, contracted during my National Service in the Far East, Blackmore phoned me. He told me he was in a pub nearby, surrounded by red-faced farmers, and—once he'd established that I had a car and could drive—asked if I would come and rescue him.

As I set off to meet him, I recalled that someone had told me that when Blackmore was called up for National Service he had 'gone religious' in rather an ostentatious way. Apparently he knelt to pray by his bedside every night, to the accompaniment of obscenities and flying boots from his fellow recruits. After three months he had been found psychologically unfit and discharged—no mean feat when you consider how familiar the military authorities were with such ploys.

He stood waiting for me outside the pub, an overnight bag at his feet. His urban pallor, long hair, velvet jacket and tight trousers looked thoroughly out of place in a country town on a summer's evening. Reluctantly I let him into the car. We drove off, I scarcely knew where, each wrestling with our own awkwardness in the presence of the other.

We stopped at a seaside pub where his appearance would not attract too much attention. There was something actorish about him that I didn't recall from our schooldays, so it didn't surprise me to learn that he was involved in theatre, or on the fringes of it, in London. He told me about a girl—not an actress, but a model—whom he'd pursued all the way from Australia, where he had been living for the past two years, only to be rejected by her in the end. He claimed to have had enough of 'pretty young things'.

I wondered what he would make of my girlfriend, Ruth, who was still at school. But I didn't mention her. We also kept off the subject of the army.

I forgot his strictures over 'pretty young things' till I took him to meet my newest friends, a schoolteacher and his wife whose sympathies were broad enough to find nothing strange in his appearance. William was out when we arrived, but Celia gave us coffee. She was a dozen years older than me and already had two children, which made her untouchable as far as I was concerned. But Blackmore set out to charm her in such a way that before long she was inviting him to stay. By the time William returned, they were already like old friends, and I was beginning to feel excluded.

Blackmore stayed there a few days. Whenever I visited, I would find them all on the lawn deep in conversation, Blackmore stripped to the waist, sunbathing. I was pleased that they should get on so well, but resented the way he seemed to be taking over my friends. Then one day I called, and he was no longer there. Finding his attentions to Celia a little too pointed, William had got rid of him.

A week or two later Blackmore wrote, explaining—or rather exculpating—himself and encouraging me to visit him in London. I did so when I went to university there, and for a while we were friends as we had never been before. In the early sixties he married a ballet dancer, and a few years later when I too got married it looked as though the school chaplain's prophecy of lifelong friendship might be fulfilled. But the break-up of my marriage, in which he was—involuntarily—involved, drove us apart again, and my still-unassuaged anger did the rest. Forgiven he might be, but the havoc he wreaked in my adolescence was never forgotten. □

GRANTA

SUSAN SWAN
SLUTS

It was Tom's contention that you could spot a slut by the colour of her complexion. The slut was the one with white skin. Not off-colour white or alabaster like the skin of heroines in old novels. But sickly white. White as chalk or a cadaver.

There were two women with chalk-white skin in Madoc's Landing, and everybody knew they slept around. The first was Mellie Sommers, an unwed mother who lived in the old Captain's House on First Street. The second was Mary Lou Heller who shot her husband through the eye with his Colt .38.

Tom said it wasn't sex that produced the tell-tale colour, but poor living habits. Sluts were girls who could stay out late because nobody cared about them. They weren't like us. They could eat plates of french fries soaked in brown oily gravy and drink cherry Cokes without anybody reminding them to eat their vegetables.

Tom and I grew up in Madoc's Landing, and so did my friend Kim. Kim's mother was Bernadette, and Tom said she was a slut too, only she was an exception to the rule because she had a healthy complexion. Bernadette's last name was Dault. Nobody in my family could say the French word right. They pronounced it dalt, which sounds like dolt with an A instead of an O, but I said it like dough, the way it was meant to be said.

Madoc's Landing is a hilly Canadian town settled by a mix of French and English. It is located at the bottom of a bay belonging to Lake Huron, the second largest of the five Great Lakes. In 1951, when I lived there, the Canadian National and the old Canadian Pacific Railway met in Madoc's Landing. It was the capital of Tecumseh, an Ontario county, and its population numbered 6,123. The judge of Tecumseh and the crown attorney came from Madoc's Landing, and we were the attorney's children. Every morning Tom and I watched a big, dark man in a Homburg hat back his Chrysler Airflow out the driveway. This man was our father, Tiff Quinn. He wheeled the car sharply on to Second Street, then squealed the tyres in front of the nuns' house on the corner. He was always in a hurry to get to the assizes.

When his tail lights vanished over the Fifth Street hill, Tom and I crossed Second Street to pick up Kim. Her mother kept house for the nuns in exchange for food and lodging. Kim's father was 'missing' (which is how my mother put it).

When Bernadette saw me at the door she didn't call me by my first name, Julie. Instead she sang out to Kim, 'Here she is *mon petit chou*, Tiff Quinn's daughter.'

The year is 1953. Tom, my father and I are posing for a photograph in the backyard of our house on First Street. We're standing by the cedar hedge where the barn used to be before Dad tore it down to hide all trace of the buggy horses he kept behind the house like a farmer. The snap was the first photograph taken with my Brownie. It was taken by my mother, Marjorie Quinn. You can see the outline of her short, wavy shadow falling across Tom and me. She had forgotten to follow my father's instructions and had taken the picture without checking the position of the sun.

It is summer, but my father, Tiff Quinn, is wearing a white shirt and bow tie and baggy flannel pants. The cuffs break on his shoes, which is the way Canadian men wore their trousers then. He is also dressed in his black court robes and one of his hands still holds the glass of gin my mother had just poured him. He is holding my shoulders, pulling me against him. I'm the dark-haired girl in a skirt that is far too short for me, and Tom is the owlish, fair-haired boy in a cowboy hat. His glasses spoil the western look he aims for, but nobody wants to tell him that. Tom is fourteen, and I have just turned eleven.

The snap was taken the day my father had obtained a conviction against Mary Lou Heller. Mary Lou claimed her husband, Frank, had shot himself by accident while cleaning his gun, but my father persuaded the jury that people don't shoot themselves in this way. Nobody looks down the barrel of a gun when they clean it. Frank, who ran the ambulance service in Madoc's Landing, knew about guns. Skeet shooting was one of his hobbies. And the coroner found powder burns on Frank Heller's left hand as if he had been trying to ward off a gunshot. My father argued that Mary Lou had murdered her husband, twenty years older than herself, as they sat drinking a cup of afternoon tea.

Of course the evidence against Mary Lou was circumstantial.

It shouldn't have been possible to convict her. But every piece of evidence is a thread, my father said. And if you gather enough threads together, you can make a hanging rope. The photograph of Frank Heller and his grotesquely shattered eye was one thread. It was taken with a Kodak Pony, a better camera than my Brownie Hawkeye. Tom stole the photograph from my father's briefcase and showed it to me. I saw Frank slumped in a chair looking at me as if he were asking for help. One eye was open, and the other eye, the bad eye, was dark and evil, a bloated bag with a rip in the middle. The defence argued that the photograph was inflammatory, but my father pointed out that the photograph was not retouched or shot in a special light. The picture was a piece of objective evidence. The photographer hadn't tried to make anything more than what the camera saw.

Mary Lou had also persuaded Frank to take out an insurance policy on his life eighteen months before his death. That was another thread. And when Mary Lou moved her boyfriend in two months later, the threads became a rope just like that.

The year is 1955, winter. Kim is eleven years old, and I am thirteen. Kim is posing for the first colour photograph I will take with my Brownie Hawkeye. I will put it on the first page of my new album. (On the first page of my old album, I put the black-and-white picture of Tom and me with our father.) The new album is a black book tied with a piece of matching black cord and inscribed with the simple title 'Photographs'. It is winter in the snapshot. You can see the snowbank rising like white frosting in front of our big turreted house on First Street. The banks also rise on either side of the cleared walk leading up to our large red-brick porch with the fanlight above our front door.

Kim, my first real best friend, is in the foreground, disguised as a fat person in a padded brown snow suit. She is patting my dog, Joe, and she is wearing my favourite flowery cotton print. I've loaned her the dress to go to Mass in, but my gift is hidden under Kim's suit which swells around her arms and legs.

Behind Kim, a woman in a hideous pair of sealskin galoshes and a raccoon coat is striking a pose, one hand on her hip. She is standing next to Tom, who is not wearing a coat, only a Maple

Leaf hockey sweater, and he is staring at Bernadette as if he wants to make it clear to me and anyone else who sees her that Bernadette is the third-most notorious woman in Madoc's Landing, next to Mellie Sommers and Mary Lou Heller. The important thing to notice about Bernadette is the colour of her cheeks. They are as pink as tea roses.

Tom said Bernadette was a slut, no matter how much rouge she wore. For one thing, Bernadette was French-Canadian and she wore skirts so tight you could crack a flea on them. For another, she dyed her hair a listless ochre, so it looked like dyed sheep's wool.

It was my contention that Tom's evidence was only prima facie. That is, it put a responsibility on Bernadette to explain herself but it wasn't enough to convict her. Tom said he was glad I was making him back up his argument because every time we fail to make the Crown prove its case, we are all a little less free.

'Tom,' I said, 'you may be the Crown, and I may be counsel for the defence, but Bernadette is not a slut because she is a good mother to my friend Kim. I'm sure,' I said, 'sluts don't take care of their children.' Of course I had no way of knowing how well Mellie Sommers treated her baby girl in private but I guessed by the way she slapped her kid's hand when she cried in her stroller, shrieking and pointing at the Coke bottle Mellie was always drinking from, that Mellie didn't deserve to be a mother.

As for Mary Lou Heller, she didn't have any children so there was no point speculating. But Tom said being a slut didn't have anything to do with children; it had to do with men, with sex, with spreading your legs for every Tom, Dick and Harry. The dictionary didn't mention Tom's meaning for the word slut. Our *Oxford* said a slut was a slattern or slovenly woman. But Tom said untidiness was not the point either.

The point was you couldn't trust a slut. A slut did the dirty deed with anybody who asked her; a slut rolled in the hay with all the boys only she didn't get paid for it. A prostitute was a slut, but a slut wasn't a prostitute, because a slut wasn't in it for the money. A slut was worse than a prostitute. She was too stupid to know she could make a living at it.

Tom said I shouldn't get on good terms with sluts. It was

tricky enough that I was a Protestant whose best friend was a dogan, a mick, i.e. a Catholic.

Of course, he said, he had no worry about me in the slut department. I know you'll never be one, he said. You're just like Mother, you're not interested in sex. Still, he told me I had to be careful; I was too sympathetic. I should stay away from girls who had double-barrelled names like Mary Lou Heller, and wore V-neck angora sweaters that smelt of Shalimar, a perfume Mom called whore's lure.

Tom also told me there were many kinds of sluts and not all of them lived in Madoc's Landing. For instance, Anne Boleyn, the wife of Henry VIII, was a slut. So was Zsa Zsa Gabor, the movie star, who married every Tom, Dick and Harry she slept with so she could pretend she wasn't a slut. Then there was our mother's cousin Lulu Marsden who lived in Vancouver. What else could you be with a name like that? You couldn't be a lady with a name that almost rhymed with cuckoo, could you?

'Are sluts capable of ordinary living?' I asked. 'Do they sometimes eat mashed potatoes instead of french fries and use a Brownie Hawkeye?'

'Of course, sluts act normal,' Tom said. 'That's how they fool you. But if you could see what they do when everybody goes to sleep,' he added, 'you would find out that sluts are every bit as disgusting as you thought.'

It is Monday, one day after I took my first colour photograph of Kim and Bernadette. Tom and I are hiding behind the lumber pile at the end of the nuns' yard. Bernadette stands by the back door, hanging out the washing.

It is a cold, overcast afternoon late in March, the time of year when the spring sun should be melting the snow into gurgling streams along Second Street. But spring is nowhere to be seen, and the icy wind blows Bernadette's scarf behind her back like a banner. The wind also makes our cheeks turn red and our noses run. We don't complain. We are used to being disappointed by the weather.

In our shiny padded jackets, Tom and I crouch behind the lumber, listening to the creak of the clothes line as the accused strings up the garments.

You slut.

I say the word to myself to test the sound of it. In my mouth, it sounds slushy, like the Popsicles Mom doesn't like me to eat in the house because they turn into cylinders of soggy ice when I suck on them.

Slut, slut, slut.

It also sounds like rut, which I know is a bad word. Deer rut and have baby fawns like Bambi. Sluts rut, and their skin decays, turns white like the lumpy paste I use in school to stick my cut-out pictures on to Bristol-board posters.

This afternoon Bernadette's arms move stiffly as she hangs up the nuns' old, mended sheets and tea towels with the insignia 'Madoc's Landing—Gateway to the Great Lakes'. It is so cold the feeling is seeping out of my toes. This familiar sensation does not scare me. I know I can stamp my plastic rubbers on the ground and scrunch up my toes to keep the blood flowing, but it's a nuisance to have to do it.

Then Bernadette hangs up something lacy and black. Tom pokes me, and I look hard to see what it is. It's a pair of panties. Now she hangs up two pairs that are named after the days of the week—Friday and Sunday. The pair in black lace makes me think of spider webs. The panties disturb me. I once peeked into my mother's lingerie drawer and saw with my own eyes that her underwear was snowy white, every piece, from the all-purpose brassières to the baggy nylon panties in the style of shorts.

Then Bernadette hangs up a black band supporting two bulbous red cups. Tom utters a strange, puffing hiss beside me. 'Ssss . . . slut,' he says, and I feel a little quake of angry excitement. In his mouth, the word slut sounds like slice. It comes out sharp and spins across the yard toward Bernadette like a hunting knife. I wait for it to strike her in the throat, for Bernadette to fall to the ground, but Bernadette couldn't have heard him because she keeps on hanging her underwear up.

Now she strings up a garter belt and several small flannel nightgowns that belong to Kim. Bernadette picks up the wicker hamper and stops. She is looking right at us, at the lumber pile. We crouch down even more and lower our heads in their knitted toques.

'Kim!' she calls. 'Are you there, *mon petit chou*?' Tom puts a mittened hand on my knee so I won't move. Kim is playing behind the Catholic church on Third Street. There is no chance Kim will hear Bernadette's cry.

At last Bernadette puts her empty laundry basket on her hip and kicks at the door of the old shed at the back of the nuns' house. It creaks open, and she disappears. Tom's hand is still on my knee. We continue to crouch behind the pile of lumber. Our breath makes foamy clouds in front of our mouths. Finally Tom lifts his hand off my knee and stands up. He moves sluggishly toward the clothes line. Then he nods at me, and I begin to march back and forth, patrolling the yard. One by one Tom removes the wooden clothes-pegs from the soft garments. He puts the pegs in his mouth and hands the underwear to me. Together we waddle back behind the pile of wood.

There we squat, going over the clothing of the accused. The underwear astonishes me. It's see-through, flimsy. I sit next to Tom, examining the scarlet brassière. Its red cups are fringed with circles sewn in black thread like the concentric circles on a dartboard. Nesting inside the cups are two rubber falsies.

Suddenly Tom hisses. The pair of black lace panties come apart in his hands, broken. He shows me how they fold together again so the crotch is intact.

'Is that so she doesn't have to take her pants off to tinkle?' I ask, and Tom looks at me in disgust—because in my shock I have used the baby's word for pee. Then he takes off his mittens so he can open the panties again. 'It's for the man, silly,' he says, his mittens dangling from under the cuffs of his snow suit on a piece of yarn. 'So he can poke it in.'

'Oh,' I say, 'oh.' And then I think slut, slut, slut—all the better to rut, rut, rut.

Then Tom unzips the front of his snow suit and takes out my Brownie Hawkeye. He doesn't look me in the eye. Instead he waves his hand to indicate that I should display the evidence so he can take a picture. I crouch down and arrange the underwear on the snow. Then I pull myself to my feet and pad slowly over and stand behind Tom. He doesn't look up; he's kneeling, so it's easy. I lean down and push Tom as hard as I can from behind.

There isn't time to look for my Brownie Hawkeye. Panting, I grab the bra and panties and run down Second Street to the Heller's house. It stands alone behind an empty school, and nobody lives there now because Mary Lou's in jail, and Frank is dead. The house is clapboard and dirty white like the snow except for the red trim around each of its narrow windows. I look closely at the front windows to make sure nobody is in the house. Then I count three breaths and go into the little yard behind the house where Frank Heller grew his vegetables. A few withered stalks of corn poke up through the icy ground.

The corn stalks were planted by a dead man, I think. Then I remember the photograph. What did he think when he saw Mary Lou pointing the gun at his face? Our father said the gun was fired only five inches from his left eye. Frank couldn't have suspected her or he wouldn't have let her come that close. Did Mary Lou sidle up to him, pelvis first, wiggling her hips as she pointed the gun in his face?

I put my hands on my hips and stick out my tongue. 'Nana-nananana—Frank Heller! The worms crawl in and the worms crawl out, up your gizzard and out your snout.'

Now I scoop up a handful of snow. To my surprise, it sticks to my mitt. It's packing snow. A soft, heavy spring wind is blowing now from the south. I pack the snow into each cup of the brassière. I press it in firmly. I hook the brassière up the way my mother hooks up hers. I put it on backwards so I can work the clasp. For a moment, two breasts stick out the back of my snow suit. Then I slide the bra around to my front. It slides easily because my snow suit is slippery. Now the cups protrude from my chest, and I have a bosom, a great big snowy bazoom. I stand in front of the side window and shake my breasts at the Heller's old house.

'Slut, slut, slut,' I shout.

A few minutes pass. I sit down in the melting snow among the dead corn stalks. The snow under the bottom of my padded suit feels wet. Soon it will soak all the way through, leaving a big wet stain, but I don't care.

'Nananana-nan-nana—Mary Lou! You're a slut who likes to rut, rut, rut!' I begin to dig purposefully behind the old stalks. The effort makes my snow suit feel heavy and hot, but at least the warm wind is making the snow soft. I keep on Bernadette's enormous brassière until the very last. Then in it goes, right to the bottom of the hole with the rest of Bernadette's things.

All at once I sit up and stare again at the old Heller place. I am sure Frank Heller is in there, spying on me, not with his single open eye, no, of course not. Spying on me with his torn, bloated one. I hold my breath and wait for his raging voice. Wait for the word to come spinning and tumbling right at me.

Slut!

The sound I hear is very small. I hear it all around me. The sound of icicles dripping from the boughs of the tree next to the Heller place and from the eaves of the broken porch. Nobody is in the old house, no one. Not a single soul is watching me from those icy, still rooms, or huddling near me among the old corn stalks.

I am all alone in the March twilight and I feel as sad as you can possibly feel.

I roll up a large, wet ball of snow and place it over the top of the hole containing Bernadette's underwear. I could make a snowman but I don't have a carrot for a nose. Or small pieces of coal for the eyes. Besides, Tom used to help me with my snowmen. And it is not much fun to make one by yourself. □

GRANTA

ALLAN GURGANUS

HE'S ONE, TOO

In Falls, North Carolina, in 1957, we had just one way of 'coming out'.

It was called getting caught.

Every few years, cops nabbed another unlikely guy, someone admired and married—a civic fellow, not bad looking. He often coached a Pee Wee League Swim Team. Again we learned that the Local Man Least Likely to Like Boys did! In our town of 2,200, this resulted in confusion to the point of nausea.

Our *Herald Traveler* was usually sedate (RECENT CHURCH GOINGS-ON OF FUN AND NOTE). It now encrusted the front page with months of gory innuendo. Circulation beefed right up.

And into jail they chucked the hearty, beautiful Dan R—, my boyhood idol.

It took me weeks to find why they'd removed him completely as a carpet stain. I was nine and prone to hero-worship. I suffered a slight stammer. I lunged at outdoor activities; accidents happened—often to bystanders. Archery from my tree house discouraged neighbours' backyard cookouts. I felt that 1957 *required* its boys to enjoy a major sport.

As soon as Dan got grabbed, my parents halted newspaper home delivery. I pedalled uphill to the public library. I spotted a stack of hometown papers set—unusual—on a shelf, above kiddies' reach. I dragged over three *Who's Who*s, one stool from Circulation. Then I hid in shadows, safe among 1921's unasked-for *National Geographic*s. I read about the public fall of my secret friend.

My index finger now traced the nine weeks and sixty column inches of Dan's descent. I read of his capture, for deeds I'd considered doing with him. I felt exactly as sick as excited.

This would become a familiar flashpoint for me and my kind. Everything we want is everything most others find the most disgusting. Your hope, their shame.

I was, at nine, confused. I am now forty-eight.

Odd, authorities never arrested our town's obvious ones. The vice squad failed to book Falls's supple florist; comically self-informed, he defined everything as 'buttery', 'heavenly', 'icky' or 'velvety'. Cops spared our insinuating, gifted organist: didn't Melvin play for the Baptists at ten, the Methodists at eleven? Also left unjailed: Falls's admired, if chunky, mama's-boy librarian.

These ones, born 'out', went genially overlooked thanks to good behaviour. They hailed from decent families; they told welcome if unrepeatable jokes to generations of mayors' wives. They were clever from surviving. And—if their humour was weekend excessive—their lives stayed weekday useful to Falls, NC. 'The Boys' would be called that well into their senilities. The Boys accepted who they'd been assigned to be.

True, they might flaunt their sexuality's effervescent side effects, but they had the sense to do the sex deed (if do it they must, and you guessed they probably must) well out of state. Sure, they got teased, and daily. Did they even hear the rednecks' sidewalk chorus—'SisterMan', 'Miss Sump Pump', 'NellieBelle', 'Velvety'? Yes. But otherwise no one bothered these vamping, mutant versions of Falls's 'good old boys'.

An artistic aunt of mine spoke fondly of these three best pals; she bought floral arrangements from one, marvelled at the Sunday Wurlitzer *crescendi* of another and—from the third—received (under the library counter) steamy best-sellers concerning tobacco-growing oversexed hillbillies.

The married fellows that our cops caught were just trying to outwit their molten (uncontainable) secret. Failing that, many hoped simply to outlive it. Couldn't you slowly lose the central urge toward men, the way your waistline painlessly, eventually, dispersed?

Your wife, your kids, sat inches away. Who would know that, while this service-station attendant shot white foam across your car window, you studied such drenching not to catch a smudge on green glass, but to observe, through it, the beautiful brown ligaments in a perfect, working, young, male arm.

Desperation for actual sex with living men led some of our brightest locals (ones with law degrees, ones passionate for clever Civil War battle strategy) direct into the crudest traps.

And the very nanosecond queer news got out, these guys fell forever.

Allan Gurganus

A man's man

I so admired Dan R—. He golfed with Dad. They partied. I guess he must've sold insurance or real estate (I never saw him actually working).

Dad's friends arrived at our house en route to their games. Our home stood in sight of the club's first hole. Foursomes gathered on our porch, drank there, paced, awaiting today's tardy partner.

Their beloved hostess was Mother, Falls's best-informed young wife. She remembered the nuances of each man's favourite drink ('Exactly three extra baby onions, please').

'Don't know how you keep so many standing liquor orders in that lovely head, Helen,' guys flirted with a woman whose IQ was 159.

Here came Dan's sporty Plymouth wagon, 'cream' and electric blue (white interior). His sound piled into our drive, activating everything. In Dan's car, young lawyers, young doctors, joshing. Behind them, leather golf bags of saddle-shoe two-tones. Bags, lumpy as boys' marble sacks grown huge, chucked atop each other like some shoulder-padded orgy—dumb, male, good will at rut.

Dan never swore; he rarely broke the speed limit. This husband and father and soon-to-be-caught queer served as deacon for the new brick Methodist church.

Jocular, adored and nearly too handsome, Dan was saved by not quite knowing it. That let you stare, let you draw maybe four inches closer than you'd risk with some dude aware of his exact market value. Dan, so visible to others, seemed half-blinded by his own inviting innocence.

People rubbed shoulders with him—'for good luck', they told themselves (if they noticed doing it at all). I noticed them doing it. At nine, I wanted to do it too.

Hidden in my tree house above his parked wagon, I gazed down upon this man; my admiration felt almost patriotic: it weakened me, but for ideal reasons.

The floor of my crow's-nest was one closet door, sacrificed in recent expansion; my father had nailed it up a maple at roughly lighthouse height. Just one closet's width held me aloft. It gave a good if sneaky overview, but offered no real living space. Suspended by rope, I kept a net sack full of ice-cold Cokes. A three-legged stool dangled. I pulled things closetward only when needed.

Today, Dan, seeing one stray line, fished a dollar bill from his wallet. Grinning, he tied it on, jerked three times. I knew to tug his green up into mine. I saluted over the ledge and, alone, sniffed dampish folding money. Its ink smelt more black than green. The smell hinted at wadded white bread, billfold's rawhide and, not Jockey shorts, but Dan's second-day-wear boxers, possibly plaid. Eyes closed, I inhaled mainly Dan, worth hundreds.

Friendly below me, he stood no more than five foot six. And yet, like certain compact guys, he appeared a giant, shrunk—someone monumental rendered wittily portable, more concentratedly male for that. He was the most perfectly made, if shortest, of my father's crowd. These men were immodest ex-soldiers of a won war. They acted as pleased with themselves as with their unearned trust funds.

Dad's group called itself the Six Footers' Club. Dan needed six more inches to qualify. These six inches caused lurid jokes I never tired of overhearing.

Men! So simple in beasty anxiousness about their size relative to other guys' vitals' sizes. 'Is it large enough?' cannot be called the subtlest question in the world, but it sure remains a biggie.

Dan, the Six Footers' mascot and pony beauty, again got teased about his runtiness and profile. A tree house was good for such eavesdropping. I knew that between guy-drink two and guy-drink three the smut would start. I waited.

Country Club North Carolina: most days after five p.m. from 1949–69 meant bottoms up, three good stiff ones downed in an hour and a half. (Not sissy white wine, either. The hard stuff.)

Men watched our driveway for the last of today's foursome. He'd soon roar up after closing some deal or suturing shut the victims of Falls's latest teen car wreck. Our house had a horseshoe of parking lot, plus hammocks and the open bar.

Mom, perfectly dressed, with a Master's degree, hovered,

warmly impersonal. Indoors, two black, uniformed maids did her heavy lifting. Dad's friends lounged and goofed right under my treetop.

After jawing through money news, after gossiping about sewage-bond issues, after the mind-numbing hit parade of their last game's best shots, ('So Dan surprises us, choosing his three iron'), they finally got dirty on me.

Stripped to shorts, my eyes half shut, breathing Dan's dollar, nose to nose with George Washington, I'd been ready.

They mentioned certain looser secretaries—those days always named Donna—and who Donna'd 'done' now, sometimes three in a hotel room at one time. Smut hushed when Mom reappeared wearing a Dior flared skirt, carrying the silver tray that—some summers—seemed jewellery fused direct to her hand's red nails. As she swept indoors, trash restarted mid-syllable.

What did a youngster hear, those corny days of sexed-up '57? Often simple dick jokes of the kind that boys my age enjoyed.

'Hey, Dean,' remarked our youngest bank president ever. 'Summer sure has bleached your hair. Or you been dipping into one of Jeanie's Clairol bottles? So tell us, Big Time Lawyer Man, is it true blonds have more cum?'

Tree high, I kept still.

'I'm not answerin' that directly, sir. But you can state your question direct into my Bone-o-Phone, Phil. Put Mouth Against Tip of Receiver and Inhale Hard . . . right here.' Much yuks. Above them, half-stiff in seersucker shorts (shorts whose very fabric's name gave me a minor-major boner), I listened in a trance of premonition, dread, desire.

At anything off-colour, Dan grew shy and pebble-kicking. The Six Footers admired him as 'too straight an arrow'. When he literally blushed, they seemed not unexcited, watching somebody so handsome redden, laugh, then hide his face behind two palms while bowing forward.

Quiet, he reigned at their group's dead centre. If any Packard or golf cart broke, Dan was first under its hood. The joke ran: he could fix an engine without getting any oil on him. Dan wore his snug, pressed clothes like some proud, poor boy, quietly defending his one good school outfit.

People included young Mr R—, though his family wasn't *from* Falls. He was token Elsewhere. Dan seemed more mysterious and attractive, being uninitiated. Locals took him aside to explain the genealogy behind some recent land deal—some webbing of tribal traits and 1790 betrayals so complex, you could see he hadn't a clue. It didn't matter. Around here, nobody new ever truly knew. Two hundred and fifty years were involved; strangers could never catch up with that many genes and so much ownership.

Dan R— (no last name, please, though it's forty-odd years later) had a charming, actorish way of planting knuckled fists on to his hips. He had this lovely way of letting his well-made head fall back as he laughed. He laughed often and—if the things he said were the things that they all said then—Dan said them in so ripened a baritone, and with such banal complete conviction, that he seemed even more a man.

Originality has never been required for admission to a Country Club. Originality would soon lose this guy his membership.

My dad was himself a chopper and clown on the links. His own ambitions for his game made him far less good at it. Dan R— played golf to relax. Golf worked my father's every nerve. 'That darn Dan.' Pop shook his head. 'Guy consistently shoots in the low seventies.' My father watched the younger man's natural swing; Dad's groans sounded close to Lust, not the simpler vice of Envy.

'I swear, Dan. I keep telling the pro—a person can't *learn* it. Guy either gots it or he don't, and, Dan? you're loaded with factory options, damnit. Maybe bottle it? For us mortals, pal? Sell me a six-pack at cost, what say?'

'Well, thanks, Richard. I do really usually try hard, I do. And sometimes, I admit, I'll get m'balls to set down at least near where I wanted 'em.'

Be careful what you wish for, Dan R—.

Wanted, dead or alive

Then Dan was not. Not in Papa's golfing party. Nowhere near our home, the couples swarming in for Friday-night bridge, arriving solemnly intent as if planning new Normandy beach landings. Something had happened.

I, a watchful boy child with the man-sized interest in him, retreated to my tree house, soon overheard tag ends of stifled driveway conversations. 'Never in a million years'd guess . . . him . . . one . . . those.'

My favourite had descended from such visibility. That same year he'd headed our Community Chest charity drive. Dan was often shown in the paper, grinning beside a giant plywood thermometer. Mercury shot up as cash poured in. He smiled a hopeful, one-sided grin; he rolled his eyes to urge our town toward generosity—a salesman's readiness to look however foolish for a sale.

Now, no photographs, no word. Missing In Action, one electric-blue Plymouth. My parents having purged our house of any tell-tale *Herald Traveler*, I grew so jumpy/bold from missing Dan, I blurted during dinner, 'Wwwwhat ever happened to . . . ?' I didn't even need to finish. They'd been waiting.

Mother stiffened from Casual to Regal. Using her linen napkin, she blotted her mouth, then—napkin stretched between her fists—studied it as if my question had just made the cloth go beautifully bloodstained.

Dad cleared his throat, public speaking, 'Someday, I'll explain, son. Once I figure it out more myself. There are certain men, often not the ones you'd expect . . . Dan went and tried something that . . . Dan's left us, basically. Nobody understands it. Pass the turnips, son, and take more or you'll never make the Six Footers' Club. Mighty good turnips tonight, Helen. Crispier. Son, I know how much you, all of us, feel so attached to, but . . . Fact is, son, around our town, what Dan tried, it's the one thing a man cannot come *back* from . . . '

This passed for clarification. I simply nodded, swallowing it whole. I would need to bike to the library. I understood I was not meant to know how bad it was, whatever Dan had chanced.

He ceased being, as Mom put it (her joke, not mine) 'The Heart-throb of Our Community Chest.' He ceased being.

Book me passage on the Fellow Ship

When Mother complained about the hours Dad squandered getting even worse at golf, he reminded her: the happiest times of his whole life had been spent at war, with other loud good boys in mobs and squadrons. 'Helen, I need my weekly fellow-ship time.' The Fellow Ship. Guys spoke of it often, as being golden. As something craved nearly as much as women were, by all real men. Me too. I heard about a local high-school athlete winning 'a full Fellow Ship to Duke University' and envied him his crowd on board, the jolly boyish voyage upriver clear to the steepled campus.

At age six, I made the Fellow Ship a pirate craft, longer than wide, a carved dragon's head snarling at its rapier tip, a barge almost too pointedly male ever to float on nebulous female water.

At nine, I pictured a torch-bearing Viking boat, its rowers shirtless doctors and lawyers, its cargo leather monogrammed golf bags, its destination the Links of America, but its true goal: grab-assing, the dirty guesses about who that slutty little Donna wouldn't 'do' dry.

At the prow, hands on hips, lit unevenly by violent orange torchlight, shirtless yet bandoliered with those leather thongs Kirk Douglas wore in *The Vikings*—stood Dan, Captain of the Fellow Ship. His deep voice calling, 'Stroke, fellows. Stroke it good, pals o'mine. Pull hard, because the Fellow Ship is for us baad boys only. Pull hard, good men, because you can.'

I imagined my tree-house closet was a Fellow Ship franchise. Or at least its outrigger offspring, the Boy Raft. Sometimes, among maple leaves, I took off my seersucker shorts.

There was a new verb, used mainly in churches then. Mother found it vulgar. 'To fellowship.' For me, that latent active word sounded like a pillage itinerary, some oar-lock means of transport and my own future port in Paradise.

PROMINENT YOUNG EXEC ARRESTED EXPOSING SELF TO YOUTH (AT PENNEY'S TOILET)

Dateline: Raleigh. A 33-year-old Falls resident, recent chair of our town's most successful Community Chest Drive ever, a four-time winner of the Broken Arrow Amateur Golf Tourney, probably did not know how much his life would change while in Raleigh, this Saturday past, on family business. It was a day of record-breaking heat, but otherwise no different from most days.

The week before, having already been elected Rotarian Young Man of the Year for 1955, he was made it for '57, too! His lovely wife had taught third grade. His three bright children are themselves valued members of their own playground community. But, within one hour of arriving in that shoppers' haven, Raleigh, Dan R— was handcuffed and already on his way to prison.

Arrest came swiftly for the young local church and business leader.

Chief Executive Officer with J & L Realty/Insurance of this city Dan R—, of 211 Elm Avenue of Falls, was caught in the Men's Room of Raleigh's new J.C. Penney's Department Store. According to authorities, he was apprehended while 'making sexual-type-suggestion-advances' to and 'having sustained manual contact with the privates of' a fifteen-year-old boy 'at the urinals of the new Penney's rest room facility, 2:32 p.m., Saturday.'

The father of the boy propositioned chanced to occupy a booth in that very rest room. He was planning to take a faulty camera to the repair shop there in Big Elk Mall. The father also happened to be an off-duty detective (still carrying his service revolver).

The resultant photographs are, according to a reliable source who asked not to be identified but has closely examined them, 'conclusive and damning'. No sooner had flashbulbs cooled than the father made a dramatic arrest. He then paraded the suspect in handcuffs the full length of Raleigh's newest luxury shopping facility, Big Elk Browse 'n Buy Mall, Lake Boone Trail (Road). The photos are now in the hands of capital police, said Raleigh Sheriff's Department spokesman, Red Furman. He would only indicate that young Mr R— was being held for 'Corrupting A Minor,' 'Soliciting,' and 'Indecent Exposure.' Other charges are being considered. A printed statement on this case ended, 'The snapshots prove past any shade of doubt—*some touching was definitely involved.*'

Mrs Dan R— would make no statement when reached by telephone at home after not answering their door during this reporter's twenty minutes of knocking.

Reverend Elmo 'Mo' Haines, of New Hope Road Methodist, is pastor to the once-popular young couple. His only comment ran, 'This is just not the Dan I know. Dan rates among the finest young gents I have fellowshipped with or ministered to, ever. I'm sure there is an explanation, though I don't yet know what it's going to be. But we're all ready. We do just pray for the R— family, and for Dan especially. Despite this being such a true and total shocker, we remember that, in the end, all things work together for the Glory of God.'

Stakeout: crime-scene pix

There was once a brand-new J.C. Penney store. It dignified an early shopping mall in glamorous Raleigh. It was built prior to four-lane highways. To reach the state capital meant a tough three-hour drive from manicured and clubby Falls.

While Dan's children made fast work of their Jumbo-Tub popcorn in the dark Mall Theater, the R— kids' dapper father, with time to kill, purchased golf balls (used and new: old for practice, new for real, for-keeps games).

Finding he'd secured himself two whole hours by his lonesome (unusual back home), maybe Dan scoped out the mall's haltered adolescent girls. They drifted to and fro across the vast space, always tacking at obliques in bright attracting schools of three to five. Not unlike the pet store's neon tetras glorifying aquarium windows of that shop exotically stinky.

It is our rarest luxury, sufficient time alone. Odd how we forget it is a hall pass we so crave. Solitude becomes especially precious to a father of three this overtaxed and hectic with blood-drives, land-closings, putter-practice, sidewalk-edging, car-pooling kids from dressage to clarinet lessons. Today, atypically wifeless (her asthma acted up each August), today, briefly unhooked from children, Dan must have felt like some once-clunky plug-in appliance suddenly retooled to be, the miracle of 1957, 'A Portable'.

Alone at last, free of wall sockets, maybe, probably, he got so doggone horny. Maybe it crunched his lower body like his wife's worst cramps coming on all at once, doubling her over. Was it a nausea of displaced attraction? What made Dan feel this strengthening weakness for some action now?

If the female genitalia can be considered (in certain magical functions) a plug-in device, the male ones remain perversely, indeed sinisterly, portable—extruded, independent, air-able, always primed for the latent test drive.

They'll get a guy—unchaperoned—into all kinds of freelance trouble, quick, even at a fluorescent mall. What to do with a healthy set of portables at two-thirty p.m. at Big Elk Browse 'n Buy, before the babysitting Disney animation ends?

Maybe, surely, Dan endured the driven sexual thoughts of a young man—in so tumid an August—just at the peak of his need to implant. Maybe these two hours among attractive strangers helped Dan admit to a more unsettling itch. It was an itch you couldn't even name, much less sate, slake or properly dig at in reputation-conscious yard-work Falls.

Itches can only go unscratched so long. Watch.

It is 2.28 p.m., 7 August 1957, in a pastel department store, and it's about to happen because Dan has got to pee.

Through Hi-Fi Stereo, past Glassware and Rec Room Needs, he wanders into the men's room at our state's flagship J.C. Penney store.

I admit, out in the open: I wish I'd been there then. I wish I could have saved him from the high price of desire fuelled by decades' sickening secrecy. Barring my helping Dan out or my feeling Dan up, I guess I wish I coulda just watched.

People later praised the two-way mirror. Some Falls gossips swore that's how cops caught Dan, and on movie film. Others claimed that this unlikely toilet had become a secret breeding place for capital-area inverts. (If, of course, they *could* breed.)

My own belated adult guess is: a restless Dan chanced into the absolute right bathroom on the absolute worst day.

If only he hadn't already seen *Snow White* four times. If only it hadn't been 1957, when you could freely park your kids in any movie house.

There were many reasons Falls condemned its ever-popular Dan R— overnight. The following is one:

Dan's children came out of the cinema, blinking, scared after seeing the witch's poisoned apple eaten. They felt spooked by so spiky a green villainess. (Always, in fables and life and in Disney movies, Evil's more photogenic than any sappy virgin dumb enough to bite an apple so obviously laced with chemo. An apple this good looking dares you not to eat it. So you really shouldn't.)

Dan's kids, perhaps with buttons of popcorn strayed into their fine silver-blond hair, were first surprised, then shocked, next hurt—not finding Dad.

'He said meet right *here*, right? And at four, I'm sure.'

Imagine them staring toward the mall's terrazzo flooring—still influenced by the movie's wishfulness. Just because they wanted it, couldn't their Dad break through this paving, hands on hips, head tipped back and rising, laughing?

The kids felt mainly ready for the long nap home in the back of their Plymouth wagon, still new-smelling, somehow male-smelling. Cross, then bored and—when an hour'd passed—irked with a first hiccup of completest fear, youngsters finally sent their oldest brother on a mission, 'Go and scout out that darn Dad of ours, Dan Jr. The car's still parked, so he's here OK. Hope he's not sick or somethin'. But, naw—Dad's never sick.'

If, in Falls, these kids had been stood up, some other

parents—friends of Dan's and Julie's (his wife)—would have spied the familiar, pretty, R— features. They would have noted the kids' worry. They'd have noted how children of such different ages—usually quite eager to appear not with each other—clung together now. But, see, this mall stood in faraway cosmopolitan Raleigh, and life was harsher here and faster and so crowded. And no one knew them.

Only later—during the mall's lock-up around ten-thirty p.m., only then did a black security guard find three children sleeping, roughly spoon-fashion, behind one huge imported palm tree. Like kids from some Grimm tale, lost in the enchanted woods, they'd stolen back among the decorative plantings nearest where Dad said to meet this afternoon at exactly four. Six and a half hours later, discovered tucked behind the fountain, back by its transformer where the rushing water's clear recycling tubes were coiled, and snuffling like Mother's asthma, three kids woke. They felt sure Dad had found them. Smiling, they turned.

But no, uh-oh, it was a worried Negro guard, chancing half a smile. And kids understood they were all in so much trouble. They'd spent their last coins on further Milk Duds. They didn't know how to phone Mom collect long-distance. And if they had, they might be getting Dad into real hot water. See, without even understanding why, they already knew to be ashamed.

The R— kids attended Methodist Sunday school; bruise-coloured consciences were forming. Starter cultures of the ethical and, when need be, the self-punishing. At home, everything usually worked on schedule, so when it didn't, somebody got blamed.

The mall guard seemed to be half-eating his foot-long walkie-talkie. People were being called, the lost kids' father's full name uttered. Then Dan's children heard a minor stir. The walkie-talkie picked up one downtown cop, 'Oh, him? Yeah, we've got him. Guy's already been printed, guy's been booked. Good riddance to bad rubbish, hunh?'

'Booked, what fo'?' the kind guard asked. Then Dan's kids, eyes large, hands laced around each others' necks and shoulders—they all knew first, knew first what their father really was.

If I'd married and stayed put in Falls, I would now teach art history at a local junior college. I'd have a smart if no-longer-slender wife named Alice, and the one son, Kyle, five—a prodigy-brat-joy.

I didn't. So I don't.

Dan, caught in public, at a Raleigh urinal, had not been as wise as the Boys. These buddies survived Falls only because they took their unusual appetites elsewhere. The good ship Fellow Ship sailed the Boys across state lines. And if they'd docked in Raleigh to seek adventures around mere malls, these experts at hiding would have known the safety code for bathroom pick-ups.

You go into a booth, you don't risk public detection as poor Dan did, standing out in the open. You take your classic position on the pot then tap your foot, setting up a signal that shoes to either side of yours can acknowledge or ignore. By the time you peek under the partition—or through a burrowed portal called, in terminology both profane and sacred, the Glory Hole (no Fellow Ship should be without one, above decks)—you have received a Morse code marriage proposal, tap-dance pre-nups from the soles next door. Everybody's implicated, notes on scrolls of toilet paper passed. 'What you into doing?' has given total strangers more up-front candid sexual info than most wedding couples know about each other. Physical description, list of fave sex acts, signed, sealed—prior to first touch, a veritable contract. If society makes your lust illegal, you might as well subvert those laws efficiently.

Men! What won't they do to get some? And guys seeking guys are spared all female indirection, all the ladies' emotional subtlety, decency and marriage-mill formality: guys'll just stick it through the hole, get 'done' in the time it's taken you to read this page. It's honest, if illegal.

The Boys judged Raleigh a bit too close to home. No telling which Falls preacher or city manager you might run into. And besides, the men you snared at Penney's would be suburban, too married, far too penitent for the Boys' intended calibre of fellowshipping.

No, weekends they travelled direct to the Ships of Many Fellows, also known as the Atlantic Fleet.

They leaned coastward—eventful weekends at rundown,

tolerant Norfolk hotels nobly named the Monticello. In formerly grand Deco lobbies, reconnoitring with other small-town escapee florists named Hiram, Buford and Earle, '*avec une* "e", please, Mary,' they drank treacherous if Windex-coloured drinks titled after ports far more exotic than Norfolk.

Then the Boys, feeling Out, wandered Water Street; two aircraft carriers, six thousand young salts, were in.

A little drunk, the Boys still talked inherited Spode.

A lot drunk, they trawled the sailor bars, and—come morning—phoned each others' hotel rooms to brag in inches.

How, at age nine, could I announce to the world that I preferred, I think, fellow sailors on the Fellow Ship? My tendencies and character were probably visible to anyone with eyes. The Boys surely guessed about me long before I did. (Just, as I later learned, they'd 'spotted' the unlikely Dan before Dan probably knew.) Instead they taught me lore about their jobs. They acted kind, familiar, courtly, but they never 'told me' about myself in a rude way, never took advantage of a ready, wistful kid, as many Republicans will tell you they *all* do, correction, *we* all do.

Coming out to my parents was tougher than going on record in *People* magazine. Telling them was like saying I had some news: I'd been arrested at J.C. Penney's pee-trough, and why? Because, the other good news was . . . They dared me to tell them. Short of clamping a hand over my mouth just as I formed the syllable, they did everything actively to prevent me. They knew all along, of course. But maybe they remembered the dreadful fate of our friend, ridden out of town for reaching toward an apple too perfect, too easily achieved, too good not to be pure poison. The very sleeping potion makes the fruit's red shine so.

They kept asking which girls I was dating most, how impending an engagement? How 'bout the promise of grand-children, when? Which likely family names for that first boy?

These were people who'd dropped a suddenly depraved young Dan. Is it any wonder I feared blurting? And they feared hearing? I told them gently at first: 'I'm married to my work.' Then: 'Don't expect me to go out with the daughter of your next-door neighbour, that plump but pretty-in-the-face personality girl you keep mentioning, the art teacher at the public school. I am not erotically interested in women, period.'

That seemed sufficient. I didn't want to be a guy who'd brutalize his parents in the guise of coming clean.

Tell it to the judge

What went on at the urinal of the brand-new J.C. Penney's at that early mall still holds me. It holds me in part because I remember how beautiful Dan's forearms were as he pressed both his fists, knuckles downward, on to the farthest points of his fine hip bones.

The arms were wound in every colour, including—near the right wrist—a sprinkling of first silver. I recall the way his dark eyebrows sent a translucent chevron (ambassadorial) to negotiate those black woolly dashes into staying perpendicular above so very Roman a nose. How blue Dan's jaw was where he shaved so often, how it looked like tempered steel—a dented ice-breaker chin, its metal neatly folded (oh, to rub my nose in that).

How openly did the young boy, in snug blue jeans, entice an itchy, married Dan, who led the Community Chest so well and made the red part of the plywood thermometer go redder, faster than any other fund-driver, ever? How did my hero fall prey to some pimply if pretty boy? And did authorities insist the boy's policeman father fill some monthly quota of morals charges? Or was this simply off-duty sport, done on spec, for the glory?

Dan's court-appointed lawyer would place most blame upon Dan's tempters. On both the young son and his hidden father, readying the camera.

Shall we blame that blazing August's having twenty-four non-raining days? Or was it Dan's depressed, asthmatic wife? Was it Julie's unwillingness to 'let him' lately, and this bad recent humidity? What drove young Dan to eye, then sidle nearer and finally touch, the secret, if offered, velvety parts of a younger and seemingly more innocent fellow male, fifteen?

All this they discussed at the hearing. It was reprinted in our local *Herald Traveler*, barely euphemized. I sat in the silent library's shady stacks, backed against the *Geographics*' egg-yolk yellows and egg-white whites. I sat reading some and crying some and reading more, in painful little sips, and not understanding how—between the lines—I understood all this so well.

They showed Dan's picture, once the trial started. It was early, a locally made portrait taken just after he arrived in town, so hopeful (the top studio of Falls's two), the file photo they'd used for all his awards as Young Man of the . . . whatever. All the drives and that big banquet he'd meant to end world muscular dystrophy. A well-intentioned guy, not yet thirty-four, smiling in his white, over-laundered shirt and with such teeth, and the starchy, believing whites of his over-laundered (unsuspecting) eyes.

This town's not big enough for both of me

Six weeks after Dan's arrest, three weeks through his jail term, his wife still lived in Falls. She repacked, hiding as well as you could in a town this small. No further church attendance. She had groceries delivered to her back door till her husband—released from his imprisonment (UNNATURAL ACTS, LIBERTIES TAKEN WITH A MINOR, INDECENT EXPOSURE)—could travel wherever they'd picked to settle next. He would get a new job—if without too many letters of recommendation.

Till Dan sent for the loved ones, his kids were kept indoors. When Julie R— dodged into some store, seeking milk, she wore a kerchief and dark wing glasses. Most people avoided her. A few confident veteran clerks did speak (if only about the weather), and later they asked others for brownie points for having treated her as a regular human being. 'After all, *she's* not the one's been going on all-fours in J.C. Penney's boys' rooms. See the bags under her eyes, even behind those glasses? To find that out about the father of your sons—poor thing, crushed-looking . . . '

Dan served a seven-week sentence. Though he'd golfed with every white-shoe-firm lawyer in Eastern North Carolina, not one stepped forward to help. And he—shamed—just accepted the court-appointed choice, a kid from Ohio fresh out of a so-so school and nothing special.

We never saw Dan again.

I, I never saw. Him.

My dad played eighteen holes a week with him for six years, but that was neither mentioned nor admitted. Dan, once considered indispensable, seemed—overnight—not just dead but unmissed, except in certain tree houses.

I would aim my bike toward the R— home, its FOR SALE stake tilted, cock-eyed, out front. Sudden weeds everywhere. A split-level brick rancher with mature evergreen plantings, it looked like most other homes on the block; it was a Duke of Clarence. Myself a little pedant, I knew the model-home names of every suburb in biking distance. I stayed seated on my bike, stopped before Dan's nice unsold home. I regretted having snubbed his three skinny kids at the club pool.

Every car approaching from behind made bristles of my crew-cut stand on end, tentacles predicting him. Sure he'd keep an implied appointment with his 'little buddy,' as he'd called me. But the sun set. It got cold. Dan never arrived.

One month later, I expected I would miss him less, not more. But it was more. So, with a certainty peculiar to the insane, I biked direct to a hanging 'colonial' sign: J & L REALTY/INSURANCE—REACHING OUT TO THE COMMUNITY.

Wearing shorts, barefoot, I approached a gargoyle secretary powdered in hopes of looking younger. She did not. She gaped at my question, rose, wedged half behind a frosted door. 'Boy, no shoes, asking ways to find Dan R—. Seems upset. Thin, well spoken . . . nervous.'

'How young?'

The lady tipped back, smiled, disappeared, 'Maybe around ten?'

'Oh dear God. Now they're coming in here to us. Where will it end?'

A man veered out, his hand extended, the smile enforced as a laminated name tag. 'Can I be of help? What do you need with him, son?'

'Nobody knows where Dan went. I miss him.'

The secretary stepped one high heel back, but the executive

bent forward, considered touching me, then thought so much better of it, his right shoulder spasmed. 'We have no address. Even if I wanted to trace him, which I don't, I could not. Who are your parents? Have you told them anythis? Because, you're going to need help with it. More help than we can give you here, son. This is a work place.' The big phone rang, and two adults practically giggled, both lurching toward one black receiver. She beat him to it.

'Who is your father?' he asked. 'Tell us who your people are.'

I turned so slow, I padded out over cold lino, then gingerly across hot pavement. Then I pedalled off so quick, swallowing all the air, eyes burning. I knew then. I could not afford to find him.

Hard evidence

The boy Dan 'touched' was the attractive youngest son of the heavy-set arresting officer. It later came out: this lieutenant tended to place his fifteen-year-old on non-school days at better-known public urinals. This ploy rarely worked, since the intended victims enjoyed communal word-of-mouth as expert as their not-unprideful oral sex. Raleigh queers were long since on to that little trick and morsel. They did acknowledge as how the cop's kid looked a bit like James Dean, and—why lie?—he was extremely well hung for a boy who'd only shaved the once, for Easter service. They nicknamed this troubled smouldering boy the James Dean Decoy, Bait Meat and, best perhaps, the Trojan Hose.

They knew to run from the sight of him (only some jerky, married out-of-towner—hiding from his own kind and their helpful information—would've gone near that infamous young beauty holding his infamous older-looking beauty).

The lieutenant encouraged his son, once stationed at busier urinals around our state's capital, to unhasp his all and, having unzipped, to what?

I find imagining this father-to-son pep talk a very tough assignment. To use your kid as other fellows' ship direct into prison. To me this seems as Martian as I might appear to any cop willing to dangle his boy as fishing bait—literally, dangle. 'Son, just maybe think of, oh, say, Marilyn Monroe. Then, nature being nature, what happens'll happen, and don't mind letting the old one near you see your . . . Not to be scared, either. 'Cause Dad's right back here. You just get the evil-doer started and, by God, Dad and the long arm of the law'll do the rest.'

I have myself experienced joyous moments in public rest rooms, commingling and looking at and more. Some moralists would say that Dan should not have touched a boy that age, even if the kid seduced him. Some readers will not have got this far because I seem to be pulling for the wrong side.

It is a medical fact: you can kill a starving man by feeding him too fast.

The life of the erotic must have consequences. Sexual urges can be exactly as memorable as they feel savage, precisely as pleasurable as they must look—to the uninvolved—pagan and utterly animal.

A kid with his pink staub in hand, face smiling, eyes drowsy, mouth gone slack, and waving his all around (as ordered), turned into a deadly fishing lure; and the Dad, wearing a trench coat to make this stake-out look more movie-like, waiting in the stall to pounce on you. (Between clients, do father and son talk ball scores, trying to fake normality and pretend that such safaris constitute everyday policing?)

Dad is about to leap and photograph. At home he has the complete incriminating snapshots stuck into a store-bought album that came stamped with the words OUR BEST MEMORIES. When he's feeling discouraged about his other work on the force, some nights late, he'll get them out and peruse the terrified faces depicted and feel . . . achievement? a quickening? The father knows that, when lurching forth, he must look only at the culprit. This'll give Junior time to hide whatever just made the malefactor (on first seeing it) jump so, made him grow so immediately culpable when, invited to reach out, he does so, *flashbulb*.

Booth's metal door is kicked wide open. First bulb fires off, blinding in a mirror four sinks long, and another one is caught . . . red-handed, red-whatevered. The yelled legalities, barked sounds so loud on tile, and silver handcuffs flashing out. They're soon cinched on to a fellow whose dick is yet quite free. The culprit's dick is yet left sticking out, it's unable to change gears that fast, belonging to a human beast, if a decent Rotarian one. Hairy wrists are bound in metal bands, but the sturdy papa hard-on is yet poking forth so far that even the cop—a fellow male after all—lets the pederast try and wedge it back in, before the officer pulls his perp through the bustle of our leading Penney's store, past MEETING YOUR KITCHEN AND BATHROOM NEEDS, UP TO 40% OFF, EVERYTHING MUST GO, where shoppers will be perplexed enough to see a handsome young man—head nodding shamefaced forward—bound in cuffs, and really shouldn't have to deal with such a boner on him too.

It's tough forcing yourself back into your breeches while wearing the cuffs that've already cut reddened slices into downy wrists. Best to deal either with your zipper or your handcuffs, but both at once is pretty much a killer.

The Fellow Ship docked below Fourteenth Street

Somehow, I've lived, grown, flourished and fled Falls, by many, many states and jobs and beaux, and somehow, it's 1990. The newest of my escape-hatch tree houses is called Greenwich Village.

We speak of a lovely Saturday night in spring, and I'm carrying sixty dollars' worth of rubrum lilies, careful that their red-black pollen not stain my pristine clothes.

I am bound for a party whose parchment invitation insists over-artfully, 'Come as you would be, and as you *are*, but, if possible, tonight, in white, dear.'

So, feeling good after a day of writing fiction that spawned four actual living, kicking sentences, I am gussied up in white bucks, white ducks, a pale tie and off-white shirt—and I'm feeling nautical but nice when I hear a passing hot rod yell one word that I, in a naval mood, believe to be '*Farragut!*'

I get hit full-face. Two paper cups, one full of warm beer, the other all cold orange crush, and I am so soaked.

I hear loud laughing as they roar off. I'm left here gasping, bent double. The shock of it has knocked the wind clear out of me, but nothing worse. I set the flowers on a stoop. Take stock. There's a small cut on my forehead. Could one piece of flying ice have managed that?

'Everything's fine. No harm done,' I tell myself. But I am so stained and sogged. I smell like someone else's four-day binge. I look down at the lightning bolt of orange from chest to my once-white crotch. I realize—even if I dash back home to change—I have nothing white left to wear.

One block north, I dodge into an alley. These lilies are trembling so, like living things. I guess they are. I hide against the hoodlums' coming back for me. I know, through friends beaten or worse, that these boys—if they get off a 'good one'—tend to circle the block and swerve back for further fun. I imagine fists next time, or hammers. This season, they've favoured hammers—the gay-bashing fashion accessory of choice. Innocence, my own, makes me wonder how they even knew I was one. Duuhh! (Probably, I overdid. All the Wildean lilies, right?)

Caught, I'm moved to explain to them, I don't usually walk around all in white like Mark Twain, who claimed to be straight. Shamed, I consider just skipping the party. Maybe I'll go late, when a spotless entrance will matter less. I pull out the invitation, double-checking the address.

Vowing to tell every-fuckin'-body how I got so orange and wet and why I smell of Hoboken brewery, I soon make myself into something of a party hit. Our specialty: a brand of bravery as flashy as some new perfume's name. Cheap yet necessary, it's a comic art that only other survivors will recognize. I am become a tale of woe transcended—I am my own sole excuse. I am the opposite of apology. Maybe I courted grief by being too far 'out'? Do I make myself look overeager to be knocked way, way back in again? I don't seek to become a nose-rubbing-in target, believe me.

I have not been tortured fully. I am in good health and have had hundreds of lovers, and I've never been arrested, yet. My heart's been broken but that's pretty normal, right? I am not sick, nor do I think of myself as 'sick'. My parents still ask for credit, having somehow heroically accepted my 'lifestyle choices'. They still remember my birthday. But they swear I've rubbed their noses in it.

Mother took me aside one year after Dan was driven from town, when she saw me still gloomy and jumpy about the speed and injustice of his going, and—trying to help, I'm sure—she said, 'There's something we never told you about Dan, when you were younger and all?' I felt scared, seizing her white wrist, begging for news. 'He was not exactly smart, Dan. He had other qualities that made up for it, and sweet as the day is . . . but not like your father or our doctor-lawyers, he was sort of always along because of his charm and the way he looked and his . . . Not re*tar*ded, just not all that swift and . . . ' She saw my face and added, 'I'm not sure why I'm telling you this. Maybe trying to make it easier for you to . . . ' And I knew, in the absolute way that we, hooked genetically, knew each other, that Mom was about to say, 'Get Over Him . . . ' but stopped. See, that sounded too much like a boy–girl romance. 'Maybe I'm trying to make it easier for you to forget him, son.' It was the wrong thing to have said. This close against my face, she saw that.

The Captain Hook

I once literally hooked literally all of him. It proved addictive. This was the year those others caught then vanished him.

He had stationwagoned over to pick up Dad for further golf. Dad, fighting his latest financial reversal, was late. Those guys never tired of golf. Maybe the dick jokes helped? I owned a new green Wilson fly-casting rod. I'd been practising alone a lot.

I felt I was getting pretty darn accurate. I could place my weighted silver hook just about where I wanted it. (Be careful what you aim for.)

Dan discovered me tossing my line at a chalked blue ring on the side of our white garage. Waiting for my father, Dan had come seeking me. On our white-frilled porch, his partners milled, swilling vodka, massacring baby onions.

'Why not cast her my way, pardner? You're gettin' good at it, I see that plain. Here, maybe try and put her about here?' Dan had spied a red plastic ring. It was the chew toy for Tuffie, our boxer. Dan lifted it free of a boxwood bush, then held it out, his arm at an exact right angle to his body. His jaw so square and blue, his face so blankly direct, he looked earnest as some model in a Red Cross diagram for boating safety. I felt weakened by appreciation.

Dan squinted in April sunlight. With his face screwed up, you saw how he must've looked as a boy, winsome if under-financed, rawer. He was not like me. He'd been born poor. Part of his sexiness came from some lasting smell of that. I once believed that dogs were the daddies, cats were the moms. I once thought all women were rich and men born poor. Go figure.

Today Dan wore fresh-pressed chinos, deck shoes, a plaid short-sleeved shirt. He smiled across sixty feet. Distance reduced him to trout size. But his hundred-watt attraction remained a lure, immense. I readied my aim. I took a bow-legged stance. It was my own approximation of the male. I posed, tough, fifty-six whole pounds.

Dan's pals played raucous twenty-one on our side porch; they gossiped hard (some young country boy who worked at Aetna Insurance had just got engaged to Donna!). Big drinks' ice cubes clinked. I readied my rod, checked all my interior devices. It was a day of birdsong, temperature in the seventies, a day as gold as blue.

Studying Dan's pale inner arm held direct off his torso, I so wanted to touch him. 'Here she comes, Dan. On your mark . . . '

I aimed. I recall the thumb release of line. 'Go!' The reel sang its precise ratcheting, pure play-out. April!

My silver line lifts a C-shape of rolling light, mid-air. Settling. Then I feel the snap of my hook find a surface firm yet yielding—springy, live, worthwhile. Not the red ring, but one pale human wrist: some excitement, some malice unaccountable, makes me jerk it anyway. Gotcha, motherfucker!

Snagging the arm of a man who's always been only kind to me is a response so male, so savage, automatic—it scares me sick. The Sports Gene! 'Owww-eesh!' Dan howls. (Might this not be Dan's exact sexual release cry?)

My rod drops to grass. I speed toward my prize. Even in pain, even after studying the wound I've caused, Dan is easing down. He's kneeling on our lawn. Readying himself, because, at my level, *he* plans to comfort *me*!

I follow line to him. Filament burns a hole in the centre of my chubby fist. He's before me, guessing how upset I'll be. The guy prepares a grin. He means, even in his shock, to protect me from embarrassment.

On his knees, Dan is just my own height fully standing. This close, his head appears enormous as a puppet's, its handsomeness gone jagged as Sherlock Holmes's hat and pipe and shoehorn nose. He receives my running weight with a little grunt. He shields me from seeing his bleeding arm. Card players have heard Dan's holler. Two lean off the porch. 'It's nothing,' Dan's baritone calls, warming my neck and ear. The one good arm cradles me against him. It pulls me closer to my target, home direct between a squatting hero's opened knees.

Tuffie's chewed red plastic ring is now suspended—bull's eye—just above my friend's clumped crotch. Other men are toasting us with bourbon, laughing, calling all their usual usuals.

Trying to keep our dealings private, Dan smiles at me, apologizing for those clods. His fibrous arm flips over, accidentally showing me white skin, powder-blue marbled veining, and one long spittle of opaque red leaving the silver beak of my own hook. That surgical hook puckers a two-inch sample of someone's bacon-fat flesh. 'Noo,' I cry. The barb looks too big ever to cut quite out of him.

We're bound together for good, flies tied. I nuzzle, sobbing, 'Didn't mean to, to you, Dan . . . '

I feel half-faint, daylight overdoing it and drenching me, accusatory. I'm pitched even deeper in a pliant vice between Dan's open sinew thighs.

Mother, seeing my latest tangled mess from her kitchen window, will soon come running. As ever, perfectly supplied, she'll hold a silver tray supporting Merthiolate, pedicure scissors, cotton balls plumped fast and hostessy into a silver salt dish (Grandmother Halsey's, 1870 or so). Plus Dan's favourite drink—a light Cutty and water. (I heard 'Cutty Shark', I liked knowing that its label showed the Fellow Ship.)

Dreading others seeing us, hating how pain alone permits our union, I cry 'Sorry' into splayed legs. They remain wide open. I've run right into their V-shape shelter, a berth. I now wedge farther between.

I am sobbing, he holds me fast. I am getting to touch good fur on one arm I failed to hook. I find that, in his pain, Dan doesn't much notice how I hold him. So, sick with boldness, I tip against the inner fabric of his much-washed chinos.

Mid-thigh, I read the Braille outline of sexual parts, his. They're presented plain, canine in guilelessness, grape-like in gentle plentiful cascade. The very symbol of abundance, Mr Dan's nearby portables.

Birds, disturbed by his wounded cry, go again all song. I hear mother clanking in the kitchen, assembling emergency gear. And me? I'm just crazed enough by guilt and proximity. Using bloodshed as my excuse, I find the nerve to cup my open right hand lightly—light as light itself—against them, against all his. Just over the top, no pressure. I simply do it, crying as distraction.

First Dan only holds my shoulders, staring at my freckles. Then pleasure—stirred, overambitious—leads me to tighten my clamp on him, his. My reach exceeds my grasp. I see his face change, slow.

(Meanwhile, back at the crotch, my subtle squirrelish fingers register: my Dan today wears no underdrawers, unusual in Falls in '57. My palm can tell: unlike Dad and me, my Dan here, is not circumcised [born poor].)

I see concern fold the brow of a squatting man, who clutches a child, holding, unexpectedly, that dude's own central credentials. No 'Ooops.' No 'Er, would ya please let 'em aloose, son?'

Instead Dan himself glances down between Dan's own mighty legs. Definitely checking on a little scoop-shaped paw now curved—familiar, hoping to remain uninsistent—quite close against his right-dressed member. Beneath my grasp, it all feels as spongy as a round home loaf of sandwich-sized Wonder.

He still half-pretends not to notice. No one near the house can see what's going on. Dan, metal-blue jaw, gives me one sleepy, dubious half-smile. In it, amused recognition, some pity maybe, much fellow feeling, a father's patience for his own kid's guileless curiosity. Oh, the Fellow Ship.

I yell, 'I didn't know it hurt. To fish. Hurt the fish, Dan.'

'Don't blame yourself. You've got the sporting touch . . . You'll land hundreds more ahead, and rainbows too. Glad to be the first in line—a great long catch o' keepers, pal. Your only problem is, your aim's too good. Every man should have such trouble. Definitely no more crying, umkay, m'buddy-ro? Promise your Dan?'

How could you not love such a fellowshipper? Had Dan talked to me in code? Did he even deeply mind or notice as I—leisurely, entranced—felt his dick's noble heft? And did Dan allow me or prevent me or invite me? Who'd had whom?

Even today, when I hear the phrase 'child molester', I think, not of One Grown-up Who Molests Children, but of some kid who diddles unsuspecting innocent adults, grown-ups who glaze over immediately, going child-passive.

I'm told that the victim adults—racked with equal parts guilt and interest—sometimes never get over it.

Dan? I count on that.

Inside your right wrist, even with the lights out, can you not still touch a little scratchy signature of scarring?

Last

Coming out, I managed. Staying out is hard.

A day in the life?

I came out at seven a.m. today—I did so just by tucking one cream-coloured silk hanky in my blazer pocket. To me, it didn't look fey, it just looked right, necessary. By three this afternoon, I was having a late lunch with two co-workers. Who told a gay-bashing 'Hear about the pit bull with Aids?' joke, one I really might've/should've protested. The lunch had been so heavy and I'm getting over a hellacious summer cold and, I just couldn't find the energy to make a scene, to force the point again and act so nunnishly doctrinaire. Didn't want to make another dreary plea for tolerance, yet again, Killjoy.

Walking back to work alone, I saw a truly great-looking boy. And—before I quite censored myself properly—I'd tossed an appreciative stare at this blond, aproned clerk. He stood spraying down the eggplants displayed before our corner greengrocer. And he offered me some visual encouragement—top lip curling back, a toughening of his flippant stance—but then, three seconds later, reverse, he flipped me the finger and muttered, 'You fuckin' *wish.*'

I crossed the street, my face neutral, spirits silenced. I was sure he'd chase me, or holler an insult (the actual name of what I am). I felt sure he'd at least aim his rubber hose at me. The Trojan Hose. At the very least, he'd ruin my best suede shoes.

See, friend, I came out at seven a.m. today. And at 2.48 I went back in.

Tentative, I re-emerged at 3.43, until that aproned blond flipped me the bird and threatened me at 3.44, till he drove me to tiptoe boldly back in yet again where many men have gone before. By 5.10, feeling stronger, I risked it again . . . but then . . .

Despite my therapy and the wish to think well of myself, I am still a subdivision of desire. Here I choose to end it.

I am the horny, guilty husband, noticing one sullen blond boy slouched at the urinal three down; I move his way, beckoned by his head wave, and one slow wink and something that he shows me.

I am the blond boy, aware of my poisonous beauty, ready for Dad to pop out of that green stall with a black camera in lieu of his pink face. For now, I'm mostly a youngster enjoying the weight of my blood-stocked dick. I am feeling the full power of being male, which means, in an odd way, being fatal for others.

And, alas, I am also the tortured ex-Marine cop, forty pounds over his Parris Island weight, a major smoker, rifle collector, registered Republican with fifteen long years till retirement, a disappointed man who—having built rabbit-catching boxes as a boy—finds entrapment lots more fun than giving speeding tickets. He is also a guy whose own sexual fantasies let him display his son (almost as pretty as he once was). He does it in order to catch the vermin he sees swarming everywhere, the shameless weirdos who'll be the death of this Great Land, the queers that he knows want, most obsessively of all, him.

Sure, he might have drinking probs and the so-so marriage and no further prospect of promotion anywhere near even assistant chief, but at least he's not *that* far gone. He is the detective about to detect. Sick behaviour like—

Mine. Like Dan's. And I keep silent, in a stall already unlatched for kicking open at lethal speed. I prepare the necessary flashbulb I'm about to insert into its reflector socket. I hear whispering. Good boy, my son is waving the perpetrator closer. I prepare the flashbulb. The glass sphere's metal tip I dampen with my tongue. I am ready, now, I breathe, kick toward desire illegal. The blast in a tile space this small is a cannon going off. I holler 'Free-eeze!' at heat. I capture for eternity the Older Me just as I touch the healthy prong of Me Young. And, armed with pictures of me molesting myself, I am going to have to turn me in. Otherwise, admit it—I'd be less than a whole man.

Hey, Dan? Missed you. □

GRANTA

JOY WILLIAMS

THE CASE AGAINST BABIES

Babies, babies, babies. There's a plague of babies. Too many rabbits or elephants or mustangs or swans brings out the myxomatosis, the culling guns, the sterility drugs, the scientific brigade of egg smashers. Other species can 'strain their environments' or 'overrun their range' or clash with their human 'neighbours', but human babies are always welcome at life's banquet. Welcome, Welcome, Welcome—Live Long and Consume! You can't draw the line when it comes to babies because . . . where are you going to draw the line? *Consider having none or one and be sure to stop after two* the organization Zero Population Growth suggests politely. Can barely hear them what with all the babies squalling. Hundreds of them popping out every minute. Ninety-seven million of them each year. While legions of other biological life forms go extinct (or, in the creepy phrase of ecologists, 'wink out'), human life bustles self-importantly on. Those babies just keep coming! They've gone way beyond being 'God's gift'; they've become entitlements. Everyone's having babies, even women who can't have babies, *particularly* women who can't have babies—they're the ones who sweep fashionably along the corridors of consumerism with their double-wide strollers, stuffed with twins and triplets. (Women push those things with the effrontery of someone piloting a bulldozer, which strollers uncannily bring to mind.) When you see twins or triplets do you think *awahhh* or *owhoo* or *that's sort of cool, that's unusual,* or do you think *that woman dropped a wad on in vitro fertilization, twenty-five, thirty thousand dollars at least . . .* ?

The human race hardly needs to be more fertile, but fertility clinics are booming. The new millionaires are the hot-shot fertility doctors who serve anxious gottahavababy women, techno-shamans who have become the most important aspect of the baby process, giving women what they want: BABIES. (It used to be a mystery what women wanted, but no more . . . Nietzsche was right . . .) Ironically—though it is far from being the only irony in this baby craze—women think of themselves as being *successful, personally fulfilled* when they have a baby, even if it takes a battery of men in white smocks and lots of hormones and drugs and needles and dishes and mixing and inserting and implanting to make it so. Having a baby means *individual*

IAN BERRY/MAGNUM

completion for a woman. What do boys have to do to be men? Sleep with a woman. Kill something. Yes, killing something, some luckless deer, duck, bear, pretty much anything large-ish in the animal kingdom, or even another man, appropriate in times of war, has ushered many a lad into manhood. But what's a woman to do? She gets to want to have a baby.

While much effort has been expended in Third World countries educating women into a range of options which does not limit their role merely to bearing children, well-off, educated and indulged American women are clamouring for babies, babies, BABIES to complete their status. They've had it all and now they want a baby. And women over thirty-five want them NOW. They're the ones who opt for the aggressive fertility route, they're impatient, they're sick of being *laissez-faire* about this. Sex seems such a laborious way to go about it. At this point they don't want to endure all that intercourse over and over and maybe get no baby. What a waste of time! And time's awasting. *A life with no child would be a life perfecting hedonism* a forty-something infertile woman said, now the proud owner of pricey twins. Even women who have the grace to submit to fate can sound wistful. *It's not so much that I wish that I had children now*, a travel writer said, *but that I wish I had had them. I hate to fail at anything.* Women are supposed to wish and want and not fail. (Lesbians want to have babies too and when lesbians have babies watch out! They lay names on them like Wolf.)

The eighties were a decade when it was kind of unusual to have a baby. Oh, the lower classes still had them with more or less gusto, but professionals did not. Having a baby was indeed so quaintly rebellious and remarkable that a publishing niche was developed for men writing about babies, *their* baby, their baby's first year in which every single day was recorded (he slept through the night . . . he didn't sleep through the night . . .). The writers would marvel over the size of their infant's scrotum; give advice on how to tip the obstetrician (not a case of booze, a clock from Tiffany's is nicer); and bemusedly admit that their baby exhibited intelligent behaviour like rolling over, laughing and showing fascination with the TV screen far earlier than normal children.

Aside from the talk about the poopie and the rashes and the cat's psychological decline, these books frequently contained a passage, an overheard bit of Mommy-to-Baby monologue along these lines: *I love you so much I don't ever want you to have teeth or stand up or walk or go on dates or get married. I want you to stay right here with me and be my baby* . . . Babies are one thing. Human beings are another. We have way too many human beings. Almost everyone knows this.

Adoption was an eighties thing. People flying to Chile, all over the globe, God knows where, returning triumphantly with their BABY. It was difficult, adventurous, expensive and generous. It was trendy then. People were into adopting bunches of babies in all different flavours and colours (Korean, Chinese, part-Indian—part-Indian was very popular; Guatemalan—Guatemalan babies are way cute). Adoption was a fad, just like the Cabbage Patch dolls which fed the fad to tens of thousands of pre-pubescent girl consumers.

Now it is *absolutely* necessary to digress for a moment and provide an account of this marketing phenomenon. These fatuous-faced soft-sculpture dolls were immensely popular in the eighties. The gimmick was that these dolls were 'born'; you couldn't just buy the damn things—if you wanted one you had to 'adopt' it. Today they are still being born and adopted, although at a slower rate, in Babyland General Hospital, a former medical clinic right on the fast-food and car-dealership strip in the otherwise unexceptional north Georgia town of Cleveland. There are several rooms at Babyland General. One of them is devoted to the premies (all snug in their little gowns, each in its own spiffy incubator) and another is devoted to the cabbage patch itself, a suggestive mound with a fake tree on it from which several times a day comes the announcement CABBAGE IN LABOUR! A few demented moments later, a woman in full nurse regalia appears from a door in the tree holding a brand-new Cabbage Patch Kid by the feet and giving it a little whack on the bottom. All around her in the fertile patch are happy little soft heads among the cabbages. Each one of these things costs $175, and you have to sign papers promising to care for it and treasure it forever. There are some cheesy dolls in boxes that you wouldn't have to adopt, but children don't want those—they want to sign on the line, want the documentation, the papers. The dolls are all supposed to be different but they certainly look identical. They've got tiny ears, big eyes, a pinched rictus of a mouth and lumpy little arms and legs. The colours of the cloth vary for racial verisimilitude, but their expressions are the same. They're glad to be here and they expect everything.

But these are just dolls, of course. The *real* adopted babies who rode the wave of fashion into many hiply caring homes are children now, an entirely different kettle of fish, and though they may be providing (just as they were supposed to) great joy, they are not darling babies anymore. A baby is not really a child; a baby is a BABY, a cuddleball, representative of virility, wombrismo and humankind's unquenchable wish to outfox Death.

Adoptive parents must feel a little out of it these days, so dreadfully dated in the nineties. Adoption—how foolishly sweet. It's so Benetton, so kind of naïve. With adopted babies, you just don't know, it's too much of a crap shoot. Oh, they *told* you that the father was an English major at Yale and that the mother was a brilliant mathematician and harpsichordist who was just not quite ready to juggle career and child, but what are you going to think when the baby turns into a kid who rather than showing any talent whatsoever is trying to drown the dog and set national parks on fire? Adoptive parents do their best, of course, at least as far as their liberal genes allow; they look into the baby's *background*, they don't want just any old baby (even going to the dog and cat pound you'd want to pick and choose, right?); they want a pleasant, healthy one, someone who will appreciate the benefits of a nice environment and respond to a nurturing and attentive home. They steer away (I mean, one has to be realistic, one can't save the world) from the crack and smack babies, the physically and mentally handicapped babies, the HIV and foetal-alcoholic syndrome babies.

Genes matter, more and more, and adoption is just too . . . where's the connection? Not a single DNA strand to call your own. Adoption signifies you didn't do everything you could; you were too cheap or shy or lacked the imagination to go the energetic fertility route which, when successful, would come with the assurance that some part of the Baby or Babies would be a continuation of you, or at the very least your companion, loved one, partner, whatever.

I once prevented a waitress from taking away my martini glass which had a tiny bit of martini remaining in it, and she snarled, *Oh, the precious liquid*, before slamming it back down on the table. It's true that I probably imagined that there was more martini in the glass than there actually was (what on earth could have happened to it all?) but the precious liquid remark brings unpleasantly to mind the reverent regard in which so many people hold themselves. Those eggs, that sperm, oh precious, precious stuff! There was a terrible fright among humankind recently when some scientists suggested that an abundance of synthetic chemicals was causing lower sperm counts in human males—awful, awful, awful—but this proves not to be the case; sperm counts are holding steady and are even on the rise in New York. Los Angeles males don't fare as well (do they drink more water than beer?), nor do the Chinese who, to add insult to insult, are further found to have smaller testicles, a finding which will undoubtedly result in even more wildlife mutilation in the quest for aphrodisiacs. Synthetic chemicals *do* 'adversely affect' the reproductive capabilities of non-human animals (fish, birds), but this is considered relatively unimportant. It's human sperm that's held in high regard and in this overpopulated age it's become more valuable—*good* sperm that is, from intelligent, athletic men who don't smoke, drink, do drugs, have Aids or a history of homicide—because this overpopulated age is also the donor age. Donor sperm, donor womb, donor eggs. Think of all the eggs that are lost to menstruation every month. The mind boggles. Those precious, precious eggs, lost. (Many egg donors say they got into the business because they didn't like the idea of their eggs 'going to waste'.) They can be *harvested* instead and frozen for a rainy day or sold nice and fresh. One woman interviewed in the *New York Times* early this year has made it something of a career. *I'm not going to just sit home and bake cookies for my kids, I can accomplish things,* she says. No dreary nine-to-five desk job for her. She was a surrogate mother for one couple, dishing up a single baby; then she donated some eggs to another couple who had a baby; now she's pregnant with twins for yet another couple. *I feel like a good soldier, as if God said to me, 'Hey girl, I've done a lot for you and now I want you to do something for Me,'* this entrepreneurial breeder says. (It's sort of cute to hear God invoked, sort of for luck, or out of a lingering folksy superstition.) Egg donors are regular Jenny Appleseeds, spreading joy, doing the Lord's work and earning a few bucks all at once as well as attaining an odd sense of empowerment (I've got a bunch of kids out there, damned if I know who they all are . . .).

One of the most successful calendars of 1996 was Anne Geddes's BABIES. Each month shows the darling little things on cabbage leaves, cupped in a tulip, as little bees in a honeycomb and so on—solemn, bright-eyed babies. They look a little bewildered though, and why shouldn't they? How did they get here? They were probably mixed up in a dish. Donor eggs (vacuumed up carefully through long needles); Daddy's sperm (maybe . . . or maybe just some high-powered NY dude's); gestational carrier; the 'real' mommy waiting anxiously, restlessly on the sidelines (want to get those babies home, start buying them stuff!). Baby's lineage can be a little complicated in this one big worldwebby family. With the help of drugs like Clomid and Perganol there are an awful lot of eggs out there these days—all being harvested by those rich and clever, clever doctors in a 'simple procedure' and nailed with bull's-eye accuracy by a spermatozoon. One then gets to 'choose' among the resulting cell clumps (or the doctor gets to choose, he's the one who knows about these things), and a number of them (for optimum success) are inserted into the womb, sometimes the mother's womb and sometimes not. These fertilized eggs, unsurprisingly, often result in multiple possibilities, which can be decreased by 'selective reduction'. They're not calendar babies yet, they're embryos, and it is at this point, the multiple possibility point, that the mother-to-be often gets a little overly ecstatic, even greedy, thinking ahead perhaps to the day when they're not babies any longer, the day when they'll be able to amuse themselves by themselves like a litter of kittens or something—if there's a bunch of them *all at once* there'll be no need to go through that harrowing process of finding appropriate playmates for them. She starts to think *Nannies probably don't charge that much more for three than for two* or *heaven knows we've got enough money or we wouldn't have gotten into all this in the first place.* And many women at the multiple-possibility point, after having gone through pretty much all the meddling and hubris that biomedical technology has come up with, say demurely, *I don't want to play God* (I DON'T WANT TO PLAY GOD?) or *It would be grotesque to snuff one out to improve the odds for the others* or *Whatever will be will be.*

So triplets happen, and even quads and quints (network television is still interested in quints). And as soon as the multiples, or even the less prestigious single baby, are old enough to toddle into daycare, they're responsibly taught the importance of their one and only Earth, taught the 3Rs—Reduce, Reuse, Recycle. Too many people (which is frequently considered undesirable—gimme my space!) is caused by too many people (it's only logical) but it's mean to blame the babies, you can't blame the babies, they're innocent. Those poor bean counters at the United Nations Population Fund say that at current growth rates, the world will double its population in forty years. Overpopulation poses the greatest threat to all life on earth, but most organizations concerned with this problem don't like to limit their suggestions to the most obvious one—DON'T HAVE A BABY!—because it sounds so negative. Instead, they provide additional, more positive tips for easing the pressures on our reeling environment such as car pooling or tree planting. (A portion of the proceeds from that adorable bestselling BABIES calendar goes to the Arbor Day Foundation for the planting of trees.)

Some would have it that not having a baby is *disallowing* a human life, horribly inappropriate in this world of rights. Everyone has rights; the unborn have rights; it follows that the *unconceived* have rights. (Think of all those babies pissed off at the fact that they haven't even been thought of yet.) Women have the *right* to have babies (we've fought so hard for this), and women who can't have babies have an even bigger right to have them. These rights should be independent of marital or economic status, or age. (Fifty- and sixty-something moms tend to name their babies after the gynaecologist.) The reproduction industry wants fertility treatments to be available to *anyone* and says that it wouldn't all be so expensive if those recalcitrant insurance companies and government agencies like Medicare and Medicaid weren't so cost-conscious and discriminatory and would just cough up the money. It's not as though you have to take out a *permit* to have a baby, be *licensed* or anything. What about the rights of a poor, elderly, feminist cancer patient who is handicapped in some way (her car has one of those stickers . . .) who wants to assert her right to independent motherhood and feels entitled to both artificial insemination into a gestational 'hostess' and the right to sex selection as a basis for abortion should the foetus turn out to be male when she wants a female? Huh? What about her? Or what about the fifteen-year-old of the near future who kind of wants to have her baby even though it means she'll be stuck with a kid all through high school and won't be able to go out with her friends any more who discovers through the wonders of amniocentesis and DNA analysis that the baby is going to turn out fat, and the fifteen-year-old just can't deal with fat and shouldn't have to . . . ? Out goes the baby with the bathwater.

But these scenarios are involved merely with messy political or ethical issues, the problematical, somewhat gross by-products of technological and marketing advances. Let the philosophers and professional ethicists drone on and let the baby business boom. Let the courts figure it out. Each day brings another more pressing problem. Implanted with their weak-cervixed daughter's eggs and their son-in-law's sperm, women become pregnant with their own grandchildren; frozen embryos are inadvertently thawed; eggs are pirated; eggs are harvested from aborted foetuses; divorced couples battle over the fate of cryopreserved material. 'We have to have better regulation of the genetic product—eggs, sperm and embryos—so we can legally determine who owns what,' a professor of law and medicine at a California university says plaintively. (Physicians tend to oppose more regulation however, claiming that it would 'impede research'.)

While high-tech nations are refining their options eugenically and quibbling litigiously, the inhabitants of low-tech countries are just having babies. The fastest growth in human numbers in all history is going to take place in a single generation, an increase of almost five billion people (all of whom started out as babies). Ninety-seven per cent of the surge is going to take place in developing countries, with Africa alone accounting for thirty-five per cent of it (the poorer the country, the higher the birth rate, that's just the way it is). These babies are begotten in more 'traditional', doubtless less desperate ways, and although they are not considered as fashion statements, they're probably loved just as much as upper-class western babies (or that singular one-per-family Chinese boy baby) and are even considered productive assets when they get a little older and can labour for the common good of their large families by exploiting more and more, scarcer and scarcer resources.

The argument that western countries with their wealth and relatively low birth rate do not fuel the population crisis is, of course, fallacious. France, as national policy, urges its citizens to procreate, giving lots of subsidies and perks to those French who make more French. The US population is growing faster than that of eighteen other industrialized nations and, in terms of energy consumption, when an American couple stops spawning at two babies, it's the same as an average East Indian couple stopping at sixty-six, or an Ethiopian couple drawing the line at one thousand.

Yet we burble along, procreating, and in the process suffocating thousands of other species with our selfishness. We're in a baby glut, yet it's as if we've just discovered babies, or invented them. Reproduction is sexy. Assisted reproduction is cool. The announcement that a movie star is going to have a baby is met with breathless wonder. A BABY! Old men on their third marriage regard their new babies with 'awe' and crow about the 'ultimate experience' of parenting. Bruce Springsteen found 'salvation' with the birth of his son. When in doubt, have a baby. When you've tried it all, champagne, cocaine, try a baby. Pop icons who trudged through a decade of adulation and high living confess upon motherhood, This Baby Saved My Life. Bill Gates, zillionaire founder of Microsoft, is going to have (this is so wonderful) a BABY. News commentators are already speculating: will fatherhood take away his edge, his drive; will it diminish his will to succeed, to succeed, to succeed? National Public Radio recently interviewed other high-powered CEO dads as to that ghastly possibility.

It's as though, all together, in the waning years of this dying century, we collectively opened the Door of our Home and instead of seeing a friend standing there in some sweet spring twilight, someone we had invited over for drinks and dinner and a lovely civilized chat, there was Death, with those creepy little black seeds of his for planting in the garden. And along with Death we got a glimpse of ecological collapse and the coming anarchy of an over-peopled planet. And we all, in denial of this unwelcome vision, decided to slam the door and retreat to our toys and make babies—those heirs, those hopes, those products of our species' selfishness, sentimentality and global death wish. □

GRANTA

KAREN E. BENDER

ETERNAL LOVE

Candlelight
WEDDING
CHAPEL
MARRIAGE INFORMATION
MAR RIAGE
WFO

After Lena and Bob were married in the Chapel of Eternal Love, Ella told them that new husbands and wives were not allowed to share a hotel bedroom. Married couples, she told her retarded daughter, learned to be married slowly, in separate rooms. For the first two days of the honeymoon, Ella shared her room at the El Tropicale with Lena, while her husband, Lou, slept in the other room with Bob. The four of them elbowed their way to the two-dollars-fifty, ninety-seven-item buffet table, piling their plates with fat-laced barbecued ribs; they lay, sun-doped, on a sparkling swath of concrete by a pale blue swimming pool. The sounds by the pool echoed, amplified by the water; even the children's shrieks were transformed into the caws of aroused, hysterical birds. Ella could pretend she didn't hear at first when Lena said very softly that she wanted to share a room with Bob.

Ella told Lena about sex in a quiet lounge off E1 Tropicale's main casino. Her thirty-year-old daughter sat patiently, twirling a pink vinyl coin purse embossed LAS VEGAS: CITY OF LUCK. 'You're a wife,' Ella began. Her daughter smiled. 'There are certain things you can do.'

'I'm called Mrs!' squealed Lena.

A cocktail waitress holding an empty tray strode swiftly across the lounge, her nylon stockings an opalescent orange under the subdued light of the chandelier.

'First,' began Ella, then stopped. 'Well, how do you feel when Bob kisses you?'

'My mouth feels wet.'

'Do you—like it?'

'I like it.' Lena paused. 'Sometimes he puts his tongue in too much. I don't like that.'

A sign by the Canary Room said: EIGHT P.M. TONITE: HILO HATTIE AND THE HAWAIIANS. Loud tourists flowed eagerly through the lounge toward the casino, flashing slabs of sunburnt skin. 'Married people—are naked in bed, Lena,' Ella said.

'Naked!' Lena said, with a tiny shriek.

Ella felt something very tall collapse slowly inside her. 'Don't be scared,' she said, trying to fit her voice around the immense gentleness that surged inside her. 'It's just—skin.'

'I liked it when he touched—here,' Lena said, reaching up

and squeezing her breast.

'Where did he do—'

'In the bathroom. At House of Pancakes.' She giggled.

'No,' said Ella. 'You don't do that in House of Pancakes. You don't do that in any—public place. You do it in your bedroom. Nowhere else.'

'In my bedroom,' repeated Lena.

'After, you take a shower. You wash your hands with soap.'

'It smelt like the ocean.'

Ella let go of Lena's hand.

'When he put his hand in my panties. I liked that. He took his hand out and he smelt like me.' She clapped her hand over her mouth and giggled, a guilty, thrilled sound.

'Lena,' said Ella, 'when did Bob do—'

'We came in through the backyard.'

'You let him do that in my backyard?'

'I liked it.'

'Soap,' said Ella, a little desperately. 'You use soap.'

'Mother,' said Lena, 'what about when we're naked?'

Ella did not want to continue. Apparently Lena and Bob were doing well enough on their own.

'If he's ever not gentle with you Lena, tell me.'

'Tell what?'

Far away Ella heard the distant clink of breakfast dishes being washed in the hotel coffee shop, the whirr of a vacuum being pushed across the lobby, the gentle sounds of maids and waiters cleaning the guests' messes of the day.

'If he ever does something you don't like.'

'Mother,' said Lena, impatiently, 'does everyone married sleep naked in a bedroom? Him?' She pointed to a porter leafing through a newspaper with the headline: WAR OF THE BOSOMS CONTINUES. 'Him?' A man pushed a rack of pink and peach-feathered costumes toward the Lido de Paris show. 'Her?' A tall showgirl, her hair in a rumpled bouffant, sipped a large glass of orange juice and blinked awake. Her feet were swollen in silver sandals, and her eyes were ringed with fatigue.

'They use soap,' said Ella. She tried to think of one more crucial rule to tell her daughter, but her mind was filled with only this—in the deep green of her backyard, somewhere amid the walnut and lemon trees, Bob had plunged his hand into Lena's panties. Now everyone flowing through the lounge seemed profoundly tainted. Ella noticed the raw nubbiness of the bandleader's ruby velvet jacket, the too-proud grip a tourist had on his white-blonde wife, the obsessive way a waitress counted her tips, turning all the green bills in the same direction, before she vanished into the dim, clockless casino again.

Bob had first called six months ago, an April day in 1961. Ella had picked up the phone and heard a male voice whisper, almost plead, 'Lena. Lena. Lena there?'

It was a question she rarely heard. 'Who may I say is calling?' Ella asked.

'Bob. Goodwill. I drive trucks—Bob—'

She knocked on Lena's door. 'Lena. There's a . . . Bob on the phone for you.'

Lena burst out of her room with a nakedly joyous expression on her face. 'Tell him to wait,' she exclaimed.

She was wearing a little rouge and perfume when, five minutes later, she deigned to pick up the phone. At first Ella couldn't figure out why her daughter smelt familiar. Then she knew. Lena had put on some of her Chanel; Lena smelt like her.

Lena had been working at the Van Nuys Goodwill for five years. Her job was to sit at a long table and sort socks and blouses that no one else wanted to own. Ella called Dolores, the coordinator of Goodwill's disabled employees, to check Bob out.

'Bob. Bob,' muttered Dolores. 'Why?'

'A Bob called Lena on the phone.'

'This is so nice!' said Dolores. 'We have five Bobs. Bob Winters is considerate, but a drooler. Bob Lanard I wouldn't let in my house, not if you care about your china surviving the night.' She paused. 'Are you sure it's not a Rob? We have a Rob who's—well—a former convict, but I think he's very nice, too.'

'It was Bob. He said he drove trucks.'

'Trucks,' muttered Dolores. 'Bob Silver.'

'Tell me about him.'

'A sweetie. Short, quiet, brown hair, good driver.'

Ella tried to feel relieved but didn't, honestly, know what she felt. Bob Silver. It was just a name, but it seemed ferocious as a comet, hurtling toward her home to do some new damage.

Bob called again that night. 'Is Lena there?'

'Lena who?' Ella asked.

She was sorry she said it; she could actually hear the terror mount in his breath. 'Lena Rose.'

'Who may I say is calling?'

'Bob.'

'Why?'

Now he was dying. She heard his breath, everything slow on his end as he struggled not to tell her why he was calling.

'I just want to talk to her,' said Bob.

Bob was half an hour early for their first date. He pulled up in an old, candy-apple red Ford that gleamed dully in the afternoon. While Lena sprayed her hair upstairs, Ella and Lou huddled in the sheer-curtained window by the door and watched him come toward them. Bob rushed up the walkway, his hands plunged deep into his pockets, head down as though he was walking into a wind.

Lou opened the door. 'Glad to meet you,' he boomed.

Bob kept his hands in his pockets, not lifting them to shake with Lou. The part in his hair was crooked.

'Bob, Lena's not ready,' Ella lied, touching his arm; she wanted to see how normal he felt. His shoulder was a little damp and surprisingly muscular. Quickly, she removed her hand.

Bob glided deftly past her into the den and plucked up the *TV Guide*. He flipped wildly through its pages for a moment, then stumbled across the room and clicked the channels until he found *Gunsmoke*.

Bob propped his feet on Lou's green vinyl footstool, sunk down into the couch and thoughtfully eyed the action in *Gunsmoke*. He looked about forty. His short, bristly hair was grey, but his feet, in blue sneakers, bounced on the footstool with the blunt, coarse merriment of a boy. Ella was used to Lena's stubbiness, the way she seemed to bump up unsuccessfully against adulthood. But it seemed strange in Bob, and she could not help thinking that, even though he was taller than she, he resembled an ageing dwarf.

Lou sat on the couch and rubbed his palms rapidly against his knees. His face looked as though it had been sculpted hurriedly into an expression of calm—the cheeks were uneven, the smile was off. He surveyed Bob as he did any stranger—as though deciding whether he would hire him. 'You like *Gunsmoke*?'

Bob clasped his hands on his lap. 'I like the man in the hat,' he said.

Lou began to lean into another question; Ella felt he would ask the wrong ones. 'How is the job?' Ella asked.

Bob arranged his hands around an invisible steering wheel and twisted it to the right until the wheel came to an abrupt stop. 'I drive,' he said. 'I like to drive.'

'Do you like—big trucks or small ones?' Ella asked.

'I just drive big ones,' he said, as though insulted.

Cowboys galloped, yelling, across a desert. Ella kept glancing at her aquamarine vase right by his elbow, pretending not to stare at him. There had to be reasons to like him. His fingernails shone. He had tied his shoes neatly. He had blue eyes. And the main point—he wanted Lena. 'How long have you worked for Goodwill?' she asked.

'Awhile.'

'And you live?'

'On a cot.'

'Excuse me?'

'With the Ensons.'

'And they are?'

'A man and a wife.'

Before she could inquire more, Lena appeared. Ella had helped her match her yellow rhinestone earrings and scarf with a yellow shift dress, the one she'd worn when she'd gotten the Goodwill job. It seemed lucky. Bob lifted his eyes from the TV. Ella had never looked at Lena the way a man would. Dressing her was like adorning a child—for a specific, decorative purpose, but not for men. Now, creamy lavender eyeshadow gleamed iridescent on her eyelids, and her hair was expansive with spray. Bob gazed at her frankly, as though he had a right to her.

Lena whisked past Ella, bumping her with her purse. 'I've been talking to your guest,' Ella began, 'and—'

'Hi, Bob,' said Lena.

Bob smiled. 'Finish your socks?'

'Shut up!' squealed Lena, clapping her hand over her mouth.

'Excuse me?' asked Ella.

'Learn to park!' Lena said.

'I'm the best parker,' Bob said. 'I'm the number-one parker. And you know it.'

Lena screeched with giggles. 'Liar!' She rushed to the door with an exuberant haughtiness. Bob ran after her, as though afraid she would disappear.

'Where are you going?'

'We're going to walk down to House of Pancakes,' said Lena.

'House of—it's going to be crowded,' said Ella, feeling vaguely hysterical. 'There'll be a long wait—'

'I'm hungry,' said Bob, tugging Lena.

'Do you have enough money? Let me give you some—'

'Bob has money.'

Bob gazed at Lena. His eyes were clear and intelligent with desire. He put his hand on her daughter's arm.

'Bye!' Lena said, waving tentatively.

Ella could not speak.

'Bye!' said Lena. 'You—you look very pretty.'

And they left.

She watched them bound across the lawn. Lena's yellow dress seemed to flutter in slow motion as she ran, as though governed by new physical laws.

Lou sprang back from the window, like a child embarrassed by what he had just seen. He pushed his hand into his glossy grey hair. 'Well,' he said, 'we're not losing a daughter—we're just gaining another mouth to feed.'

Lou had never owned Lena the way she had. For thirty years, he had tried hard not to look too closely at their daughter, instead cultivating a relentless optimism that Ella had found incomprehensible, yet also necessary. Now it made her feel alone.

'We're not gaining anything,' said Ella. She grabbed her sweater and followed the two figures walking down the street.

She walked briskly, but casually, keeping a block between herself and her daughter. When Lena and Bob turned into a shopping centre at the corner, Ella stopped beside a hefty Buick that was parked at one end of the lot.

They walked through the empty parking lot. It spread, like a dark lake, between House of Pancakes and a Hallmark, an ice-cream parlour, a laundromat and a pet store. It was Sunday, and all the stores were closed, but Bob and Lena stared hard at the windows as though willing them to open. Ella waited for something to go wrong. Bob went over to cars, rubbed their dusty tops, nodded like an expert, returned to Lena. She put coins into a newspaper rack, removed a paper and handed it to him; he rolled it up and tapped it against his leg.

Lena and Bob walked around the parking lot slowly, once, twice, three times. The orange flanks of House of Pancakes loomed, unreal, candied in the pale light. Customers left the restaurant and walked toward their cars with a casual confidence; Bob and Lena watched them walk. As the two of them finally went through the coffee shop's glass doors, Bob touched Lena's back, just for a moment; his hand reached for the yellow fabric, trying, gently, to hold on.

Bob began to come to the house once a week. Lena was always dressed and ready an hour beforehand; she sat absolutely still on her bed, as though the fact of his imminent arrival was so fragile she had to take care not to disturb even the air. But she always made him wait. One night, while Bob installed himself in the den and waited for Lena to join him, Ella swept in to quiz him about his life. 'Where is your cot?' she asked.

'Near the garage.'

'Who are the Ensons?'

'A man and a wife.'

She dragged out of him the following scintillating facts: he preferred lamb chops to chicken, and peas to potatoes.

Ella ruled that Lena and Bob had to spend part of the date

somewhere in the house. They sat on the patio while Ella washed the dishes, observing them through the kitchen window. Toward nine o'clock, when the sky had turned dark, Ella heard a jump and rustle and the sound of running; she looked out a window on to the shining, moon-silver lawn. Lena and Bob were not kissing or touching but just chasing each other, endlessly, like large, slow bears. Their sound was of the purest joy, a soft, hushed giggling as they followed each other through the dark yard.

Dolores told her that Bob lived with the Ensons—a couple—in Sherman Oaks, and had a brother in Chicago, Hugh, who paid them rent. Ella got Hugh's number and called him up.

When she told him that Bob was dating her daughter, there was a silence so hostile she wondered what she had actually said.

'I'm sending money,' Hugh said irritably. 'I'm sending money.'

'I'm not asking—'

'It's not easy, lady. Do you think it's easy sending—'

'Sir,' she said, 'I'm not asking for money. I just want to know what he's like.'

Another silence. 'Well, you see what he's like.'

'For the last few months. What about before?'

'What is there to know? He's forty-one. Three years older than me.'

'Where has he lived?'

'The folks had him at an institution for awhile. They didn't know what the hell to do with him. He's been at the Ensons six years, since the folks died. They got him to Goodwill. He likes driving, I hear.'

'What else?'

'You might want to know this. He had a vasectomy.'

She pressed the phone more firmly to her ear.

'They did that early. When he was sixteen, seventeen. No little Bobs running around.'

Ella did not know how to digest this fact, so she decided to move on. 'Anything else? Health problems, disorders, anything?'

'No, he's just real slow.'

'And you?' she asked, in spite of herself.

'Me?'

'You, what do you do?'

'I'm in insurance. Life and homes. I just got married two years ago. I've got a son now,' he said, his voice suddenly soft and eager to please.

'How nice,' she said coolly.

'I hope he and your daughter get along real well,' he said, his voice high-pitched with false sincerity. 'I'll call back to see how he is—' He hung up. She never heard from him again.

One night, as Ella put on her sweater, preparing for her usual reconnaissance mission to House of Pancakes, she felt Lou's hands on her shoulders. He turned her around.

'I have to go,' she said.

'Have dinner with me.'

'Dinner?' she asked. 'But they're—'

'They're just going to House of Pancakes.' He looked away from her. 'Who else is going to marry her?' he asked.

He was wearing an undershirt, and his shoulders were thinner now at sixty-two, almost girlish. She followed him to the kitchen. Lena had discovered her own perfume now—a chirpy, lavender scent from Sav-On—and the scent floated through the hall. In the kitchen the shiny appliances hummed.

Lou paced around, while Ella heated chicken with mushrooms. 'What do you think they're doing?' she asked him.

'Eating,' he said.

'They'll forget to pay,' she said.

'Then they'll get arrested,' he said. He folded his arms. They were caramel-coloured, dusted with silver hair. His gaze stopped on her, held her. 'Let's fool around,' he said, a soft huskiness in his voice.

She stopped; she wished she could feel interested. 'If you want to,' she said, a little hopefully, 'then come over here.'

She turned away from him and, gently, he wound her long hair into his hands. His aftershave smelt drugstore-blue and sharp. His breath was a hot current against her neck. His hands slid down her bare arms and gently cupped her breasts, and Ella tried to let herself go against him, but she couldn't.

Lou stopped, sensing her resistance. 'She's fine,' he said.

Delicately Ella disentangled herself from him.

'I need you too,' Lou said. He lightly slapped her hip, as though she were a cow, and she heard him walk away from her.

Lena and Bob marched into the kitchen one evening, their fingers wound together tightly, as though they had been assigned to each other as buddies on a school trip. Lena held up their hands. A plastic yellow ring encircled her index finger.

'I'm married!' said Lena.

Bob swiped a bruised pear off the table and took a big, juicy bite.

'You're what?' Ella asked.

'He gave me a ring!'

'You're engaged,' said Ella.

'I'm going to have a husband!' screeched Lena. She pulled Bob to her side, like a purse.

Ella slowly laid her dishtowel on the sink. She touched Lena's taut hand, the yellow ring; it was the type that fell, encased in a plastic bubble, out of a gumball machine. Bob's breath was loud and puppyish, and his bristly hair seemed a harder silver than before. Lena giggled. She said to Bob, 'Say what I said to—'

'Do I have to?'

'Yes.'

Bob slowly got to his knees in front of Ella. He rubbed his hands on the sides of his grey pants and looked at the floor.

'I forget,' he said to Lena.

'You know,' said Lena. She whispered, loudly, 'I want to—'

'I want to propose a marriage,' Bob said, addressing Ella's knee.

'Lena,' Ella said, 'honey, he's supposed to kneel in front of you, not me.'

'But he's asking you.'

Ella looked down at the rosy, bald circle on Bob's scalp. He looked like a gardener sprawled across a patch of lawn, pressing seeds into a plot of dirt. He was inevitable, and perhaps because of that, she felt an unexpected rush of love for him.

'Lou,' Ella called carefully. 'Lou.'

'I'm married!' Lena shrieked as her father came into the room and then rushed into his arms. It was something she rarely did; Lou was unsure how to hold her, and his arms curved awkwardly around her. He stepped away and looked at her, blinking.

'Married,' Lou said.

'Stand up,' Ella said. Bob rocked back on to his feet and stood, slowly, grabbing Lena's hip for balance. He was standing up, one of them now.

'We have to have a toast,' said Lou slowly.

Ella lifted a pitcher of cranberry juice from the refrigerator and filled the glasses. Lou arranged Lena and Bob's arms into the gesture of a toast. Lena and Bob clutched their glasses fiercely as though expecting them to rise to the ceiling, pulling them, legs kicking, off the floor.

'*L'chayim*,' Lou said.

It was Lou's idea that they get married in Las Vegas. They had a nine p.m. appointment at the Chapel of Eternal Love, at the other end of South Fifth, but Bob played the slots too long and almost made them late. Lena played right beside him, a little wobbly in her heels, her veil plopped on top of her machine.

The four of them walked down the Strip to the Chapel of Eternal Love, past Stardust and the Thunderbird and the Riviera. The streets glowed with the hotels' gaudy pink and orange and white light. Lena wore a polyester, puff-sleeved ivory dress which they had purchased off a mannequin in the window of Treasureland, a discount emporium. The mannequin rose grimly out of a litter of golden ashtrays and inflatable palm trees. Lena had stopped by the window, pointed to the mannequin and said with great assurance, 'Her.'

Ella held Lena's hand in hers; with the other, she touched Lou's arm. 'They do know we're coming?'

'Yes.'

'What about flowers? Do they provide them?'

'Relax.' He did not look at her. 'It's going to be beautiful.'

She wanted to ask him if love was truly good, if marriage made you safe, if the right man or woman would make anyone happy. She wanted to ask Lou if she had, in fact, given birth to

Lena—if her daughter truly lived outside her body.

Outside the chapel Ella took Lena to the far corner of the parking lot, drew Red Plum lipstick across her trembling lips.

'Ready?'

Lena nodded.

'Scared?'

Lena shrugged.

Ella took her hand. She wanted to tell her something. Marriage, she thought, was not simply choosing your mate, but the person you wanted to be for the rest of your life. There were other wives Ella could have been. Ella's marriage had shaped her, firmly and precisely, but she could not see the marks of her own evolution; she could not see how the love she gave and took made her what she was.

And here was her daughter with one suitor, one choice.

'Do you understand what this means, Lena?'

'It means that Bob and I will be together and we will be happy.'

Ella adjusted Lena's veil with trembling fingers. 'Where's your bobby pin?' she asked. 'Don't let this fall off. Don't keep touching it.'

Lena swatted her hand away. 'I want to get married now.'

The justice of the peace looked worn down by all the eternal love he'd seen that day. His assistant, wearing a red sequined dress and a sparkly name tag that said WITNESS, took the wedding fee of twenty dollars from Ella, then flung open the door to a large refrigerator. Rows of cold bouquets were lined up like a silent, aloof audience inside. She shivered. 'What colour roses, hon? Red, pink, white or silver?'

'I would like silver, please,' Lena said.

Lena stood beside Bob, their elbows touching. She tugged her wedding dress straight and nodded obediently at the justice. Her hand gripped the refrigerated spray of silver roses, which were the colour of a dull nickel. Her face had the alertness of true happiness.

Ella stood, the maid of honour, beside Lena; Lou removed his navy fedora and held it as he stood beside Bob.

'By the power invested in me by the state of Nevada, I pronounce you man and wife,' said the justice. He coughed. He suddenly seemed uncomfortable, as though just realizing he was intruding upon a family gathering.

Lena moved first. She raised her hand to Bob's face with a great tenderness, her fingers spread as though to capture as much of him as she could. Ella stared at Lena's fingers, which looked eerie and remote as a sea animal, and she did not know where Lena had learned to touch someone like that.

The witness hauled over a large, blue-sequined sack of free gifts for the newly-weds. 'Something to start off your new home,' she said. It was brimming with boxes of detergent, spatulas, colanders. The justice thrust his arm inside and brought out a box of Tide.

'Yuck,' Lena said.

'This is your free gift,' the assistant said.

'I don't want that one,' Lena said, pouting.

'You don't want it?' asked the justice.

'Let them pick,' Ella said.

The justice glared at Ella and checked his watch. 'Lady, I'd like to stay here all night, but—'

'Let them pick,' Ella hissed. She would not let them walk back into the streets of Las Vegas with a bad gift. Lena and Bob plunged their hands into the sack together. They began to bring out another box of Tide, pale detergent flowing out through a crack in the top. Ella pushed in front of Bob and Lena and slapped the box back into the bag. She grabbed hold of a spatula and pushed it into Lena's trembling hand.

'Congratulations,' Ella said.

Out by the pool, the Las Vegas sun hammered on to their faces. Ella watched her daughter spread herself on a bright, plastic chaise lounge. Lena's eyes were masked by her horn-rimmed sunglasses, and her nipples were visibly erect under her lemon-yellow bathing suit. She lay on the chaise in an aloof silence, as though she were spinning quiet, magnificent thoughts.

'Do you want some lotion?' Ella asked.

Lena did not answer. She stood up regally and walked over to the pool. Standing, a little unsteady, on its edge, she looked down at Bob in the water. Bob yanked her leg, and Lena crashed in.

Ella was not the only one who watched while Lena and Bob tumbled and splashed, cheerful, muffled bellows rising from their mouths. Their slick arms smacked the surface and swooped under the water, and their faces butted and kissed, but it was not exactly clear what they were doing to each other, and the crowd around the pool was riveted. Ella felt the backs of her knees tense. She got ready to stand up.

But after a minute Lena swung herself casually out of the pool. She glittered like an unearthly creature, with water shining on her arms, her hair. Lena came right to her chaise and sat beside her.

'I would like to share a room with Bob,' Lena said.

That night the four of them stood in El Tropicale's dim hallway. Bob's arm circled Lena's shoulder with a brave attempt at propriety.

'Honey, may I have your key,' Ella said.

Lena handed her mother the key. Lou was silent. Bob's fingers fluttered on Lena's shoulder, and Ella tasted fear, metallic, in her throat.

'Lena,' Ella started, as her daughter took Bob's hand, 'Lena, knock if you need anything.' Lena whisked into her room and closed the door.

Lou had assumed a posture of odd, formal politeness. 'Do we want to go sit at the piano bar?' he asked.

'I don't feel like it.'

'Do we want to play the slots?'

'No,' she said, opening the door to their own room next door.

They went inside, twitchy as a couple meeting each other illicitly for the first time. With a sharp, definite motion, Lou shrugged off his wine-coloured jacket. His white shirt stuck to his shoulders in the heat.

'Have you noticed the footwear they sell here?' he asked.

'Footwear?'

He tossed his jacket over a chair. 'People are on vacation, they lose their shopping sense.' He took a deep, sharp breath.

'Pink loafers. They take them home and they realize, where the hell am I going to wear pink loafers?'

'They're going to have to live with us,' said Ella.

'They probably don't want to.'

'She can't cook or clean,' said Ella.

'I don't think he'd notice.'

She thought she heard the TV's muffled garble start in the other room. 'I hear them,' she said.

The two of them froze, listening. 'No,' he said. 'You don't hear them.'

She put her hands on the wall dividing their room from Lena's. It was strangely cool. She heard only a faint, staticky wave of audience laughter.

'Look!' said Lou. He knocked on the wall sharply, twice. 'Hello!' he called. Breathless, they awaited an answer; there was none. 'See?' he said. 'They can't hear us.' He turned abruptly and walked away from the wall. 'Come away from there,' he said.

She wanted, vaguely, to accuse him of something; she wanted to see pain on Lou's face, a sorrow she could recognize.

'Leave her alone,' he said, not sounding entirely convinced. He sank wearily into the sofa and rubbed his hands vigorously over his face. 'Let's have a drink.'

She couldn't. Instead Ella pulled the ice tray out of the refrigerator and, in a gesture that felt both normal and alien, shook out cubes of ice and dropped them into a glass. She sat on the bed and crunched the ice cubes slowly and deliberately, trying to listen only to the hard clink they made as they fell back into the glass.

At about one a.m. there was a sharp knocking. Ella opened the door to Lena, who was shivering in her nightgown. Bob was right behind her, naked, holding a white towel across his waist with only middling success.

'What?' Ella demanded. 'What's wrong?'

'I'm bleeding, Mother. There's blood—'

Ella yanked Lena into the bedroom. Bob toddled in behind her, wearing the frozen, frightened smile of a child unsure what he was expected to do. Lou stood up. 'What's—' he began, and she saw his face melt to alarm.

'I've got her,' Ella announced. She pulled Lena into the bathroom. 'Sit,' she said. Ella wound a long ribbon of toilet paper around her hand. 'Show me where.'

Lena sat on the toilet and daintily flipped up her nightgown. Ella saw a smear of blood on Lena's large beige panties; she reached up, grapped the elastic and pulled the panties down to the floor. Ella dabbed Lena's vagina with the toilet paper; it came back pale red.

Ella knelt and peered critically between her daughter's legs. She had no idea what she was looking for; there was just a little blood. She held a towel under warm water and gently dabbed Lena's pubic hair.

'Am I OK, Mother?'

Ella didn't speak.

'Am I OK?'

'I don't know.' Ella let Lena wonder a moment. 'Answer me. Was he nice to you?'

'I think so.'

'Does it still hurt?'

'I started bleeding.'

'Do you feel better now?'

Lena touched her vagina tenderly, then stood up.

Ella knelt before her daughter and reached for her hands. 'You've had—' Ella spoke slowly—'intercourse now, Lena.'

Lena slapped Ella's hands away, impatient. 'I have to go see my husband.'

Bob was waiting in a chair, the towel arranged, like a large white napkin, across his lap. Lou was sitting in a chair on the other side of the room. They each had the alert demeanour of someone trying very hard not to speak.

'I stopped bleeding,' Lena said proudly to Bob.

Bob folded the towel around his waist and jumped up; he hurried out of the room. Lena bounded after him, and Ella followed into the hallway. 'The TV's still on,' he called to Lena.

'Leave it on,' said Lena.

As Lena began to follow him into their room, Ella saw Lena's nightgown sticking, indecent, over her hips; she reached forward to tug it down. But Lena pushed grandly past her mother. The pink door shut, and Ella was left standing in the corridor alone.

Back in the room, Lou looked at her. 'Is she all right?'

Ella nodded.

He gingerly lifted Lena's beige lace panties off the floor. 'She left these,' he said.

She remembered when she had bought these panties for Lena—on sale at Henshey's, two for one. Lou folded them gently, barely touching the edges, then handed them to Ella. She was moved by the way he folded them. She went to the bathroom and threw them out.

She opened the refrigerator and took out a perfect, tiny bottle of Dewar's. She unscrewed the cap, swallowed half the bottle and handed it to her husband.

There was only one thing she could think to do.

She went to Lou and kissed him.

They kissed in the strange, clean room, surrounded by lampshades and bedspreads and dressers that were not their own.

Ella let her husband kiss her neck, her breasts, her knees, hard enough to erase Lena. Ella had not expected to feel abandoned. She had not expected that Lena's closing the door would make her turn to Lou. The kindest thing he could do was make her forget. And as Lou had been, since Lena's birth, second place to her daughter, Ella sensed, in the muscular trembling of his fingers, how much he wanted to make her forget. She felt the nakedness of their lips in the deep, cooling dark.

Long after Lou had fallen asleep, she sat awake beside him. Then she went to the window and looked down at the street. It was the street Lena had walked down to her wedding, and it burnt with the hotel's twenty-four-hour lights. She watched the lit messages—BINGO and POKER and WIN!—that flashed a brilliant display of pink and orange and yellow into the empty street. Ella believed, suddenly, absolutely, that Lena was also looking out her window. She saw her daughter leaning naked on the ledge, her hair streaming over her bare shoulders, gazing at the bright casino lights and their strange, insistent attempts to illuminate the sky. □

ABRAHAM BRUMBERG
THE LAST JEWS IN WARSAW

Children at the Medem Sanatorium in Miedzeszyn, near Warsaw, in the 1930s

The Last Jews in Warsaw

One day late last summer I took a walk in Warsaw's Jewish Cemetery. It is a bleak place, with narrow paths winding their way between the gravestones, some of them still standing, others lying on the ground, defaced, overgrown by weeds. I am not partial to cemeteries, but I have come back to this one again and again over the past twenty-five years: it is one of the few remaining links to my childhood in pre-war Poland.

I paid only one visit to the Jewish cemetery before the war, sometime in the spring of 1939. I was twelve years old. My parents and I were part of a huge crowd accompanying the funeral cortège of a leader of the Jewish socialist Bund. The procession moved sombrely towards the cemetery gates, which were flung open to accommodate the mourners. The huge number of people, the band playing Chopin's Funeral March, the black, red and white flags fluttering in the breeze, the speeches at the burial site, all left an indelible impression on me.

Both Jewish and Polish (that is gentile) socialists addressed the crowd: an example of the 'internationalism' which the Bund prized so highly, yet which was often undermined by the local *shkotsim* (gentile boys) with their scowling faces, shouted insults and threats of beatings for offences such as failing to doff one's cap when passing a Catholic church. I was young and idealistic and I desperately wanted to believe in the slogan 'Workers of the world unite!', sacred to socialists and communists alike, however much they may have despised each other. The anti-Semites, I reasoned, were nothing but the flotsam and jetsam of capitalist society. They caused trouble, but would eventually disappear.

The thousands of marchers have long since been burnt to cinders. All that remains of the Bund is a monument to several of its leaders who fell in the Ghetto uprising in the April and May of 1943. Their tombstones carry no biblical motifs; instead the leaders' faces are carved in stone (a practice forbidden by religious law), and their names, birthdates and dates of death are inscribed in Yiddish and in Polish. This monument is what has drawn me repeatedly to the burial grounds. And so once more I stared intently upon the youthful faces of the Ghetto fighters, imagining their owners coming back to life, their revolutionary rhetoric echoing around the cemetery.

Eventually I turned away from the monument and proceeded to the exit. There I met the caretaker of the cemetery, Boleslaw Szenicer, and it was then, in the course of a brief conversation that something I had surely known for many years became newly, wrenchingly clear to me.

Szenicer is a man in his mid-thirties who looks more like a ticket salesman at a Coney Island concession booth than a man in charge of burials. The visor of his cap sits high upon his nose; his clothing is a ragbag of nondescript, mud-coloured garments; and his language wanders freely from halting Yiddish to uncertain English and fluent Polish, with a few German and Russian words thrown in. I found him standing near his office, surrounded by a group of American tourists. 'Here,' he was saying to them, 'put on the yarmulkes and don't forget to return them—some always seem to go missing. And we also sell postcards, only twenty groszy each.'

Several years ago, when I first met Szenicer, he told me that he had taken on the cemetery job only to keep the promise he made to his late father, the former keeper. 'In about ten years' time,' he told me then, 'I shall bury the last Jew in Warsaw, lock the cemetery and leave for Israel.'

His words had had an elegiac quality. But what he now told me made me think about their literal meaning. 'How many Jews are there in Warsaw?' I asked him. 'Oh,' he replied, shrugging his shoulders, 'probably no more than about six hundred.'

'Six hundred?' I exclaimed. 'Are you sure?'

He smiled. 'Why such surprise? Well, maybe one thousand. How many Jews do you think there are in Poland altogether? Probably no more than three thousand, perhaps three and a half. That's all.'

I was having some trouble assimilating what he said. 'That means that in a few years, as you once told me . . . '

'Four at most,' replied Szenicer, matter of factly. 'The Jews who are left are in their eighties. Over the past few months I have seen to more funerals than ever before. This means that the rate of attrition is higher than before—a natural process. So . . . '

Six hundred. Or a thousand. Not enough to fill a concert hall. And in all of Poland three and a half thousand—one tenth of one per cent of the pre-war population of three and a half million.

These statistics shouldn't have shocked me: I have entertained no illusions that Poland is anything but *Judenrein*. Yet somehow I had never fully come to terms with them.

Why? Perhaps I did not want to face the horror behind the numbers. Perhaps I wanted to hold on to some shards of false consciousness. Why, after all, there *are* some Jews left in Poland. There are even faded relics of an organized Jewish life: a Society of Polish Jews, a Yiddish theatre, a Jewish Historical Institute and, as of last year, a functioning synagogue in Warsaw. There is talk about founding a Museum of Jewish Life in Poland. A special emissary is sent by the foreign ministry to Polish embassies in the West to bring the tidings of renewed Jewish cultural activities in Poland; delegations of Jews, devout and secular, come to Poland from all over the world to attend special events (such as 'a week of Jewish culture', the yearly commemoration of the Warsaw Ghetto uprising) or to visit some remote *shtetl* where their ancestors came from.

Now, in the course of one brief conversation, it came to me with the force of a revelation that these embers of survival are nothing but an exercise in nostalgia, a clutching at historical memories, a mirage. Polish Jewry belongs to the past, and nothing—no pious wishes, no solemn meetings of Polish diplomats with representatives of Israel or Jewish communities in the West, no attempts to construct a Jewish school or to organize Jewish student associations—can possibly bring it back.

I was brought up in a secular Yiddish-speaking environment and went to school where the language of instruction was Yiddish. Yiddish was the language I heard on the streets, at home, in school, in the theatre, and it was the language spoken by most of my friends. I read works by European authors in Yiddish translation—Dickens, Kipling, Selma Lagerlöf, Knut Hamsun, Jack London and others. *The Call of the Wild* was the favourite of generations of Jewish schoolchildren, as was the more horrific *The Sea Wolf*. A friend of mine, now in the United States, had all the works of Jules Verne in Yiddish prominently displayed on his bookshelf. I read them, one by one. (Not surprisingly, my favourite was *Michael Strogoff*: Tsarist Russia was more part of my universe than the moon, the jungles of Borneo or the depths of the Pacific Ocean.)

I also devoured books by Polish authors—Henryk Sienkiewicz, Boleslaw Prus, Stefan Zeromski; we were expected to be good Yiddishists but also loyal Poles. Reading late nineteenth- and early twentieth-century novels bolstered our patriotism. (My fascination with Polish literature did not abate even after we arrived in the States in 1941. Every Saturday I would take the subway all the way from our house in the West Bronx to Avenue A in lower Manhattan, where a branch of the New York Public Library boasted a wide selection of Polish novels.)

I took it for granted that my friends and I—firm both in our Jewishness and our allegiance to Poland—took pride in Poland's European standing (number five in coal production); we gloried in the exploits of Tadeusz Kosciuszko or in the fact that Marie Sklodowska Curie was a Pole. But oddly enough I never seemed to crave the friendship of Polish children, and young gentiles seemed hardly to notice us except to shout abuse—abuse that I sometimes didn't fully understand. Once when returning from school with my friends I heard a group of young boys shouting derisively '*Starozakonni, starozakonni!*' and had to ask my father what it meant. 'Followers of the Old Testament,' he explained, but I was still baffled. We were Jews, of course, but not followers of the Old Testament—whatever *that* was; surely they meant those Hasidic boys one saw on the streets with their side curls and long black coats.

Poland in the late 1930s was awash with anti-Semitic passions. Jewish stores were attacked, and their owners beaten up; Jewish students were forced to occupy special 'ghetto benches' in the universities and were preyed upon by razor-wielding bands of hoodlums. The government advocated policies designed to make the country *Judenrein*. So how, in such conditions, did we manage to combine our assertive Jewishness and our Polish patriotism? Even more curiously, how did so many of us grow up in so ambivalent a climate without suffering irreparable emotional damage?

I believe the explanation lies in the third ingredient in my upbringing—'internationalism', which is to say, socialism. Not

Soviet-style socialism—a betrayal, I was taught, of true socialism's most sacred beliefs—but a doctrine rooted in equality, individual freedom and democracy: this, we were assured, was what the true followers of Marx espoused, and this was the future they believed in. 'Daddy,' I greeted my father at age eight, as he stepped down from the train that brought him back to Warsaw from a long stay in France, 'I am now class conscious.' My father smiled gently and greatly enjoyed telling his friends of the charming surprise that awaited him upon his return from abroad.

A few weeks earlier I had joined the SKIF (*Sotsialistisher Kinder Farband*—socialist children's association), the children's branch of the Bund. I told my father about it, adding that the new circle would be named—at my suggestion—after Karl Marx. My father, a generous man, refrained from commenting on this novel suggestion.

As a *skifist*, I attended bi-weekly meetings, though I don't remember anything about them. I wrote some doggerel called 'May Day' which the editor of the children's page of the Bundist daily *Folkstsaytung* (People's Gazette) thought (inexplicably) fit to publish. I joined the Bund youth athletic club *Morgnshtern* (Morning Star), and every Monday and Thursday afternoon, together with my friends, would join in strenuous physical exercises or a game of soccer. One Sunday morning we marched, eight abreast, in our blue shirts and red ties (outfits the same colour as, but never to be confused with, those worn by our adversaries on Red Square) to the Warsaw Circus, where hundreds of *skifistn* and members of the Bund's Youth Organization *Tsukunft* (Future) displayed their athletic skills before a cheering crowd.

Like other European youth organizations, the SKIF had an affinity for the Great Outdoors. I longed to join one of its summer camps, but was considered too young. I did, however, somehow manage to get into a winter camp held one bitterly cold week in late 1938 or early 1939. The participants—about thirty young boys and girls—were housed in a simple villa somewhere in the countryside. I remember getting up every morning at five-thirty to the piercing sound of a bugle, making my bed, hurriedly dressing and then running through the snow to a nearby forest. The sun was barely out, the air a curtain of ice; we would then return to the villa and burn our mouths on cups of scalding cocoa.

Our leader was a young man by the name of Emanuel Pat, who later became a well-known physician in the Bronx. Our daily programme consisted of gymnastics, revolutionary songs and the odd lecture delivered by Pat and other speakers from the Bund sent down from Warsaw for that purpose. The winter camp lasted ten days, and, despite the daily morning maledictions, we returned home invigorated, our ideological batteries recharged.

As a pupil of a secular Yiddish school-cum-*skifist*, I was also offered a minor role in a play about the French Revolution, probably stitched together by some of our teachers and acted by pupils of the Yiddish schools. The play was performed on the stage of the Nowosci Theatre in Warsaw—a Jewish-owned establishment where many Yiddish plays were produced. All I remember of that rousing drama was running around in torn trousers, one of many sans-culottes, and singing '*O, ça'ira, ça'ira, ça'ira—les aristocrats aux lanternes!*' French was reserved for the refrains only; the play's dialogue was entirely in Yiddish.

We looked forward immensely to the annual May Day demonstrations. Some were sponsored jointly by the Bund and the *Left Poalei Zion* (Labour Zionists)—the only Jewish political grouping with which the Bund would collaborate; some included the PPS (Polish Socialist Party). The Communists, who did not command a big following before the war, were forbidden by law from marching under their own banner; many would march instead under the banners of the trade unions they dominated.

It was exhilarating to see: the earnest faces of the marching men and women, the massed red flags, the banners proclaiming LONG LIVE THE FRIENDSHIP OF ALL WORKERS and DOWN WITH FASCISM, the procession flanked by cane-swinging members of the Bund's defence militia. The Zionist socialist groups, such as *Hashomer Hatzair*, were also accompanied by their own defence units, as was the PPS. The police were everywhere but did not interfere, and almost all demonstrations passed without incident.

I was usually taken to watch the procession by my mother, whose maternal feelings seemed to outweigh her party loyalty, but I was always on the lookout for my father marching by. Once, in front of the huge Polish National Theatre which still stands in

Warsaw today, I detached myself from my mother, and, breaking through the ranks of the militia, joined the marchers. A militiaman turned me around, pushed me towards the spectators and sternly admonished me not to do it again.

During these years, my father was the deputy director of the Medem Sanatorium in Miedzeszyn, near Warsaw, and it was an important part both of my upbringing as a *skifist* and our family life. Founded in the late 1920s, the sanatorium had come to fulfil two functions. As a health institution, it was staffed by doctors and nurses who looked after between one and two hundred poor Jewish children suffering from respiratory ailments, who required above all good food, clean air, plenty of rest and basic medical attention. My mother was a nurse, and her role was to conduct preliminary interviews with the children's parents. At each day's end she would come home exhausted from the interminable conversations, bringing to our supper table chilling tales of misery and despair.

At the same time—and more importantly—the sanatorium was the embodiment of a socialist dream. It was the proudest creation of the Bund, a veritable children's republic, thought of as a model of the future socialist state. Many of the activities were carried out by the children themselves, such as looking after the sanatorium's chickens and incubators, attending to its Biological Station (plants, fish, meteorological instruments), checking on cleanliness and composing a daily news report to be read at the breakfast table.

The *sanatoristn*, as the children were called, also participated in regular assemblies and elected a 'children's council' (*kinderrat*) responsible for coordinating the various activities and adjudicating cases of minor disciplinary infractions. In 1935 a leading Polish film director, Alexander Ford, made a film about the sanatorium called *Mir Kumen On* (Here We Come). The film was banned by the Polish authorities, which considered it anti-Polish and pro-communist. This was nonsense, but right-wing politicians have always been prone to blurring the differences between democratic socialism and communism. The film was shown abroad to great acclaim and even won the first prize at a festival of documentary films in France. I appeared in it for two breathless moments.

In the summers my father would rent a room in a villa nearby, and I was allowed to play in the grounds of the sanatorium, proud to enjoy this privilege while all the other children had to observe the daily regimen, but also smitten with guilt. I made sure not to miss out on the plays and festivals and recall one in particular—a game based on the capture and destruction of the Bastille, held (naturally) on 14 July.

My childhood seems rather a conundrum now, half a century later. In pre-war Poland, a poor and fairly backward country where a great many people believed that Jews had killed Christ and used gentile children's blood for baking matzo on Passover, lived thousands of Jewish youngsters who were fervently dedicated to the liberating truths of socialism, internationalism and solidarity with the Polish 'masses'. We were deeply respectful of the country's history and culture, and passionate about its unspoilt countryside. Our ideology combined the belief that Jews had the right to remain in Poland with the belief that we also had the right to build our lives and institutions in our own language, Yiddish. It was an odd mélange, this creed, yet it worked.

Both my parents were typical *intelligenty*. They had broken away from traditional homes to become dedicated secularists and socialists. Their values were grounded in rational considerations. The sense of security that I derived from their beliefs made it easy for me to reject the temptations of other ideologies swirling around me at that time.

After my brief exchange (the last, I wondered?) with Boleslaw Szenicer, I boarded the bus that would take me back to my hotel, and it occurred to me that perhaps my astonishment at Szenicer's words was the price paid for wilful naivety. I have been writing and speaking about Poland's Jews, Polish–Jewish relations and anti-Semitism for nearly fifteen years. I have given the figure of 'approximately three thousand' for the number of Jews in Warsaw, and 'about seven to eight thousand' in the country as a whole, figures which, I would point out, did not necessarily include the 'undeclared Jews', those who never denied their ancestry but cared little about it, nor those fully 'assimilated' Jews who wanted to pass themselves off as pure Poles (no easy task, given the propensity of Polish anti-Semites for denouncing the 'Jewish traitors' in their midst).

In the course of my lectures and articles, I have often referred to 'anti-Semitism without Jews'—yet even while using the phrase, and the word *Judenrein*, I resisted the implications of both. Yes, Poland was virtually devoid of Jews, but those seven or eight thousand who remained seemed to constitute a community—tragically small, but a functioning community nevertheless. It was a notion that made it easier to come to terms with discomfiting realities: a Yiddish theatre in Warsaw, most of whose actors are Polish and speak no Yiddish, and whose audience is provided with taped translations; a Yiddish newspaper that comes out three times a week and is more widely read outside Poland than in; the Jewish Historical Institute staffed largely by Polish gentiles. In addition, the handful of religious Jews in Warsaw have recently been offered the services of a resident rabbi, the first in twenty years, and a number of young Jewish parents in Warsaw have recently founded a Jewish school, with Polish, of course, as the language of instruction. (The school, only two years old, is so successful that Polish parents are clamouring to have their children accepted there: the beginning of the end, I wonder?)

My assumption—that Poland still was home to an authentic, if minuscule, Jewish community—may have been reasonable twenty years ago. Now, as Szenicer's brutal words made clear, it is not. As I sat in my hotel room after returning from the cemetery, my ruminations turned first into vexation, then anger. For haven't I, too, been caught up in and perhaps contributed to this myth-making exercise? And shouldn't I have known better?

I should. In 1958, during my first post-war visit to Poland, I went down to Miedzeszyn to visit the sanatorium. The buildings were still standing, though to my chagrin their present inhabitants, officials from the Ministry of Education, did not know anything about the history of the place. Thirty-one years later, in 1989, I read an account by Wiktor Kulerski, a teacher and former Solidarity leader, of the *Umsiedlung* (deportation) of thousands of Jews from villages and towns near Warsaw in July 1942—the so-called great *Aktion*, which left 40,000, out of a 1940 population of 450,000 Jews, in the Warsaw Ghetto, the rest having been sent to the gas chambers in Treblinka.

Kulerski described in searing terms the round-up of the children and staff of the Medem Sanatorium. I had left the sanatorium with my parents and a few others on 6 September 1939 in a horse-drawn wagon, heading east, like thousands of Polish citizens, to escape the advancing German army. The news of the eventual fate of the children and personnel reached us in the United States in the summer of 1942: all of them, including those who could have saved themselves, were rounded up and sent to Treblinka.

Thirty years on, having read Kulerski's shattering description of the sanatorium's liquidation, I decided to go to Miedzeszyn again. I went with Marek Edelman, the one Bundist leader of the Ghetto uprising who has remained in Poland; as a former *sanatorist*, he wanted to see what was left of it.

We drove to Miedzeszyn, but found not a trace of the buildings both of us remembered so well. Our inquiries got us nowhere; no local inhabitant, young or old, could tell us anything. At one point Marek said excitedly: 'It was *here*, I remember, where the train would stop. We would walk ten minutes or so through a small wood, then come out in a meadow and there, a hundred metres ahead of us, stood the sanatorium!' The railroad station was long gone, the meadow had disappeared and the small wood, apparently, had turned into a large forest.

Two days later Wiktor Kulerski himself drove me to Miedzeszyn. He had been there only a few years ago and had taken some pictures of the buildings. After an hour we stopped. 'Here it is,' announced Kulerski. Except that the 'here' was, in effect, nowhere. There was *nothing* to see. No trace of the old buildings remained. Kulerski recognized the grounds only by the location of a small pond with water lilies dating back to the early 1930s. Clearly, for reasons unknown, the authorities, whoever they were, had razed all the facilities to the ground.

'Nothing' is not quite accurate. Nearby, on a small mound, stood a memorial stone with a brief inscription: HERE, UPON THESE

GROUNDS, THE HOME ARMY MAINTAINED A HOME FOR POLISH CHILDREN 1942–45. This, and nothing more: no reference to the fact that, before the Home Army took over the now-destroyed buildings, they had housed more than a hundred Jewish children of the Medem Sanatorium, all sent to be gassed in Treblinka. The very last thread linking me to Poland had, I felt, been severed for good.

Nevertheless, instead of acting upon these words, I continued to take part in a game of make-believe. The obscene Home Army plaque should have cured me of the attempt to find some remnants of real Jewish life in Poland. But it didn't. The myth still worked.

The persisting anti-Semitism, too, contributed to the myth. I did not lull myself into believing that anti-Semitism, as so many Poles have insisted, had been a 'marginal phenomenon', 'atypical', the offal of the guttersnipe press. Only last year Lech Walesa—the now ex-president—made a long speech to commemorate the liberation of Auschwitz, while managing not to mention the fact that more than ninety per cent of its victims were Jews. On another occasion he refused to condemn his chaplain and confessor, the 'Solidarity priest' Henryk Jankowski, who declared, in a sermon and then on television, that Jews had spawned the 'Bolshevik menace' and were responsible for World War Two. He continued to stand by him until the Vatican itself had to interfere, forcing Father Jankowski to apologize and say he 'had been carried away' (by what, one wonders?) and henceforth would tend only to his 'priestly duties'.

In the meantime yet another priest, the Chaplain of the Armed Forces, Bishop Leszek Glodz, announces that seventy-five per cent of the Polish press is effectively 'under the domination' of the 'Polish-language' (read: Jewish) press, and that there are only two papers with pure Polish credentials, one Catholic and the other the paper of the Armed Forces; and Archbishop Tadeusz Goclowski announces he is 'pained' by Father Jankowski's words only inasmuch as 'declarations of a strictly political character have no place in religious services'.

When workers march under the banner of Solidarity and call for their enemies, Jews and 'friends of Jews', to be sent 'to the gas ovens'—as they did in the spring of 1995—Jews and a great many Poles are horrified. The indignation aroused by such incidents is rooted in the assumption that they are not only odious, but positively harmful to the remaining Jews in Poland. Hence the demands that Walesa denounce Jankowski (made by Shevakh Weiss, chairman of the Israeli Knesset, by the American Jewish Committee, by Marek Edelman and others)—as if such denunciations would make any difference to Walesa's own views (they haven't in the past), to the anti-Semitic lumpen or to the Jews themselves.

In fact such incidents have hardly any impact on the microscopic number of Polish Jews, their lives, their work, their relations with other people. They do not quake in their boots and look out of their windows for the first sign of a pogrom.

Those days are gone. There are no 'Polish–Jewish relations' in Poland today because there are, in effect, no Jews in Poland today. The indignation, anger, concern: all are a matter of simple morality, of Poland's political health, a *Polish* matter—above all, a matter of History.

I had been aware of this before, but never as forcefully as now, after my visit to the cemetery, after Szenicer's remarks. As soon as I fully absorb these truths, I told myself in my hotel room facing the square where thousands of May Day paraders once filled the air with their shouted slogans and hurrahs, I shall be able to shed the illusions that have plagued me so long.

Perhaps I shall return to the cemetery one day. But it will be only when Boleslaw Szenicer locks its heavy gates and departs. I shall stand outside, look in through the fence and remember. □

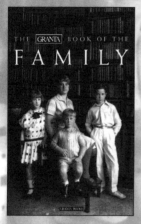

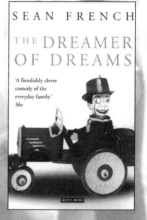

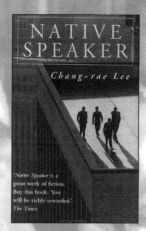

Notes on Contributors

Karen E. Bender lives in New York City and is working on a novel.

Leila Berg is best known for her children's books, among them *Little Pete*, *My Dog Sunday* and *Nippers*. 'Salford, 1924' is taken from her memoir *Flickerbook*, to be published by Granta Books next year.

Abraham Brumberg has written widely on Russia and Eastern Europe. He lives in Washington, DC.

Tony Gould's most recent book, *A Summer Plague: Polio and its Survivors*, was published last year. He is now working on a book about the Gurkhas, to be published by Granta Books.

Allan Gurganus's books include *Oldest Living Confederate Widow Tells All*, a novel, and *White People*, a collection of stories. 'He's One, Too' is taken from an anthology *Boys Like Us*, to be published in the US by Avon, and will also appear in his next book, *On Tattered Wings*. He lives in North Carolina.

Brian Hall is author of *The Impossible Country,* on former Yugoslavia, and *The Saskiad*, a novel, to be published this autumn by Houghton Mifflin in the US and Secker & Warburg in the UK. 'I Am Here' is taken from *Madeleine's World*, a 'biography' of his elder daughter.

David Mamet is a playwright, film director, screenwriter and novelist. His most recent book is a novel, *The Village*.

Adam Mars-Jones's books include *Lantern Lecture*, *Monopolies of Loss* and *The Waters of Thirst*. A fuller version of 'Blind Bitter Happiness' will appear in *Sons and Mothers*, an anthology to be published by Virago.

Todd McEwen's previous novels are *Fisher's Hornpipe* and *Max*. His latest, *Arithmetic*, from which 'Arithmetic Town' is taken, will be published by Jonathan Cape next year.

Blake Morrison is the author of *And when did you last see your father?* His next book, *As If*, will be published by Granta Books next year.

Jayne Anne Phillips's books include *Black Tickets*, *Machine Dreams, Fast Lanes* and *Shelter*. 'Mother Care' is taken from a novel in progress.

Susan Swan grew up in Midland, Ontario. She is the author of three novels, most recently *The Wives of Bath*. 'Sluts' is taken from her new short-story collection *Stupid Boys are Good to Relax With*.

Joy Williams is the author of three novels, two collections of short stories and a guide to the Florida Keys. She lives in Connecticut.